THE PREFERENTIAL OPTION
FOR THE POOR

Rohan Michael Curnow

THE PREFERENTIAL OPTION
FOR THE POOR

A SHORT HISTORY AND A READING BASED
ON THE THOUGHT OF BERNARD LONERGAN

MARQUETTE
UNIVERSITY

PRESS

MARQUETTE STUDIES IN THEOLOGY
NO. 81
ANDREW TALLON, SERIES EDITOR

© Copyright by Rohan Michael Curnow
Sydney, Australia, 2012

LIBRARY OF CONGRESS CATALOGING-IN-PUBLICATION DATA

Curnow, Rohan Michael, 1976-
The preferential option for the poor : a short history and a reading based on the thought of Bernard Lonergan / Rohan Michael Curnow.
    pages cm. — (Marquette studies in theology ; No. 81)
Includes bibliographical references and index.
ISBN 978-1-62600-700-0 (pbk. : alk. paper)
1. Church work with the poor—Catholic Church. 2. Poverty—Religious aspects—Catholic Church. 3. Lonergan, Bernard J. F. 4. Doran, Robert M., 1939- 5. Liberation theology. 6. Catholic Church. Consejo Episcopal Latinoamericano I. Title.
BV639.P6C87 2013
261.8'325—dc23

                                                        2013016135

Feeding of the 5000, 1999 (acrylic on canvas),
James, Laura (Contemporary Artist) /
Private Collection / The Bridgeman Art Library

♾The paper used in this publication meets the minimum requirements of the American National Standard for Information Sciences—
Permanence of Paper for Printed Library Materials, ANSI Z39.48-1992.

Association of American
University Presses

MARQUETTE UNIVERSITY PRESS
MILWAUKEE

The Association of Jesuit University Presses

For my Ma and Da, Cheryl and Greg (1946–2004) Curnow

"Remember that you owe your birth to your parents; how can you repay them for what they have done for you?" (Sir 7:28)

CONTENTS

ABSTRACT

This book situates the doctrine of the Preferential Option for the Poor within the field of Lonergan Studies. To do so, it draws primarily upon the work of Bernard Lonergan and Robert Doran.

The book is divided into six chapters. Chapter 1 begins with an historical account of the emergence of the doctrine of the Preferential Option of the Poor. It covers the time period from the opening of the Second Vatican Council in 1962 to the meeting of the Latin American Episcopal Conference at Puebla, Mexico, in 1979. Chapter 2 continues this narrative, beginning in the period after the Puebla meeting, and illustrates the process by which the doctrine of the Preferential Option of the Poor actually bifurcates into ecclesial (Roman Magisterium) and theological (Latin American) forms. Chapter 3 introduces the key concepts from Lonergan Studies that are required to appropriate the Preferential Option for the Poor within a critical-realist framework. Chapter 4 employs these concepts, particularly the understanding of religious and moral conversion outlined in Chapter 3, to begin to situate the Option for the Poor within the framework of Lonergan Studies. Concurrently, it engages major Liberation Theologians on the topic of the Option. Chapter 5 continues in the vein of Chapter 4 and addresses two further elements of integral conversion—intellectual and psychic. Chapter 6 uses Doran's theology of history, as outlined in his *Theology and the Dialectics of History*, to demonstrate some of the potential of Doran's achievement with respect to the constructive task of understanding the Option for the Poor.

ACKNOWLEDGEMENTS

This is one of those books that begin life as a doctoral thesis. Doctorates are often a function of a lifetime's support. And mine most certainly was. As a result, there are very many people I need to thank. Indeed there are too many to list. Those I do not mention by name below, I thank here now. I suspect you know who you are.

I would particularly like to express my heartfelt gratitude to my thesis directors, Professors Robert Doran (Marquette University) and John Dadosky (Regis College, University of Toronto), for the support and incisive feedback they provided during the writing process. I also thank Dr. John Charles Beer and the Board of the Travelling Fellowship that bears his name for the financial support that aided my doctoral studies so significantly.

I am grateful to Professors Peter Beer, SJ, Raymond Canning, Fr. Gerard Kelly, Patrick McArdle, Gilles Mongeau, SJ, Neil Ormerod, Gordon Rixon, SJ, and Michael Vertin for their guidance over the years.

Those who proofread the text, particularly Julia Lauwers, Rev. Andrew Murray, SM, and Dr. H. Daniel Monsour – who also worked on the index – I thank for dedicatedly completing one of the most onerous tasks in academia. The errors that remain, of course, are my own.

Professor Andrew Tallon of Marquette University Press welcomed the original manuscript. He and his staff worked carefully and efficiently to massage it into its final state. I am most grateful for their work.

Rev. Fr. Brendan Quirk provided me with a place to complete this book. I thank him and the parishioners of St Mary MacKillop's Parish, Rockdale City, Sydney, for their generosity. I also thank Fr. Quirk, Brendan Freeman, and Matthew Low for their friendship; without it, I am sure, this book would have been completed much faster.

My siblings, all my niblings, and all my friends – even the Canadians – I thank for their ongoing succor and forbearance. Explicit thanks must go to Lyndall Evans for her support and limitless kindness. The Evans Clan I thank for toleration. And I also thank Bentley and Paprika for their company during some of the more lonely stretches of writing.

Lastly, but by no means least, I thank my mother and father. Words cannot say it. I hope deeds do. This book is dedicated to them.

The next book's acknowledgements will be shorter. I promise.

INTRODUCTION
CONTENT AND PARAMETERS

I. INTRODUCTION

Frederick Crowe once noted that the topic of Bernard Lonergan and Liberation Theology might seem like Melchizedek; that is, without contextual father or mother.[1] Indeed, the reception Lonergan's thought received at a 1975 congress in Mexico City illustrated a pronounced divergence in opinion of its relevance to political theology.[2] Two liberation theologians of some esteem—namely, Hugo Assmann and José Comblin—were unsympathetic towards Lonergan's conception of the theological task.[3] However, as Crowe further notes,[4] the same confer-

---

1 Frederick E. Crowe, "Bernard Lonergan and Liberation Theology," in *Appropriating the Lonergan Idea*, ed. Michael Vertin (Washington, D.C.: Catholic University of America Press, 1989), 116.

2 The proceedings were published as Enrique Ruiz Maldonado, ed. *Liberación y cautiverio: Debates en torno al método de la teología en América Latina* (Ciudad de México: Comité Organizador, 1975).

3 Assmann contended that Lonergan's theology does not lead to history. Ibid., 296. Comblin made two negative assessments: one glib, and the other scathing. The first claimed that if medieval theologians had to engage in the task of theology as Lonergan envisaged it, they would not have stuck at the theological task for even fifteen minutes. The second suggested that Lonergan's thought was made to order for the task of supporting the ideologies of Latin America's juntas and dictatorships. Ibid., 517-19. Ignacio Ellacuría, whose work is often cited in this book either directly or via the work of Jon Sobrino, once wrote that subjectivity "is an impoverished sign of what God and man are in history. It has value insofar as it attempts to give an immanent base to God's presence among human beings; but it tends to conceive human transcendence in individual terms, and hence in itself does not lead to praxis in societal life and history." Ignacio Ellacuría, *Freedom Made Flesh: The Mission of Christ and His Church*, trans. John Drury (Maryknoll, NY: Orbis Books, 1976), 92. This book hopes to allay such fears.

4 Crowe, "Bernard Lonergan and Liberation Theology," 116-17.

ence also witnessed an undercurrent of thought that was not only less hostile to Lonergan's thought, but even cautiously optimistic about the relevance his work may hold to the challenges facing Liberation Theology.[5] In the three decades since the congress, academics such as Robert Doran,[6] Matthew Lamb,[7] Frederick Lawrence,[8] and Stephen Martin[9] have helped illustrate that Lonergan's thought can in fact shape a potent understanding of progress, decline, and redemption within history.

This book functions as a contribution—albeit a limited one— made in the same vein as the works by the aforementioned academics. Specifically, this book is an attempt to locate the doctrine of the Preferential Option for the Poor within the field of Lonergan Studies. It is more a work of theological foundations than it is of systematic

---

5   Maldonado, ed. *Liberación y cautiverio: Debates en torno al método de la teología en América Latina,* 375, 408, 531-38, and passim.

6   Robert M. Doran, *Psychic Conversion and Theological Foundations: Toward a Reorientation of the Human Sciences* (Chico, CA: Scholars Press, 1981), 41-67; Robert M. Doran, "Theological Grounds for a World-Cultural Humanity," in *Creativity and Method: Essays in Honor of Bernard Lonergan, S.J.* (Milwaukee, WI: Marquette University Press, 1981); Robert M. Doran, "Suffering Servanthood and the Scale of Values," in *Lonergan Workshop 4,* ed. Frederick Lawrence (Missoula, MT: Scholars Press, 1983), 41-67; Robert M. Doran, "The Analogy of Dialectic and the Systematics of History," in *Religion in Context: Recent Studies in Lonergan,* ed. Timothy P. Fallon and Philip Boo Riley (Lanham, MD: University Press of America, 1988); Robert M. Doran, *Theology and the Dialectics of History* (Toronto: University of Toronto Press, 1990); Robert M. Doran, *What Is Systematic Theology?* (Toronto: University of Toronto Press, 2005).

7   Matthew L. Lamb, "Methodology, Metascience and Political Theology," in *Lonergan Workshop 2,* ed. Frederick Lawrence (Missoula, MT: Scholars Press, 1981), 281-403. And, Matthew L. Lamb, *Solidarity with Victims* (New York: Crossroad, 1982).

8   Frederick G. Lawrence, *Communicating a Dangerous Memory: Soundings in Political Theology* (Atlanta, GA: Scholars Press, 1987). And, Frederick G. Lawrence, "Lonergan as Political Theologian," in *Religion in Context: Recent Studies in Lonergan,* ed. Timothy P. Fallon and Philip Boo Riley (Lanham, MD: University Press of America, 1988), 1-34.

9   Stephen Martin, *Healing and Creativity in Economic Ethics: The Contribution of Bernard Lonergan's Economic Thought to Catholic Social Teaching* (Lanham, MD: University Press of America, 2008).

theology,[10] although by relating the Preferential Option for the Poor to Lonergan's understanding of the converted subject it begins to move towards an appropriate 'system of conceptualization' and also towards eradicating inconsistencies in various understandings of the Option for the Poor.[11] This book does not function as a critique of either Liberation Theology or the Roman Catholic Magisterium's stance regarding the Preferential Option for the Poor. Rather, it is a contribution that takes a core doctrine of Liberation Theology—perhaps the core doctrine, that is, the doctrine of the Preferential Option for the Poor—and seeks to demonstrate the fecundity of Lonergan Studies as a means of expressing its full significance. In this sense, it is a piece of work that I hope will prove useful to liberation theologians as their field of theology, in the words of the Superior General of the Society of Jesus—the Very Reverend Dr. Adolfo Nicolás, SJ—continues to mature.[12]

---

10   This book does not engage with Lonergan's economic theory and its focus remains more directly theological. However, as Michael Shute and Gerard Whelan have noted, Lonergan constructed his theology of history—a theology which Doran extends—with his understanding of economic theory in mind. See Michael Shute, "The Origins of Lonergan's Notion of the Dialectic of History: A Study of Lonergan's Early Writings on History, 1933-1938" (Doctor of Theology, Regis College and University of Toronto, 1990). And Gerard Whelan, "The Development of Lonergan's Notion of the Dialectic of History: A Study of Lonergan's Writings 1938-53" (Doctor of Philosophy, University of St Michael's College, 1997).

11   For Lonergan, the working out of such systems of conceptualization belongs to the functional specialization of 'systematics'. See Bernard J. F. Lonergan, *Method in Theology* (London: Darton Longman and Todd, 1972), 132.

12   In his interview with Spanish *El Periodico* on 14 November, 2008, Fr Nicolás defended Liberation Theology by noting that it is a "... courageous and creative response to an unbearable situation of injustice in Latin America." He continued, "As with any theology, it needs years to mature. It's a shame that it has not been given a vote of confidence and that soon its wings will be cut before it learns to fly. It must be given more time." Jordi Casabella, "Adolfo Nicolás: "No sé si abrir fosas y beatificar mártires ayudará a reconciliar"" http://www.elperiodico.com/es/noticias/sociedad/adolfo-nicolas-abrir-fosas-beatificar-martires-ayudara-reconciliar-34712 (accessed 14-June 2011). The translation is that of the author of this book.

2. A REFLECTION ON POVERTY:
THOUGHTS FROM LIBERATION THEOLOGY

The question of who exactly constitute the poor—or, what exactly constitutes poverty—is of no small significance in any discussion on the Preferential Option for the Poor.[13] It is an issue with which worker-priest Paul Gauthier (whose influence on the Second Vatican Council is discussed in the first chapter of this work) and liberation theologian Gustavo Gutiérrez, among others, have struggled.[14] This section seeks to clarify the nature of poverty, as used in Liberation Theology, by: (a) flagging the fact that the word 'poverty' can be employed to denote something positive or negative; (b) noting that material poverty is always an evil; and, (c) discussing the existence of a hierarchy of poverty.

First, the term 'poverty' itself can be employed to connote something either positive or negative. For example, the terms 'spiritual poverty' and 'cultural poverty' can both be employed in positive and negative senses. Spiritual poverty, in the sense of its usage in the phrase 'the poor in spirit' does indeed connote a virtue.[15] Moreover, cultural poverty in the sense Cardinal Lercaro employed the idea is also a positive. Giuseppe Alberigo writes that Lercaro

> proposed the Church's need for cultural poverty, obviously not in
> the sense of ignorance, but rather as a renunciation of the covetous

---

13 Employing an adjective (such as 'poor') as a noun is usually considered incorrect. However, the phrase 'the poor' is used prolifically within much theological reflection and as such the terminology holds a precise theological provenance (such as the Hebrew *anawim*). For this reason, the usage of 'the poor' is perpetuated in this book.

14 Paul Gauthier, *Christ, the Church, and the Poor*, trans. Edward Fitzgerald (Westminster, MD: The Newman Press, 1965), 15-51. Gustavo Gutiérrez, *A Theology of Liberation: History, Politics, and Salvation*, trans. Caridad Inda and John Eagleson (Maryknoll, NY: Orbis Books, 1988), 163-73.

15 Gutiérrez, drawing on the documents of Medellín, refers to this form of poverty as what is intended by the word 'preference' in the phrase 'Preferential Option for the Poor': this is the element of Christian spirituality that allows us to recognize God as God and all others as siblings. Gustavo Gutiérrez, "Option for the Poor: Reviews and Challenges," *Promotio Justitiae* 57 (1994): 14. See also, Gustavo Gutiérrez, *The Truth Shall Make You Free: Confrontations*, trans. Matthew O'Connell (Maryknoll, NY: Orbis Books, 1990), 161.

possession of a finished and closed conceptual system. The Church would, instead, place itself in a posture of openness toward all cultures as equally capable of receiving the gospel message and widening the horizons of faith.[16]

This use of the term 'cultural poverty' can be seen in positive light as a call for the Church to make the shift from a normative understanding of culture to one that is empirical.[17] These uses of the term 'poverty' in a positive sense differs with John Paul II's use in *Centesimus annus*, where he writes, employing the same terminology: "[the] Option [for the Poor] is not limited to material poverty, since it is well known that there are many other forms of poverty, especially in modern society—not only economic but cultural and spiritual poverty as well (§57)."[18] So it is that 'cultural poverty' and 'spiritual poverty' may refer to virtuous dispositions or to privations. The context will usually clarify which sense is intended. In liberation thought, as in John Paul II's thought, the usage is normally in the sense of a privation. And this is also the sense in which the term is employed throughout this book.

Secondly, there exists a question of whether material poverty—the lack of goods required for human existence—is an evil or a virtue. It may seem unusual to suggest any positive value to such deprivation, but Gutiérrez notes that some Christians have a tendency to view material poverty as a positive human and religious ideal.[19] This approach, according to Gutiérrez, however well intentioned, must be discarded. Otherwise, those people who seek to free themselves from subjugation to material deprivation are seeking an anti-Christian goal. Gutiérrez considers such a proposition unacceptable and argues that therefore all material poverty, in the sense of the deprivation of the goods required to exist, must unambiguously be denounced as an evil.

16   Giuseppe Alberigo, *A Brief History of Vatican II*, trans. Matthew Sherry (Maryknoll, NY: Orbis Books, 2006), 80.

17   For an outline of such a shift, see Bernard J. F. Lonergan, "The Transition from a Classicist World-View to Historical Mindedness," in *A Second Collection: Papers by Bernard J. F. Lonergan, S.J.*, ed. William F. Ryan and Bernard Tyrrell (Toronto: University of Toronto Press, 1996), 1-9.

18   Pope John Paul II, "Centesimus annus" http://www.vatican.va/holy_father/john_paul_ii/encyclicals/documents/hf_jp-ii_enc_01051991_centesimus-annus_en.html (accessed 4 September 2012).

19   Gutiérrez, *A Theology of Liberation: History, Politics, and Salvation*, 163.

Thirdly, there is a question of a hierarchy of privations with respect to poverty: how do liberation theologians relate the different kinds of poverty? For example, as already noted, John Paul II refers to cultural and spiritual poverty as well as to the materially deprived.[20] Furthermore, Benedict XVI also calls for material, cultural, moral, affective, and spiritual poverty to be fought in attempts to establish peace on earth.[21] How do the different kinds of poverty relate to one another? John Paul II, relatively early in his Pontificate, suggested that spiritual poverty is in fact worse than material poverty. He wrote, "Because poor are those who lack material resources, but more so are those not familiar with the way God marks for them, who do not have his adopted Son, who ignore the moral path which leads to the joyous eternal destiny to which God calls humanity."[22] Benedict XVI has likewise written that, "As Blessed Teresa of Calcutta frequently observed, the worst poverty is not to know Christ."[23] Such stances can be contrasted with the writings of liberation theologians who acknowledge that there are a range of situations that can be defined as poverty[24] but insist on a certain priority for economic poverty. For them, mate-

20   Pope John Paul II, "Centesimus annus"., §57.

21   Pope Benedict XVI, "Message of His Holiness Pope Benedict XVI for the Celebration of the World Day of Peace: Fighting Poverty to Build Peace" http://www.vatican.va/holy_father/benedict_xvi/messages/peace/documents/hf_ben-xvi_mes_20061208_xl-world-day-peace_en.html (accessed 17-May 2010).

22   Pope John Paul II, "Celebración de la palabra: Homilía del Santo Padre Juan Pablo II" http://www.vatican.va/holy_father/john_paul_ii/homilies/1984/documents/hf_jp-ii_hom_19841012_celebrazione-santo-domingo_sp.html (accessed 5-April 2009). The original Spanish reads, "Porque pobre es quien carece de recursos materiales, pero más aún quien desconoce el camino que Dios le marca, quien no tiene su filiación adoptiva, quien ignora la senda moral que conduce al feliz destino eterno al que Dios llama al hombre" (§4).

23   Pope Benedict XVI, "Message of his Holiness Benedict XVI for Lent 2006" http://www.vatican.va/holy_father/benedict_xvi/messages/lent/documents/hf_ben-xvi_mes_20050929_lent-2006_en.html (accessed 14-June 2011).

24   Virgilio Elizondo, "Culture, the Option for the Poor, and Liberation," in The Option for the Poor in Christian Theology, ed. Daniel G. Groody (Notre Dame, IN: University of Notre Dame Press, 2007), 157-68. Gustavo Gutiérrez, "The Option for the Poor Arises from Faith in Christ," Theological Studies 70:2 (2009): 322.

rial poverty is not the only form of oppression, but it is foundational. As Clodovis Boff notes, "[the poor] do not simply exist alongside the other oppressed, like the black, the Indian, or the woman. ... A black taxi driver and a black soccer star are not the same thing. Similarly, a female domestic servant and the first lady of the land are not the same. An Indian whose land is stolen and an Indian still in possession of it are not the same."[25] Not only does material poverty mean "death,"[26] but it also is usually concomitant with a lack of access to cultural, social and political goods.[27] Material poverty can cause cultural poverty and it places acute pressures on the spiritual life. Here it is sufficient to note that Liberation Theology prioritizes material poverty as in some sense the most basic while acknowledging, and also seeking to overcome, other forms of privation on both cultural and spiritual levels.

Jon Sobrino's phenomenology of bread—a concept that is referred to a number of times in this book—illustrates Liberation Theology's stance on the idea of a hierarchy of poverty. Speaking of the basic goods required for life as the foundation of the Reign (or Kingdom) of God,[28] he argues that life is always open to more. Life points always to a fuller life, to being more than merely existing. Bread, he contends, is food. But it is not only food. It is also activity and toil, that is, it is work. Moreover, bread needs to be shared within a local community, and with other groups, and so becomes the focus of a spirit of community. It moves into the cultural realm in the festival of maize where poetry, art, and singing occur, and bread also has something of the sacramental about what it conveys. Bread means the possibility of life, and the possibility of life in all its fullness.[29] So Sobrino argues that the religious life begins with bread. The material life is the germ of a fuller life, and this is precisely why Liberation Theology speaks

---

25 Clodovis Boff, *Theology and Praxis: Epistemological Foundations* (Maryknoll, NY: Orbis Books, 1987), 77.

26 Gutiérrez, "Option for the Poor: Reviews and Challenges," 15.

27 Gutiérrez, *A Theology of Liberation: History, Politics, and Salvation*, 163.

28 The terms 'Kingdom of God' and 'Reign of God' are used interchangeably in this book. No differentiation of meaning is intended when either term is used.

29 Jon Sobrino, "Central Position of the Reign of God in Liberation Theology," in *Mysterium Liberationis: Fundamental Concepts of Liberation Theology*, ed. Ignacio Ellacuría and Jon Sobrino (Maryknoll, NY: Orbis Books, 1993), 380-81.

of integral liberation: social, cultural, and spiritual liberation are only possible if life exists.[30]

For this reason, Sobrino argues that poverty is a complex phenomenon and there is no need to "develop a chemically pure concept of poverty as a genus to be divided, according to the old logic, into distinct species."[31] Rather, "the generic term 'poverty,' with all its historical fluidity, is irreplaceable as an expression of the denial and oppression of humanness, and expression of the need, the contempt, the voicelessness, and anonymity that millions of human beings have suffered."[32]

Without seeking to develop a 'chemically pure concept of poverty,' the reflections in this short introduction do serve to add some clarity to the usage of the term 'poverty.' Material poverty is always an evil. And while the term 'poverty' can be used to denote something positive, the sense in which it is usually employed by liberation theologians and in papal encyclicals is as referring to a privation. Liberation Theology does prioritize material poverty,[33] but it does so out of a concern to avoid cultural and spiritual poverty. This is to say, Liberation Theology seeks the integral liberation of the poor from all oppression, whether such oppression is spiritual, cultural, or material, and it does so from the 'underside of history.'

3. BOOK STRUCTURE

Chapters 1 and 2 of this book contain an historical account of the process by which the doctrine of the Preferential Option for the Poor emerged in Catholic thought. Chapter 1, specifically, focuses on the initial ecclesial impetus for development and traces the process from

---

30   Ibid., 381.

31   Jon Sobrino, "Depth and Urgency of the Option for the Poor," in *No Salvation Outside the Poor: Prophetic-Utopian Essays* (Maryknoll, NY: Orbis Books, 2008), 23-24.

32   Ibid., 24.

33   It is outside the ambit of this book to conclusively establish the nature of the biblical understanding of poverty. What should be noted here, however, is that the eminent biblical scholar, Benedictine Jacques Dupont, argues that Jesus' original addressees of the Reign of God are the materially poor. This is not a focus that is in opposition to Matthew's emphasis on 'the poor in spirit' as a spiritual disposition, but rather the foundation upon which Matthew's stance is built. See Jacques Dupont, "Introduction aux Béatitudes," *Nouvelle Revue Théologique* 108:2 (1976): 97-108.

Vatican II—in particular the ideas of the Group of the Church of the Poor at the Council—through a period of tentative support from the Roman Magisterium, until the Latin American Episcopal Conference's (*Consejo Episcopal Latinoamericano* or CELAM) explicit affirmation of an Option for the Poor at its meeting in Puebla, Mexico, 1979.

Chapter 2 continues to trace the trajectory of development of the doctrine of the Preferential Option for the Poor. It recounts what is identified in this book as the 'Bifurcation of the Preferential Option for the Poor'. That is, Chapter 2 contains an account of the process by which the Preferential Option for the Poor splits into two distinct forms: an ecclesial form adopted by the Roman Magisterium—particularly by John Paul II and Joseph Ratzinger (the latter's thought is treated both in his capacity as the Cardinal Prefect of the Congregation for the Doctrine of the Faith and as Pope Benedict XVI)—and a theological form as adopted by liberation theologians such as Gustavo Gutiérrez and Jon Sobrino. The stance of CELAM is identified as tending to function as a middle term between the Vatican and theological positions, and in doing so confirms the bifurcation of the Option for the Poor.

Chapter 3 introduces the thought of Bernard Lonergan and of Lonergan scholar Robert Doran. Specifically, it focuses on the subject in her integrity.[34] That is, it introduces Lonergan's appropriation of the philosophical 'turn to the subject' and his focus on conversion. This third chapter: (1) summarizes Lonergan's theory of conscious intentionality and introduces his understanding of patterns of experience and realms of meaning; (2) presents Lonergan's understanding of the horizon of the subject; and, (3) sets forth Lonergan and Doran's combined stance on religious, moral, intellectual and psychic conversion.

Although Chapter 2 established the foundational role of conversion in any understanding of the Option for the Poor, the precise nature of conversion remains clouded in the writing of many liberation theologians. In light of this context, Chapter 4 begins to situate the Option for the Poor in the field of Lonergan Studies, particularly

---

34 With respect to issues of inclusive language and gender, in this book the original language of any quoted author is preserved even in instances where such language is considered outdated. The present author, however, adopts the practice of writing in a manner that alternates between feminine and masculine pronouns rather than adopting periphrastics such as 'him or her' or 'she or he'.

with reference to Lonergan's understanding of conversion. It employs Lonergan's concepts of religious and moral conversion to begin to build a structure that is able to interrelate liberation theology's understanding of the elements involved in the Option for the Poor. Concurrently, this chapter demonstrates how it is that moral conversion overcomes egoistic and group bias in history and how this relates to the Option for the Poor.

Chapter 5 continues in the vein of Chapter 4. But whereas Chapter 4 dealt with religious and moral conversions as largely spontaneous, Chapter 5 considers intellectual and psychic conversion as self-reflexive. It then continues to elaborate the structure of integral conversion as it relates to the Option for the Poor. The claims seminal liberation theologians make regarding the Option for the Poor's significance extending beyond the realm of Social Ethics and into hermeneutic and methodological matters is provided with a solid foundation. Moreover, this chapter also demonstrates how intellectual and psychic conversions are able to overcome the common-sense and dramatic-affective biases that impede the healing and progress of history.

Chapter 6 concentrates more narrowly upon the issue of the Preferential Option for the Poor and the mission of the Church. That is, while Chapters 4 and 5 treated conversion and the Option for the Poor, Chapter 6 will focus more specifically on an instance of great importance to Liberation Theology: the development of a systematic account of the Reign of God that is able to guide the mission of the Church in a manner that incorporates the Preferential Option for the Poor. To illustrate the capabilities of Lonergan Studies to meet such an exigence, in this final chapter the theology of history developed by Doran in his *Theology and the Dialectics of History* is elucidated. This theology of history is then related to the issue of the mission of the Church in terms of hermeneutics and praxis, terms that are integral to the theological understanding of the Preferential Option for the Poor.

CHAPTER I

THE ʻGROUP OF THE CHURCH OF THE POORʼ AT VATICAN II AND THE POST-CONCILIAR EMERGENCE OF THE DOCTRINE OF THE PREFERENTIAL OPTION FOR THE POOR IN OFFICIAL CHURCH TEACHING

I. INTRODUCTION

On 11 September, 1962—one month before the opening of the Second Vatican Council—Pope John XXIII delivered a radio address in which he claimed: "Confronted with the underdeveloped countries, the Church presents itself as it is and wishes to be, as the Church of all, and particularly as the Church of the poor."[1] Almost seventeen years later, on 13 February, 1979, the Latin American Episcopal Conference (*Consejo Episcopal Latinoamericano* and henceforth CELAM) declared, "We affirm the need for conversion on the part of the whole Church to a Preferential Option for the Poor, an option aimed at their integral liberation."[2] This chapter is concerned with the trajectory of thought which links these two events; that is, the historical process by which an explicit doctrine of the Preferential Option for the Poor emerged as a teaching of the Bishops of Latin

---

1 The full quote reads, "In faccia ai paesi sottosviluppati la Chiesa si presenta quale è, e vuol essere, come la Chiesa di tutti, e particolarmente la Chiesa dei poveri." See Pope John XXIII, "Radiomessaggio del Santo Padre Giovanni XXIII ai fedeli di tutto il mondo a un mese dal concilio ecumenico Vaticano" http://www.vatican.va/holy_father/john_xxiii/speeches/1962/documents/hf_j-xxiii_spe_19620911_ecumenical-council_it.html (accessed 3 September 2012).

2 See the final documents of CELAM III, at §1134, in John Eagleson and Philip Scharper, eds., *Puebla and Beyond: Documentation and Commentary* (Maryknoll, NY: Orbis Books, 1979), 264.

America. It considers the period stretching from the beginning of
Vatican II (1962) until the third meeting of CELAM in Puebla,
Mexico (1979). It is divided into two sections. The first focuses on the
Group of the Church of the Poor, which formed from among the bishops at the Second Vatican Council. It uses a presentation of the Group
of the Church of the Poor's complexion, activities, and achievements
at Vatican II to recount the reemergence into ecclesial consciousness
of the constitutive role of the poor in the Church's understanding of
both itself and God. This first section also considers how this awareness of the role of the poor is evident in the final documents of the
Council. Then, the second section takes up the issue of the emergence
of an explicit Option for the Poor in official Church teaching in the
post-conciliar period. It traces this process by considering two stages
of development: the first of these movements—from Pope Paul VI's
Populorum progressio to CELAM II at Medellín—is characterized
by Jon Sobrino as a "giant leap forward"; and, the second—from the
post-Medellín period until CELAM III at Puebla—he considers "a
dainty step forward."[3]

2. THE IRRUPTION OF THE POOR: VATICAN II AND THE GROUP OF THE CHURCH OF THE POOR

During the opening months of the Council, the schema *De Ecclesia*
came under intense scrutiny. On December 6, 1962, during his intervention on the schema, Giacomo Cardinal Lercaro, Archbishop of
Bologna, called to mind the radio address of John XXIII some three
months earlier. He argued that

> ... the Mystery of Christ in the Church is always, but particularly
> today, the Mystery of Christ in the poor, since the Church, as our
> Holy Father Pope John XXIII has said, is truly the Church of all,
> but is particularly 'the Church of the Poor'. ... None of the schemata
> which have been put before us, or which are to be put before us,
> seem to take this essential and primordial aspect of the Mystery of
> Christ into account in any explicit and formal project which accords
> with historical circumstances. ... In all the subjects the Council will
> deal with, may the ontological connection between the presence
> of Christ in the poor, and the two other profound realities of the

3 Jon Sobrino, "The Significance of Puebla for the Catholic Church in Latin
America," in *Puebla and Beyond: Documentation and Commentary*, ed. John
Eagleson and Philip Scharper (Maryknoll, NY: Orbis Books, 1979), 302.

Mystery of Christ in the Church, namely the presence of Christ in the Eucharistic action by means of which the Church is made one and is constituted, and the presence of Christ in the sacred hierarchy which instructs and governs the Church, be brought out and clarified.[4]

This moment in history, Lercaro declared, was "the hour of the poor."[5] Though profoundly prophetic, this intervention was overwhelming for many of the Council Fathers in that it proved "too advanced for [their] general consciousness."[6] But outside the official Council structures, its calls were taken up by an informal working group known as 'The Group of the Church of the Poor'[7] or the 'Belgian College Group' after the place in which it met.[8] This section of the chapter narrates the history of the Group of the Church of the Poor in an attempt to illustrate that the poor broke into the Church's consciousness at the Council in a new way. To do so, it focuses on the Group of the Church of the Poor's: (a) origins and complexion; (b) aims and activities; and, (c) achievements and shortcomings at the Council.

2.1 THE GROUP OF THE CHURCH OF THE POOR: ORIGINS AND COMPLEXION

Although Lercaro's intervention provided high-level legitimization to the Group of the Church of the Poor, its spiritual roots were more humble. These roots can be found in the French worker-priest movement of the mid-1940s.[9] More specifically, Father Paul Gauthier,

4   Gauthier, *Christ, the Church, and the Poor*, 153-55.

5   Guiseppe Ruggieri, "Beyond an Ecclesiology of Polemics: The Debate on the Church," in *History of Vatican II: The Formation of the Council's Identity, First Period and Intersession, October 1962 – September 1963*, ed. Giuseppe Alberigo and Joseph Komonchak (Maryknoll, NY: Orbis Books, 1997), 346.

6   Ibid.

7   This is not to say that Lercaro's intervention inspired the formation of the Group of the Church of the Poor—the Group had already formed and had met three times before Lercaro's famous speech—but it provided fuel for the Group as it was beginning to gather momentum.

8   Hilari Raguer, "An Initial Profile of the Assembly," in *History of Vatican II: The Formation of the Council's Identity, First Period and Intersession, October 1962 – September 1963*, ed. Giuseppe Alberigo and Joseph Komonchak (Maryknoll, NY: Orbis Books, 1997), 201.

9   Ibid.

a French-born priest and former seminary professor, had issued a challenge to the Council in the form of an appeal from the community he founded, 'The Companions of Jesus the Carpenter of Nazareth'.[10] This text had been made possible by the patronage of Georges Hakim, Archbishop of Akka-Nazareth in Israel.[11] And although it was not an official document of the Council, it was circulated in an *ad hoc* manner among the fathers.[12]

Gauthier's theological reflections begin with Christological issues, and then move to the ecclesiological. Christologically, Gauthier's chief contention is that Jesus identifies himself with the poor and the subsequent Christian tradition continues this identification. One can grasp something of the nature of Gauthier's theology when he writes, "Why did Jesus identify himself with the poor? Perhaps because together with him they carry the burden of this world's sin, because they are more closely associated with the Redemption, both as saved and saviours?"[13] When this Christological claim is held in conjunction with the established theological principle that there is an identity between the reality of Jesus and the Church, an ecclesiological claim emerges: there is at least a partial ontological identity between the Church and the poor.[14] This leads Gauthier to a position whereby he can conclude that

> [t]he division between the Churches is certainly a scandal to unbelievers and a source of dismay for believers, who are aware of the prayer of Christ: "That they may all be one so that the world may believe that thou hast sent me." But the separation between the Churches on the one hand and the poor peoples of the world on the other is a much graver scandal and a source of still keener sorrow.[15]

And further, he writes, "The fact that there is a chasm between the hierarchical Church and poor people is a scandal every bit as great as

10   The book had the French title *Les pauvres, Jésus et l'Église*. The English version is referred to in this chapter, Gauthier, *Christ, the Church, and the Poor*. Part II of the English text, "Christ, the Church and the Poor," contains the material which was circulated to the Council Fathers.

11   Ruggieri, "Beyond an Ecclesiology of Polemics: The Debate on the Church," 345.

12   Raguer, "An Initial Profile of the Assembly," 201.

13   Gauthier, *Christ, the Church, and the Poor*, 68.

14   Ibid., 69.

15   Ibid., 58.

the disunity of the Churches, because it too is a schism, a gash in the body of Christ. Jesus is, in fact, indissolubly one both with his Church and with the poor."[16] This is, in essence, the challenge Gauthier and his community issued to the fathers of the Council. They asked, how is the Council going to acknowledge more fully the identity of the Church, the poor, and Christ?

Although the Group of the Church of the Poor appears to have been in some sense spiritually rooted in Gauthier's experience as a worker-priest in France and Nazareth, it was a diverse association whose membership numbered almost fifty during the third session of the Council.[17] Lercaro himself was not significantly involved in the

16 Ibid., 61.

17 Norman Tanner, "The Church in the World (Ecclesia ad Extra)," in *History of Vatican II: Church as Communion, Third Period and Intersession, September 1964 – September 1965*, ed. Giuseppe Alberigo and Joseph Komonchak (Maryknoll, NY: Orbis Books, 2003), 382. More fully, Desmond O'Grady notes "The following had participated in the Group's meetings: Patriarch Maximos IV, Cardinals Lercaro and Gerlier, Monsignors Hakim (Galilee, Israel), Himmer (Tournai, Belgium), Ancel (Lyons, France), Angerhausen (Essen, West Germany), Blomjous (Mwanza, Tanzania), Helder Câmara (Rio de Janeiro, Brazil), Coderre (Saint-Jean, Canada), Nguyen-Kim-Diem (Cantho, Vietnam), González Moralejo (Valencia, Spain), Larraín Errázuriz (Talca, Chile), Mercier (Laghouat, Algeria), Riobe (Orléans, France), Yago (Abidjan, Ivory Coast), Austregesilo Meaquita (Afogados da Ingàzeira, Brazil), Văn Bình (Saigon, Vietnam), Boillon (Verdun, France), Botero Salazar (Medellín, Columbia), Bejot (Rheims, France), de la Brousse (Dijon, France), Bueno Couto (Taubaté, Brazil), Charbonneau (Ottawa, Canada), Cuniberti (Florenica, Columbia), Darmancier (Wallis and Futuna Islands, Oceania), Devoto (Goya, Argentinia), Dupont (Lille, France), Fauvel (Quimper, France), Fragoso (Sao Luis de Maranhao, Brazil), Franić (Split-Makarska, Yugoslavia), Golland Trinidade (Botucatú, Brazil), Gouvêa Coelho (Olinda and Recife, Brazil), Guyot (Coutances, France), Hirata (Oita, Japan), Huyghe (Arras, France), Hypolito (Salvador, Brazil), Iriarte (Reconquista, Argentina), Leuliet (Amiens, France), Loosdregt (Vientiane, Laos), Marcos da Oliveira (San André, Brazil), Thangalathill (Trivandrum, India), Martin (New Caledonia, Oceania), Marty (Rheims, France), Maury (Dakar, Senegal), Maziers (Lyons, France), Mazerat (Angers, France), Motta e Albuquerque (Vitoria, Brazil), Muñoz Duque (Nueva Pamplona, Columbia), Monte Nivaldo (Arseufra, Brazil), Nuer (Luxor, Egypt), Puech (Carcassonne, France), Renard (Versailles, France), Sales (Natal, Brazil), Santos Ascarza (Valdivia, Chile), Valencia (Buenoventura, Columbia),

Group of the Church of the Poor and he attended only one session of its meetings. However, he was treated by Paul VI as a point of liaison with the group.[18] Committed members of the group—those who, along with Gauthier, can perhaps be considered its nucleus—included: Helder Pessôa Câmara, Auxiliary Bishop of Rio de Janeiro, Brazil; Georges Mercier, Bishop of Laghouat in Algeria, who with Câmara would be one of the Group of the Church of the Poor's spokesmen; Charles-Marie Himmer, Bishop of Tournai in Belgium; Pierre Cardinal Gerlier, the Archbishop of Lyons, France; and, Monsignor Alfred-Jean-Félix Ancel, Gerlier's auxiliary.[19]

2.2 THE GROUP OF THE CHURCH OF THE POOR: AIMS AND ACTIVITIES

The first formal meeting of the core of the Group of the Church of the Poor was on October 26, 1962. Cardinal Gerlier presided and it is worth quoting him at length

> The duty of the Church in our age is to adapt itself in the most responsive way to the situation created by the suffering of so many

Távora (Aracajú, Brazil), Toussaint (Idiofa, Congo), van Melckebeke (Singapore, Malaysia), Vieira (Salvador, Brazil), Viola (Salto, Uruguay), Zambrano Camader (Facatativá, Colombia), Zazpe (Rafaela, Argentina); in addition, Canon Diot, secretary of Cardinal Feltin, Archbishop of Paris; Don Dossetti, on behalf of Cardinal Lercaro; Father Dournes on behalf of Monsignor Seitz, Bishop of Kontum, Vietnam; Monsignor Duarte, secretary of the Bishop of Aracajú, Brazil; Father le Guillon on behalf of Bishop Rouge of Nîmes, France; Monsignor Bonnet of the Mission Ouvrière, Paris; Father Congar of Strasbourg and Father Dupuy of Le Saulchoir; Father Diez Allegria and Father Mollat, both of the Gregorian University, Rome; Monsignor Glorieux, secretary of the Concilia Commission on the lay apostolate; Monsignor Rodhain, secretary of the Secours Catholique; Father Deschamps, Mission de France, Pontigny; Father Laurentin of the Catholic faculty, Angers; Father Jullien of the Quimper seminary; Father Pecriaux of Rome; Father Tillardo from Brazil; Father Timko Imre from Budapest; and Father Villain of Paris." Desmond O'Grady, *Eat from God's Hand: Paul Gauthier and the Church of the Poor* (London: Geoffrey Chapman, 1965), 138-39. It is apparent from this list that Francophone and Latin American participants dominated the make up of the Group of the Church of the Poor.

18   Tanner, "The Church in the World (Ecclesia ad Extra)," 382.

19   John McCormack, "The Church of the Poor," *The Furrow* 17:4 (1966): 215.

human beings and by the mistaken idea, fostered by certain appear-
ances suggesting that these human beings are not a primary concern
for the Church. ... If I am not mistaken, it seems that no room was
allowed for this, at least directly, in the program of the Council.
Now, the effectiveness of our work is bound up with this problem.
If we do not tackle it, we leave aside some of the most relevant aspects of evangelical and human reality. The question must be raised.
We must insist with the authorities that it be raised. Everything
else is in danger of remaining ineffective if this problem is not studied and dealt with. It is indispensable that the Church, which has
no desire to be rich, be freed from the appearance of wealth. The
Church must be seen for what it is: the Mother of the Poor, whose
first concern is to give her children bread for both body and soul,
as John XXIII himself said on September 11, 1962: "The Church
is and wishes to be the Church of all, and particularly the Church
of the poor."[20]

In preparation for this meeting Cardinal Mercier had composed a
note in which he identified three main problems on the issue of "The
Church of the Poor": (1) the development of the poor countries; (2)
the evangelization of the poor and workers; and, (3) giving the Church
once again its poor 'face'.[21] As a means of meeting the needs these problems raise, Mercier advocated: (a) establishing the teaching on the social presence of Jesus to humanity; (b) encouraging poverty within
the Church; and, (c) enlightening public opinion and holding a world
congress akin to a hybrid of a Eucharistic congress and the Bandung
international development conference.[22] The problems Mercier identified were non-trivial; the proposed means of rectifying them were
theoretically and politically complex. It is perhaps then understandable that in the face of these difficulties the Group of the Church of
the Poor sought the creation of a secretariat or special commission to
facilitate their resolution. The Group of the Church of the Poor presented a petition to Ameleto Giovanni Cardinal Cicognani, Secretary
of State and President of the Secretariat for Extraordinary Affairs,
suggesting the creation of a secretariat or special commission to address four key topics: (1) the exercise of personal and social justice,
especially towards developing peoples; (2) the peace and unity of the

---

20   Raguer, "An Initial Profile of the Assembly," 202.
21   Ibid.
22   Ibid.

human family; (3) the evangelization of the poor and alienated; and, (4) a call for an evangelical renewal of pastors and faithful especially by means of poverty.[23] Unfortunately, the Group of the Church of the Poor failed in its attempt to have such a special commission or a secretariat created. But a commission was created to develop a schema on the Church's presence in the world, Schema XVII (later called Schema XIII), that would become *Gaudium et spes*.[24] Furthermore, even though it lacked official apparatus, the Group of the Church of the Poor continued to work between the first and second session ensuring that the themes of poverty and service were related to the whole range of Council topics.[25]

> During the second session, the Group of the Church of the Poor's activities continued at an accelerated rate. They met six times at the end of 1963, namely, on October 18 and 25; November 8, 15, 22, and 29. It was decided that the ideas of the Group of the Church of the Poor needed to be more thoroughly grounded in doctrine, and to achieve this end, three study groups were set up: 'dogma', 'pastoral', and as a foretaste of the coming direction of social teaching, 'sociology'.[26] Lectures were given to all interested bishops, and texts and ideas were inserted into the various schemata being developed.[27] As an example of the tenor of the Group of the Church of the Poor's activities, in his intervention at the general congregation of the Council on October 25, 1963, Bishop Pierre Boillon of Verdun, France, claimed,

> The Church ... is a stranger to the poor. Marxism has captured the attention of the poor because it speaks to them of their dignity as men. Why is the Church not heard? Because the exterior signs of wealth deceive the poor. ... Let the Council declare ... that the poor have a divine right to first place in the Church. Let the Church be

---

23   Ibid., 203.

24   O'Grady, *Eat from God's Hand: Paul Gauthier and the Church of the Poor*, 128.

25   Ibid., 129.

26   Joseph Famerée, "Bishops and Dioceses and the Communications Media (November 5 – 25, 1963)," in *History of Vatican II: The Mature Council, Second Period Intersession, September 1963 – September 1964*, ed. Giuseppe Alberigo and Joseph Komonchak (Maryknoll, NY: Orbis Books, 2000), 164-65.

27   Ibid., 165.

poor and appear poor. Vatican II cannot be silent on this question. The rich will not enter the Kingdom of Heaven.[28]

In this way, work behind the scenes and, wherever possible, on the floor at the Council continued throughout the second session. As it came to a close, the Group of the Church of the Poor sent another petition to the pope expressing concern that Schema XVII had not been discussed. They sought to have its examination brought to the beginning of the next session.[29] Mercier, moreover, pressed forward in the petition with his idea that the Eucharistic congress due to be held in Bombay (November 28, 1964), lest its opulence give the wrong impression, ought to also be a congress on social issues.[30] Pope Paul VI replied to the Group of the Church of the Poor through Lercaro: the pope wanted the Council to conclude its considerations of the Church *ad intra* before it addressed the issue of the Church *ad extra*. Paul VI assured the Group of the Church of the Poor that the schema would be discussed during the third session, and a special commission—including specialized laity—would work on the schema during the intersession.[31]

The third session saw a reduced role for the Group of the Church of the Poor and even fragmentation within the group. At the outset of the third session, Ancel and Mercier, both leading members of the group, circulated programs to the Group. Mercier's was titled, "On the Eve of the Third Session"; Ancel's was simply, "Church of the Poor". Whereas Mercier developed a pastoral program and urged symbolic gestures and a living of the mystery of poverty, Ancel was not only practical but also theoretical. He opposed any gestures that did not result in long-term change and was interested in converting the whole Church to poverty. For Ancel, the task required serious academic theological work.[32] One can add to this tension the fact that Lercaro—arguably

---

28   Henri Fesquet, *The Drama of Vatican II: The Ecumenical Council June, 1962 – December, 1965*, trans. Bernard Murchland (New York: Random House, 1967), 193.

29   Famerée, "Bishops and Dioceses and the Communications Media (November 5 – 25, 1963)," 165.

30   Ibid.

31   O'Grady, *Eat from God's Hand: Paul Gauthier and the Church of the Poor*, 140.

32   Tanner, "The Church in the World (Ecclesia ad Extra)," 382. Denis Pelletier, "Une marginalité engagée: le groupe Jésus, l'Église et les Pauvres,"

not a member of the Group of the Church of the Poor, but closely related to it—preferred mystical theology and an evangelical Church of the Poor. Moreover, Lercaro seemed to have no real clarity on the issue of the nature of poverty such that he considered poverty as a virtue and poverty as a path to God in the same breath as poverty as an abomination.[33] Varied viewpoints and a confusion of ideas were operative both within the Group itself and in Lercaro's reading of its activities.

Nonetheless, the Group of the Church of the Poor composed a document addressed to the pope that contained two distinct motions: "Simplicity and Evangelical Poverty" and "Primacy in Our Ministry for the Evangelization of the Poor." The first motion dealt with embracing evangelical poverty such as the eschewing of solemn titles and the adoption of pastoral ones. The second suggested a priority in the apostolate so that those furthest from the Church, often in the Third World, would be reached.[34] Along the same lines, the second motion argued for a renewal of the worker-priest movement.[35] The Group of the Church of the Poor collected over 500 signatures in support of these two motions.[36]

Despite the Group of the Church of the Poor's achievement of submitting the two motions and petition to the pope, it was Lercaro's report on poverty that Paul VI wanted to see.[37] Moreover, Paul VI asked

in *Les Commissions Conciliaires à Vatican II*, ed. M. Lamberigts, C. Soetens, and J. Grootaers (Leuven: Peeters, 1996), 63-89.

33   Ian Linden, *Global Catholicism: Diversity and Change Since Vatican II* (New York, NY: Columbia University Press, 2009), 94.

34   Tanner, "The Church in the World (Ecclesia ad Extra)," 383.

35   The Group of the Church of the Poor seems to have succeeded in this aim, if numbers alone are indicative. At the height of the worker-priest controversy in the 1950s, there were no more than 100 such priests. In 1979, there were at least 950 worker-priests in France. See Viet Straßner, "Die Arbeiterpriester: Geschichte und Entwicklungstendenzen einer in Vergessenheit geratenen Bewegung" http://www.con-spiration.de/her-wartz/texte/arge.html (accessed 30-March 2010).

36   Tanner, "The Church in the World (Ecclesia ad Extra)," 384.

37   To what extent the Group of the Church of the Poor's activities had an impact upon Paul VI's thinking is debatable. Arguably, it had some: he declared to the media—as he departed for the Holy Land on 4 January, 1964—that he was taking the concerns of the sick, refugees and the oppressed back to the 'source'. These comments had been preceded by Paul

Lercaro to review the material produced by the Group of the Church of the Poor. An overcommitted Lercaro had to be reminded twice by the pope to produce the report. When he managed to complete the task, it seemed that he had either ignored or disregarded most of the Group of the Church of the Poor's own preparatory piece, "*La pauvreté dans l'Eglise et dans le monde*". Lercaro's report was comprised of a preface and two subsequent parts. The preface acknowledged the lack of preparation among Catholics to deal with the issue of poverty. The first part argued that an opulent society increases socio-economic stratification and decreases the sense of the sacred and results in an outcome worse than Marxism. Lercaro called for an increase in the practice of evangelical poverty, and a deepening of the theological understanding of poverty in both its biblical and Christological dimensions. The second part argued for practical reforms in the Church. Evangelical poverty was to be practiced with respect to titles, dress, and style of life. Worker-priests or clergy were to be selected specifically for work among the poor. Fasting and abstinence were to be replaced by offerings for the poor and needy. And Lercaro suggested a greater openness and lay involvement in the management of Church property.[38] Tragically, though perhaps indicative of the Church's lack of preparedness to deal with the issues involved, the report on poverty was received by the Secretary of State, Cicognani, and then forwarded to Eugène Cardinal Tisserant in his role as the President of the Commission for the Review of the Dress and Ornaments of Prelates. The report then "disappeared into the sands of time."[39] This was the end of the official treatment of poverty as a distinct issue at the Council.

VI's laying the papal tiara on the altar of St Peter's Basilica at the close of the second session of the Council, a tiara that has never since been worn by a pope. Whilst he was in no way oblivious to the Group of the Church of the Poor's concerns, only limited headway in bringing about their aims was made with Paul VI. See Linden, *Global Catholicism: Diversity and Change Since Vatican II*, 95.

38 Tanner, "The Church in the World (Ecclesia ad Extra)," 385.
39 Ibid.

2.3 THE GROUP OF THE CHURCH OF THE POOR: ACHIEVEMENTS AND SHORTCOMINGS

The question arises—given the treatment of Lercaro's report on poverty, and indeed Lercaro's treatment of the Group of the Church of the Poor's report on poverty—as to what effect the Group of the Church of the Poor had on the outcomes of Vatican II. There is evidence of the impact of the Group on the final documents of the Council, and when one looks at them one can see the issue of poverty addressed—largely Christologically or in terms of mission—in: *Lumen gentium* §§8,[40] 23; *Gravissium educatinus* §9; *Apostolicam actuositatem* §8; *Gaudium et spes* §§1, 15, 63, 69, 71, 81, 86, 88, 90; *Christus dominus* §§13, 30; *Presbyterorum ordinis* §6; *Optatam totius* §§8, 9; *Ad gentes* §12; and, *Perfectae caritatis* §13. Indeed, *Lumen gentium* reveals several themes pertinent to the work of the Group of the Church of the Poor. It reads,

> Differences crop up too between races and between various kinds of social orders; between wealthy nations and those which are less influential or are needy; finally, between international institutions born of the popular desire for peace, and the ambition to propagate one's own ideology, as well as collective greeds existing in nations or other groups. ... What results is mutual distrust, enmities, conflicts and hardships. Of such is man at once the cause and the victim (§8).

> There are, indeed, close links between earthly things and those elements of man's condition which transcend the world. The Church herself makes use of temporal things insofar as her own mission requires it. She, for her part, does not place her trust in the privileges offered by civil authority. She will even give up the exercise of certain rights which have been legitimately acquired, if it becomes clear that their use will cast doubt on the sincerity of her witness or that new ways of life demand new methods (§76).

> The Council, considering the immensity of the hardships which still afflict the greater part of mankind today, regards it as most opportune that an organism of the universal Church be set up in order that both the justice and love of Christ toward the poor might be

---

40   Alberigo identifies *Lumen gentium*, §8, as the section in which the Group of the Church of the Poor makes its clearest mark on the final documents. Giuseppe Alberigo, "Major Results, Shadows of Uncertainty," in *History of Vatican II: Church as Communion, Third Period and Intersession, September 1964 – September 1965*, ed. Giuseppe Alberigo and Joseph Komonchak (Maryknoll, NY: Orbis Books, 2003), 620.

developed everywhere. The role of such an organism would be to stimulate the Catholic community to promote progress in needy regions and international social justice (§90).

The dual concerns of poverty and development are clearly present, as is a motivation to break—or at least permit a break—with the way things have been. In noting that the Church ought to be willing to set itself against the State if circumstance required that it do so, the hitherto accepted relationship of prestige the Church sought with the State became forfeitable. *Gaudium et spes* made explicit the link between the social mission of the Church and ecclesiology (§§63–72). It also suggested that the expectation of a new earth should spur us on to develop creation, that is, it argued that building upon what the earth has given us in a co-creative manner is not demeaning the significance of the coming Reign, but contributing to it (§39).[41]

Nonetheless, although the final documents made some attempt to engage with the issue of poverty, there is as Donal Dorr notes, lack of cohesion and synthetic wholeness to these presentations.[42] Dorr further notes that whilst Vatican II spoke of being for the poor, it had not yet discovered what it meant to be with the poor.[43] Not surprisingly, most authoritative assessments note that "Vatican II did not deal in any depth with the issue [of poverty]."[44] And in that regard, the Group of the Church of the Poor's successes at the Council must be considered as limited: it kept the theme of poverty in the minds of the fathers but its own position was unclear, and this lack of clarity was manifested in the final documents. Not that the fault was the Group of the Church of the Poor's own, or, at least, not entirely its own. The *ad intra* concerns of the Church had dominated to such an extent that "there was time to discuss indulgences in the Aula, but no time to inform

---

41   David Hollenbach, "Gaudium et spes," in *Modern Catholic Social Teaching: Commentaries & Interpretations*, ed. Kenneth Himes (Washington, D.C.: Georgetown University Press, 2005), 273-79.

42   Donal Dorr, *Option for the Poor: A Hundred Years of Catholic Social Teaching* (Blackburn, Vic.: CollinsDove, 1992), 390-91n.29.

43   Ibid., 170-76.

44   See *The New Dictionary of Catholic Social Thought*, s.v. "Poverty." Gutiérrez echoes these sentiments. See Gutiérrez, *A Theology of Liberation: History, Politics, and Salvation*, 162.

bishops about the problems of underdeveloped nations."[45] For some, this would make a certain sense: until the Church knows what exactly it is *ad intra*, its relationship with the world *ad extra* cannot be precisely determined. To the Group of the Church of the Poor, however, the logic is flawed. The Poor enter the discussion at the level of *ad intra* considerations. Gutiérrez goes further in that he does not rule out a bias against the Third World. He writes,

> It is not difficult to understand why the theme of the Church of the poor was largely neglected in Vatican II, despite the efforts of many bishops and other persons during the Council. ... [I]n the process of Vatican II, the issue of poverty attained only a tiny presence. ... It is easy to understand (painful but easy): the majority of bishops and experts came from important countries, rich countries that had entered the modern world; they were citizens of the modern world. Poverty, in spite of the empathy and profundity of many who attended the Council, remained a distant question.[46]

Evidently, the Group of the Church of the Poor had struggled valiantly against not only its own, but also the Council's limitations. It had sown seeds and perhaps this was enough; they were to sprout after the Council.

As a parting contribution to its enrichment of the theological landscape—and not least because of the limited treatment of poverty in the final Council documents—the Group of the Church of the Poor released a final document on the issue of poverty. It was titled Schema 14. It was much clearer than many of its previous reflections. It reads, in part:

> *We will give whatever is needed* in terms of our time, our reflection, our heart, our means, etc., to the apostolic and pastoral service of workers and labour groups and *to those who are economically weak and disadvantaged, without allowing that to detract from the welfare of other persons or groups of the diocese*. We will support lay people, religious, deacons, and priests whom the Lord calls to evangelize the poor and the workers by sharing their lives and their labors. See

---

45   Fesquet, *The Drama of Vatican II: The Ecumenical Council June, 1962 – December, 1965*, 780-81.

46   Gustavo Gutiérrez, "Church of the Poor," in *Born of the Poor: The Latin American Church Since Medellín*, ed. Edward Cleary (Notre Dame, IN: University of Notre Dame Press, 1990), 12-13.

Luke 4,18-19; Mark 6,4; Matthew 11,4-5; Acts 18,3-4; 20,33-35; 1 Corinthians 4,12; 9,1-27.

Conscious of the requirements of justice and charity and of their mutual relatedness, *we will seek to transform our works of welfare into social works based on charity and justice,* so that they take all persons into account, as a humble service to the responsible public agencies. See Matthew 25,31-46; Luke 13,12-14; 13,33-34.

We will do everything possible so that those responsible for our governments and our public services establish and enforce the laws, social structures, and institutions that are necessary for justice, equality, and the *integral, harmonious development of the whole person and of all persons, and thus for the advent of a new social order, worthy of the children of God.* See Acts 2,44-45; 4;32-35; 5,4; 2 Corinthians 8 and 9; 1 Timothy 5,16.[47]

Henri Fesquet reports that this document was considered by many as one of the "precious fruits of Vatican II."[48] Clodovis Boff and George Pixley suggest that Schema 14 is one of the strongest links between Vatican II and the CELAM conferences of Medellín and Puebla.[49] Coupled with Schema 14, one can note that, despite a lack of clarity on the issue of poverty in the official documents of Vatican II, *Lumen gentium* acted, in a way, as enabling legislation for trends that had already begun in the Latin American Church.[50] The next section addresses those trends, and the gradual unpacking and clarification of the ideas present but underdeveloped in the documents of Vatican II.

---

47   The emphases are added by the present author. The document, Schema 14, is reproduced in full by Jon Sobrino, "The Urgent Need to Return to Being the Church of the Poor" http://ncronline.org/news/justice/urgent-need-return-being-church-poor (accessed 4 September 2012). See also, Fesquet, *The Drama of Vatican II: The Ecumenical Council June, 1962 – December, 1965,* 800. The document is reproduced in the Appendix.

48   Fesquet, *The Drama of Vatican II: The Ecumenical Council June, 1962 – December, 1965,* 799.

49   George V. Pixley and Clodovis Boff, *The Bible, the Church and the Poor,* trans. Paul Burns (Maryknoll, NY: Orbis Books, 1989), xvi. Twomey also draws attention to this link. See Gerald S. Twomey, *The 'Preferential Option for the Poor' in Catholic Social Thought from John XXIII to John Paul II* (Queenstown, ON: The Edwin Mellen Press, 2005), 98.

50   Linden, *Global Catholicism: Diversity and Change Since Vatican II,* 97.

3. THE EGRESSION OF THE DOCTRINE OF THE PREFERENTIAL OPTION FOR THE POOR: POST-CONCILIAR DEVELOPMENTS

Ian Linden observes that, despite the best efforts of the Group of the Church of the Poor and Cardinal Lercaro, the Church of the Poor was to be championed in the city slums and impoverished villages of Latin America rather than at the Vatican.[51] This is perhaps ironic considering that the Latin American bishops represented 22% of the total number of bishops at Vatican II—and were shepherds to 40% of the world's Catholics—but were so unvocal that they were dubbed by the media as leaders of a "Church of silence."[52] Whilst not vocal at the Council in a manner proportionate to their significance, after returning home the Latin Americans adopted the Church of the Poor as a key theological motif. This section of the chapter focuses largely on this Latin American development of the Church of the Poor theme and its transformation into the doctrine of the Preferential Option for the Poor. There are two parts to this presentation: (a) the first section considers the period from *Populorum progressio* until the conclusion of CELAM II at Medellín; and, (b) the second section considers the cautious affirmation of Medellín by the Church hierarchy and the conclusions of CELAM III at Puebla including the first use of the phrase 'Preferential Option for the Poor'.

3.1 FROM *POPULORUM PROGRESSIO* TO CELAM II AT MEDELLÍN

In *Populorum progressio* Paul VI's key focus is on development and it therefore contains a number of reflections on poverty. The pope was aware of the dated nature of official social teaching and he sought, with *Populorum progressio*, to bring that teaching up to date. The document, like much of Paul's thought, is commonly regarded as being well ahead of its time. It opens,

> The progressive development of peoples is an object of deep interest and concern to the Church. This is particularly true in the case of those peoples who are trying to escape the ravages of hunger, poverty, endemic disease and ignorance; of those who are seeking a larger

51   Ibid., 88.

52   Twomey, *The 'Preferential Option for the Poor' in Catholic Social Thought from John XXIII to John Paul II*, 109.

share in the benefits of civilization and a more active improvement of their human qualities; of those who are consciously striving for fuller growth (§1).[53]

The document contained no naïve defence of the status quo. He wrote, "Knowing, as we all do, that development means peace these days, what man would not want to work for it with every ounce of his strength?" (§87). In his use of the term, 'development', Paul VI clearly intended the development of the whole human being and the development of all human beings (§14). Both liberal capitalism and Marxism were subjected to vigorous critiques (§§26, 39). And there was a sense in the document that the conflict between North and South was of greater significance than the conflict between East and West. The growing distortion between the industrialized and non-industrialized world required a global solidarity in order to heal the disparity (§§17, 49, 64, 65). Again, as at Vatican II, development was the guiding idea on social matters. But here it was considerably more sophisticated.[54]

The document made significant advances over previous official social teaching. For example, Paul employed an heuristic account of the human good rather than one that was content specific. He also coupled personal sin and personal responsibility with a sense of social sin and an acknowledgement of the moral relevance of social structures (§81). He attempted to shift away from paternalistic approaches to development by noting that it is something people do for themselves, not something imposed from outside (§65). There is realism present in the approach, despite a tendency to optimism.[55] And although he is focused on peace, it is not peace at all costs:

> Everyone knows, however, that revolutionary uprisings—except where there is manifest, longstanding tyranny which would do great damage to fundamental personal rights and dangerous harm to the common good of the country—engender new injustices, introduce new inequities and bring new disasters. The evil situation that exists, and it surely is evil, may not be dealt with in such a way that an even worse situation results (§31).

---

53   Pope Paul VI, "Populorum progressio" http://www.vatican.va/holy_father/paul_vi/encyclicals/documents/hf_p-vi_enc_26031967_populorum_en.html (accessed 3 September 2012).

54   Dorr, *Option for the Poor: A Hundred Years of Catholic Social Teaching*, 179-85.

55   Ibid., 203.

For Paul VI, justice is of such importance that it is a higher good, in a limited number of situations, than social stability.[56] Given this acute focus on justice, the *Wall Street Journal*—ignoring Paul VI's criticism of Marxist thought—considered the capitalist system under attack and the pope was accused of serving "warmed-over Marxism."[57] But most commentators observed, on the whole, the approach to poverty was more advanced than anything developed at Vatican II. Gutiérrez has noted it was the theme of "integral development" in *Populorum progressio* (§21)—a theme also present in the Group of the Church of the Poor's Schema 14—that opened a door to Liberation Theology and the work of CELAM at Medellín.[58]

In Latin America by 1968 the United Nations' Decade of Development was drawing to a close. In reality, it had been a decade of oppression, and Pablo Richard notes that in contradistinction to the European situation, the key theological issue in Latin America in the 1960s was not the death of God but the death of people.[59] It is within such a context that CELAM met at Medellín. It is not surprising that, given the widespread impoverishment in Latin America, the final documents of Medellín were to make central what the documents of Vatican II—which had closed only three years prior—addressed in an *ad hoc* and peripheral manner. Poverty was the central theme of the meeting. By adopting this theme, the bishops of CELAM did not see themselves as doing anything other than applying the insights of Vatican II to the Latin American milieu. The final documents are published in English by CELAM as *The Church in the Present-Day Transformation of Latin America in the Light of the Council*.[60]

56   This caveat is all the more remarkable when one considers that Paul VI was steadfastly against conflict and always seemed to hold out hope that a peaceful consensus would ultimately prevail.

57   Allan Figueroa Deck, "Commentary on *Populorum progressio* (*On the Development of Peoples*)," in *Modern Catholic Social Teaching: Commentaries & Interpretations*, ed. Kenneth Himes (Washington, D.C.: Georgetown University Press, 2004), 308.

58   Gutiérrez, *The Truth Shall Make You Free: Confrontations*, 119-20.

59   Pablo Richard, *Death of Christendoms, Birth of the Church* (Maryknoll, NY: Orbis Books, 1987), 5. As cited in Twomey, *The 'Preferential Option for the Poor' in Catholic Social Thought from John XXIII to John Paul II*, 132.

60   Latin American Episcopal Conference, *The Church in the Present-Day Transformation of Latin America in the Light of the Council: Position Papers* (Bogatá: General Secretariat of CELAM, 1973). Latin American

The Magisterium initially feared that Medellín, with its focus on concrete living conditions on the continent and its adoption of a Jocist (Young Christian Workers) inspired 'see—judge—act' methodology, would undermine the traditionally understood mission and structure of the Church. Specifically, as Linden records, Paul VI warned of the dangers of subversive criticism arising from historicism.[61] But these concerns proved to be unfounded. Although Base Ecclesial Communities and historically attuned theology garnered an official seal of approval at Medellín, CELAM was not seeking to jettison Church tradition but simply to arrive at an integral vision of the Church's role in Latin America that did not segregate from each other the social and spiritual missions of the Church. This is clear in the *Introduction to the Final Documents*, when the bishops declare their "eager desire to integrate the scale of temporal values in a global vision of Christian faith" which links to the "original vocation" of Latin America: "A vocation to create a new and ingenious synthesis of the old and the new, the spiritual and the temporal."[62]

In keeping with their holistic vision, the bishops supported grassroots efforts among the people of the continent to achieve and maintain human rights,[63] not on the basis of social ethics, but because such concrete conditions are "intimately linked to the history of salvation."[64] Regarding these concrete conditions, the bishops wrote that the "aspirations and clamours of Latin America are signs that reveal the direction of the divine plan."[65] As such, these aspirations could not simply be passed over but were 'signs of the times' which had to be scrutinized for their theological significance. The bishops steadfastly argued against any position that separates the temporal and the spiritual from one another when they asserted, "In the search for salvation we must avoid the dualism which separates temporal tasks from the work of

---

Episcopal Conference, *The Church in the Present-Day Transformation of Latin America in the Light of the Council: Conclusions* (Bogatá: General Secretariat of CELAM, 1973).

61   Linden, *Global Catholicism: Diversity and Change Since Vatican II*, 114.

62   Latin American Episcopal Conference, *The Church in the Present-Day Transformation of Latin America in the Light of the Council: Conclusions*, 36-37.

63   Ibid., 64.

64   Ibid., 25.

65   Ibid.

sanctification."[66] They employed a unified vision of the human good
in which religious ends are not set against natural ends but rather are
intimately related. They were thus able to argue that, in the economy
of salvation, "The divine work is an action of integral human development and liberation which has love as its sole motive."[67] Rooted in
the transformation engendered by faith and baptism, such love com-
pels the Christian to a more profound relationship with God, fellow
humans, and the whole of creation.[68] In support of its approach to
reconciling the social and religious mission of the Church, CELAM
cited *Gaudium et spes*, "We do not confuse temporal progress and the
Kingdom of Christ; nevertheless, the former, 'to the extent that it can
contribute to the better ordering of human society, is of vital concern
to the Kingdom of God.'"[69] Within the purview of the Kingdom—as
at Medellín—the poor hold a special place.

Not only did poverty guide the bishops' reflections at Medellín,
it was studied in a more systematic manner than it had been by the
Group of the Church of the Poor or elsewhere at Vatican II. One of
the sixteen final documents was titled "Poverty of the Church."[70] This
document distinguishes and interrelates three kinds of poverty—material poverty, spiritual poverty, and poverty as a commitment.[71] In anticipation of directions and terminology to come, the document states
that the Church must henceforth adopt a pastoral orientation in order
to "bring us to a distribution of resources and apostolic personnel that
effectively gives preference to the poorest and most needy sectors and
to those segregated for any cause whatsoever, animating and acceler-

66   Ibid., 43.

67   Ibid., 42.

68   Ibid.

69   Ibid. The quotation from *Gaudium et spes* can be found at §39.

70   The final documents were divided up into three sections. In the section on
      'Human Promotion', there were five documents: Justice, Peace, Family and
      Demography, Education, and Youth. In the second section, 'Evangelization
      and Growth in the Faith', there were four documents: Pastoral Care of
      the Masses, Pastoral Concern for the Elites, Catechesis, and Liturgy. In
      the final section, 'The Visible Church and its Structures', there were seven
      documents: Lay Movements, Priests, Religious, Formation of the Clergy,
      Poverty of the Church, Joint Pastoral Planning, and Mass Media.

71   Latin American Episcopal Conference, *The Church in the Present-Day
      Transformation of Latin America in the Light of the Council: Conclusions*,
      189-90.

ating the initiatives and studies that are already being made with that goal in mind."[72] The document facilitated these actions of solidarity with the poor by opening the door to a dialectical social hermeneutic: solidarity "has to be concretized in criticism of injustice and oppression, in the struggle against the intolerable situation which a poor person often has to tolerate."[73] However, this was no reductionist or secularized understanding of solidarity as the "Document on Justice" makes clear. At the root of all considerations is the conversion of the Christian:

> Thus, for our authentic liberation, all of us need a profound conversion so that 'the Kingdom of justice, love and peace,' might come to us. The origin of all disdain for humankind, of all injustice, should be sought in the internal imbalance of human liberty, which will always need to be rectified in history. The uniqueness of the Christian message does not so much consist in the affirmation of the necessity for structural change, as it does in an insistence on the conversion of men and women which will in turn bring about this change. We will not have a new continent without new and reformed structures, but, above all, there will be no new continent without new people, who know how to be truly free and responsible according to the light of the Gospel.[74]

The "Document on Peace" and the "Document on the Poverty of the Church" also highlight the relevance of conversion to grounding all action for justice in defence of the oppressed.[75] It is not a simplification to argue that at the root of liberation, for Medellín, is conversion. It is not simply a matter of structural change, though this is essential to the process and it flows from conversion. New people, it argued, will bring about a new society more in keeping with the values of the Reign of God.

Despite opposition from the upper classes and accusations of Marxism, the Latin American Church reinvented itself at Medellín. Immersion in the world—use of the 'see—judge—act' contextual approach to theology—dominated the new methodology espoused by the bishops.[76] They stated, "We believe that we are in a new histor-

---

72   Ibid., 189-92.
73   Ibid., 192.
74   Ibid., 41.
75   Ibid., 59, 194.
76   *The New Dictionary of Catholic Social Thought,* s.v. "Medellín."

ical era. This era requires clarity in order to see, lucidity in order to diagnose, and solidarity in order to act."[77] Alongside a new methodology, new terminology was introduced at Medellín: 'structural injustice,'[78] 'liberation,'[79] 'participation,'[80] 'conscientization,'[81] 'institutional violence,'[82] and, 'preference for the poor.'[83] These developments indicated that for the first time, after being allied for five centuries with the ruling classes, the Church in Latin America renounced all privilege and declared its solidarity with the poor over and above all else. The Church now called Christians on the continent to see with newly converted eyes, to judge from the perspective of the poor, and to act in solidarity with the poor to rectify distortions in history. Much remained to be nuanced and clarified, but a leap forward had indeed been made.

3.2 THE TENTATIVE AFFIRMATION OF MEDELLÍN, AND CELAM III AT PUEBLA

The conclusions of Medellín became questions addressed to the broader Christian community. What was the Universal Church going to make of them? In a world then dominated by the East-West conflict, was the spectre of Marxism going to prove Medellín's undoing? There was not a long wait to find out. The year 1971 saw the publication of two significant works, Paul VI's *Octogesima adveniens* and the Synod of Bishops' document *Justitia in mundo*. When Paul VI wrote *Octogesima adveniens*, he again condemned Marxism but acknowledged that Marxist social analysis could be useful to Christians.[84] Paul VI also argued that "In teaching us charity, the Gospel instructs us in the preferential respect due to the poor and the special situation they have in society: the more fortunate should renounce some of their rights so as to place their goods more generously at the service

---

77   Latin American Episcopal Conference, *The Church in the Present-Day Transformation of Latin America in the Light of the Council: Conclusions*, 25.

78   Ibid., 41.

79   Ibid., 41, 82-84, 97, 122, 40, 42, 44, 88, 90.

80   Ibid., 43, 44, 45, 46, 47, 48.

81   Ibid., 48, 51, 62.

82   Ibid., 61.

83   Ibid., 191.

84   Christine E. Gudorf, "Octogesima adveniens," in *Modern Catholic Social Teaching: Commentaries & Interpretations*, ed. Kenneth R. Himes (Washington, D.C.: Georgetown University Press, 2005), 325.

of others" (§23).[85] Paul deferred consideration of the mission of the
Church so that the Synod could address the issue: "It will moreover be
for the forthcoming Synod of Bishops itself to study more closely and
to examine in greater detail the Church's mission in the face of grave
issues raised today by the question of justice in the world" (§6).

When it did treat the topic of the Church's mission, the Second
World Synod of Bishops added its collegial weight to the conclu-
sions of Medellín by linking the spiritual and social missions of the
Church.[86] It argued:

> The uncertainty of history and the painful convergences in the as-
> cending path of the human community direct us to sacred history;
> there God has revealed himself to us, and made known to us, as it
> is brought progressively to realization, his plan of liberation and
> salvation which is once and for all fulfilled in the Paschal Mystery of
> Christ. Action on behalf of justice and participation in the transfor-
> mation of the world fully appear to us as a constitutive dimension
> of the preaching of the Gospel, or, in other words, of the Church's
> mission for the redemption of the human race and its liberation
> from every oppressive situation (§6).[87]

In 1975 in *Evangelii nuntiandi* Paul VI cautioned against a reduction
of the Church's mission to the purely temporal (§32). But he then
went on to argue that

> ... the man who is to be evangelized is not an abstract being but is
> subject to social and economic questions. They also include links
> in the theological order, since one cannot dissociate the plan of cre-
> ation from the plan of Redemption. The latter plan touches the very
> concrete situations of injustice to be combated and of justice to be
> restored (§31).[88]

---

85 Pope Paul VI, "Octogesima adveniens" http://www.vatican.va/holy_fa-
ther/paul_vi/apost_letters/documents/hf_p-vi_apl_19710514_octoges-
ima-adveniens_en.html (accessed 4 September 2012).

86 Kenneth R. Himes, "Justitia in mundo," in *Modern Catholic Social
Teaching: Commentaries & Interpretations*, ed. Kenneth R. Himes
(Washington, D.C.: Georgetown University Press, 2005), 355.

87 World Synod of Catholic Bishops, "Justitia in mundo" http://catholic-
socialservices.org.au/Catholic_Social_Teaching/Justitia_in_Mundo (accessed 4 September 2012).

88 Pope   Paul   VI,   "Evangelii   nuntiandi"   http://www.vati-
can.va/holy_father/paul_vi/apost_exhortations/documents/

And

> When preaching liberation and associating herself with those who are working and suffering for it, the Church is certainly not willing to restrict her mission only to the religious field and dissociate herself from man's temporal problems. Nevertheless she reaffirms the primacy of her spiritual vocation and refuses to replace the proclamation of the Kingdom by the proclamation of forms of human liberation—she even states that her contribution to liberation is incomplete if she neglects to proclaim salvation in Jesus Christ (§34).

In both *Justitia in mundo* and *Evangelii nuntiandi*, by linking the social and religious missions of the Church, there is a cautious but clear confirmation of the trajectory of thought initiated by Medellín.

The language used by the Second Synod of World Bishops and by Paul VI is also reminiscent of Medellín. *Justitia in mundo* mentions: "the cry of those who suffer violence and are oppressed by unjust systems and structures" (§5); "conversion of hearts" (§16); "every group or people suffering persecution—sometimes in institutionalized form" (§22); and, "among peoples themselves there is arising a new awareness which shakes them out of any fatalistic resignation and which spurs them on to liberate themselves and to be responsible for their own destiny (§4)." In *Evangelii nuntiandi*, Paul likewise employs such terminology when he writes:

> The Church considers it to be undoubtedly important to build up structures which are more human, more just, more respectful of the rights of the person and less oppressive and less enslaving, but she is conscious that the best structures and the most idealized systems soon become inhuman if the inhuman inclinations of the human heart are not made wholesome, if those who live in these structures or who rule them do not undergo a conversion of heart and of outlook (§36).

And further,

> The Church, as the bishops repeated, has the duty to proclaim the liberation of millions of human beings, many of whom are her own children—the duty of assisting the birth of this liberation, of giving witness to it, of ensuring that it is complete. This is not foreign to evangelization (§30).

---

hf p-vi exh 19751208 evangelii-nuntiandi en.html (accessed 4 September 2012).

The support given to Medellín by the pope and the Second World Synod of Bishops may have been couched with cautious clarifications, but it was undeniably support they gave.

Despite the Second Synod of World Bishops and Paul VI's support of Medellín, its conclusions were not accepted without opposition. The Belgian Jesuit Roger Vekemans—who left Chile in haste after the election of Salvador Allende—and Archbishop Alfonso López Trujillo fought against Medellín from the day its final documents were promulgated. Vekemans had set up a rightwing think-tank, CEDIAL (*Centro de Estudios para el Desarrollo e Integración de América Latina*), and established a periodical *Tierra Nueva* with the financial support of, among other sources, the West German Catholic Episcopal Conference. Vekemans's major concerns regarded the use of Marxist analysis, and *Tierra Nueva* was devoted almost entirely to attacking the theology of liberation. According to José Comblin, everything that appeared in the "Roman documents can already be found in *Tierra Nueva* ten years earlier."[89] Trujillo was fearful that the Base Ecclesial Communities would divide the hierarchical Church from the Church of the Poor, and he used his powerful position—he was elected as General-Secretary of CELAM in 1972 and then became its President in 1979—to conduct his campaign against Medellín. The period between Medellín and Puebla also saw the dismissal of Antonio Cardinal Samoré who had been the Holy See's delegate at CELAM II: Comblin suggests that Samoré was held responsible for the perceived excesses of Medellín.[90] Hélder Câmara, Paulo Arns, Oscar Romero and Raúl Silva were also marginalized.

It appears that those who supported the achievements of Medellín were justifiably anxious at the opening of CELAM III in Puebla; by this time a counter-trend was fully developed. Gustavo Gutiérrez, Juan Luis Segundo, Hugo Assmann, Jon Sobrino, Ignacio Ellacuría, Raúl Vidales, Enrique Dussel, Segundo Galilea, Pablo Richard, and José Comblin were not present at the conference.[91] Not only were they not asked to act as *periti*, they were not engaged to work on the

---

89   José Comblin, "The Church and Defence of Human Rights," in *The Church in Latin America 1492-1992*, ed. Enrique Dussel (Maryknoll, NY: Orbis Books, 1992), 449.

90   Ibid., 441.

91   Robert McAfee Brown, *Gustavo Gutiérrez: An Introduction to Liberation Theology* (Maryknoll, NY: Orbis Books, 1990), 38.

preparatory documents. Conference organizers claimed that any accusation of a pattern of exclusion of progressive theologians and prelates was paranoia. Then a dictated cassette message emerged in which Trujillo called to arms his fellow Brazilian, Bishop Luciano Duarte. Twomey cites an excerpt: "... get your bombers ready, then, and a little of your 'sweet poison,' because we will need you to be in top form both at Puebla and in the CELAM assembly. It is my belief that you ought to undergo training just as boxers do before stepping into the ring."[92] The opponents of Medellín were manifold at Puebla and there was no chance of Puebla making as strident a set of gains as had Medellín. Dorr suggests that one question stood out above all others, would Puebla reaffirm Medellín or kill it with a thousand qualifications?[93]

Perhaps remarkably, given the build-up, the conference was dominated by a floating middle rather than by so-called conservatives or progressives.[94] John Paul II was present and for his part he did not seem to support or denounce Medellín forthrightly in any of his addresses. He did modify phrasing, and terms like 'constitutive' from *Justitia in mundo* became 'indispensable'. His approach to the Option for the Poor followed the same tack: "primarily committed to those in need"; "preferential yet not exclusive love of the poor"; and, "you, being poor, are entitled to my particular concern."[95] From the new pope there were concessions to opponents of Medellín, but not submission to them. This 'centrist' position in support of Medellín was also evident in the final documents. Despite the heightened hostility towards Marxism encouraged by Trujillo and Vekemans, the fact that the term 'Option' appeared and rang throughout the document was telling. At Puebla, a clear articulation of a preferential, but not exclusive, solidarity with the materially poor and oppressed is presented as the crux of the Church's mission. And Sobrino argues that at Puebla it is the

---

92   Twomey, *The 'Preferential Option for the Poor' in Catholic Social Thought from John XXIII to John Paul II*, 212.

93   Dorr, *Option for the Poor: A Hundred Years of Catholic Social Teaching*, 261.

94   Penny Lernoux, *Cry of the People: United States Involvement in the Rise of Fascism, Torture, and Murder and the Persecution of the Catholic Church in Latin America* (Garden City, NY: Doubleday & Company, Inc., 1980), 436.

95   Dorr, *Option for the Poor: A Hundred Years of Catholic Social Teaching*, 265-66.

Option for the Poor that is "the theoretical reference for the mission of the whole Church and an essential element of all those missions without exception."[96] Even an arguably rigged CELAM meeting was intent on reaffirming Medellín, and on the floor at the assembly the progressives were "able to hold serve."[97] No liberation theologian was condemned, and Medellín's denunciation of injustice was perhaps even strengthened. It marked the first use of the phrase 'Preferential Option for the Poor'. Though no systematic account of it was provided, it appeared seven times in the final document, and this usage served to provide its generative core.[98]

The Option for the Poor was so salient in the thinking of the bishops that a chapter of the final document bore the title 'A Preferential Option for the Poor' (§1134–§1165).[99] Despite the absence of a technical definition of the Option, the document provides a functional description of it that facilitates a grasp of its core meaning. Gregory Baum argues that the Option as presented at Puebla mirrors the dual focus of Christian discipleship: "To analyze society from the perspective of the marginalized—the hermeneutical dimension—and to stand in solidarity with their struggle—the activist dimension."[100] These elements are certainly evident in the concrete actions the chapter recommends: "We will make every effort to understand and denounce the mechanisms that generate this poverty" (§1160); and, "Acknowledging the solidarity of other Churches, we will combine our efforts with those of people of goodwill in order to uproot poverty and create a more just and fraternal world" (§1161). But the core of Puebla's understanding—like Medellín before it—is conversion. The chapter on the Preferential Option opens:

> With renewed hope in the vivifying power of the Spirit, we are
> going to take up once again the position of the Second General

---

96   Jon Sobrino, "Puebla, serena afirmación de Medellín" *Christus* 44:521 (1979): 50.

97   Twomey, *The 'Preferential Option for the Poor' in Catholic Social Thought from John XXIII to John Paul II*, 212.

98   Ibid., 209.

99   The translation of the Puebla documents provided in *Puebla and Beyond* are used in this book. See Eagleson and Scharper, eds., *Puebla and Beyond: Documentation and Commentary.*

100   Gregory Baum, *Essays in Critical Theology* (Kansas City, MO: Sheed & Ward, 1994), 157.

Conference of the Latin American episcopate in Medellín, which adopted a clear and prophetic option expressing preference for, and solidarity with, the poor. ... We affirm the need for conversion on the part of the whole Church to a Preferential Option for the Poor, an option aimed at their integral liberation (§1134).

The notion of conversion is present throughout the chapter on the Preferential Option for the Poor and it appears six times within four pages. For example: service to the poor calls for constant conversion and purification (§1140); the poor challenge the Church and call it to conversion (§1147), and, re-examining what constitutes the ideal of human life in dignity and happiness is suggested to dispose the Christian to conversion (§1155). In other parts of the document, the relevance of the Option for the Poor is evident when conversion or the two-fold nature of discipleship are linked to the radical need for structural and societal change in solidarity with the poorest of the continent (§§12, 134, 438, 642, 1055, 1119). But it is in the chapter on the Option for the Poor that Puebla's fully-fledged Option for the Poor emerges: Christian conversion, a hermeneutics of solidarity, and transformative praxis.

4. CONCLUSION

This chapter has sought to illustrate the trajectory of development of the doctrine of the Preferential Option for the Poor from the Second Vatican Council, and particularly from the Group of the Church of the Poor, up to its emergence as an explicit doctrine at Puebla. What was partial and confused in the work of the Group of the Church of the Poor, and underdeveloped in the documents of the Council, became clearer in *Populorum progressio* and reached unparalleled expression in the CELAM meeting at Medellín. The poor moved from the periphery of the Church's focus to the center. Moreover, despite opposition and hesitation after Medellín, Paul VI and the Second Synod of World Bishops took CELAM's vision forward until CELAM met again in Puebla. Puebla resulted in the resounding affirmation of Medellín, and the explicit doctrine of the Preferential Option for the Poor became a permanent part of the Latin American theological landscape. But as with Medellín, the conclusions of Puebla functioned as a set of questions addressed to the Universal Church. John Paul II's response to CELAM III would prove decisive in the shaping of the Preferential Option, and tensions between the Magisterium and liberation theologians would be manifest in the struggle to understand the Option for the Poor. Indeed, subjected to these forces, the understanding of the Option was to diverge into separate ecclesial and theological doctrines. It is this process of bifurcation which is the focus of the next chapter.

CHAPTER 2

THE BIFURCATION OF THE DOCTRINE OF THE PREFERENTIAL OPTION FOR THE POOR

I. INTRODUCTION

In 1979, at Puebla, Mexico, the Latin American Episcopal Conference (CELAM) affirmed the Latin American Church's Option for the Poor in terms that grounded it in Christian conversion, related it to hermeneutics, and argued that it was actualized in Christian activity in the world. But the global context, the conflict between East and West, cast a shadow upon this achievement. Would the Universal Church—led by a Polish pontiff with direct experience of the horrors of Communism's claimed option for the proletariat—embrace the Option for the Poor, and if so, what would it look like as a universal doctrine? It would take over a decade for this question to be answered.

In the 1980s the Roman hierarchy grew increasingly vocal in its opposition to the influence of Marxist thought on Catholic theology. The Vatican was concerned that it may both distort the faith and provide a foothold for Communism. On the other side of the globe, many Latin American theologians were scandalized by the scale and extent of the poverty and oppression they witnessed. Rooted in these different concerns, tension between the Roman hierarchy and liberation theologians in Latin America lasted throughout the 1980s: in 1983, Gustavo Gutiérrez's work was called into question, and John Paul II chided Father Ernesto Cardenal for his involvement with the Sandinistas; in 1984, the Congregation for the Doctrine of the Faith (CDF) issued a document highly critical of Liberation Theology; in 1985, Leonardo Boff was silenced; and, in 1986, the CDF again issued an instruction aimed at Liberation Theology.

Representative of the tensions between the Roman Magisterium and liberation theologians is the fact that during the twelve years following Puebla the doctrine of the Preferential Option for the Poor bifurcates into ecclesial and theological forms. This chapter seeks to present an account of this process of bifurcation. It is divided into three sections. The first section recounts the manner in which Pope John Paul II appropriated the Option for the Poor and then demonstrates that Pope Benedict XVI's encyclicals confirm the trajectory of John Paul's thought. The second section argues that liberation theologians have appropriated the Preferential Option for the Poor in a manner that is in concert with Medellín and Puebla, but which is distinct from the Roman Magisterium's position. The third and final section of the chapter illustrates that the CELAM meetings at Santo Domingo (Dominican Republic, 1992) and Aparecida (Brazil, 2007) produced final documents which, when compared with each other, confirm the existence of a bifurcation of the doctrine of the Preferential Option for the Poor: Santo Domingo represents the Roman Magisterium's affirmation of the nature of the Option, whereas Aparecida stands in the line of thought represented by Medellín, Puebla, and mature Liberation Theology.

2. THE ECCLESIAL DOCTRINE OF THE PREFERENTIAL OPTION FOR THE POOR: THE ROMAN MAGISTERIUM'S GRADUAL APPROPRIATION OF THE CELAM POSITION

This section of the chapter traces the Roman Magisterium's gradual appropriation of the doctrine of the Preferential Option for the Poor. It begins by recounting John Paul II's initial reticence to employ the Latin American terminology 'Preferential Option for the Poor'. It moves on to consider the CDF's two instructions on Liberation Theology (1984 and 1986) and the Extraordinary Synod's Final Report (1985). It then presents John Paul II's definition of the Option for the Poor as it is contained in two of his social encyclicals, *Sollicitudo rei socialis* and *Centesimus annus* (1987 and 1991). Finally, it demonstrates that Benedict XVI does not deviate from John Paul II's understanding of the doctrine of the Preferential Option for the Poor.

2.1 UNCERTAIN BEGINNINGS:
JOHN PAUL II'S INITIAL RETICENCE TOWARDS
EMPLOYING THE LATIN AMERICAN TERMINOLOGY

Whilst the Latin American bishops unambiguously affirmed the Preferential Option for the Poor at Puebla, John Paul II was reticent to embrace the Option unequivocally or, at least, to do so using the Latin American terminology. This is not to say that John Paul was unaware of the Option's deep roots in the Christian tradition or that he was not in favour of an Option for the Poor. Jean-Yves Calvez suggests that John Paul II was chagrined in 1984–85, by the thought that he had been giving the impression that he did not believe in a Preferential Option for the Poor.[1] Throughout the height of the controversies surrounding Liberation Theology, John Paul II explicitly and forthrightly expressed his abiding concern for the poor: at Toronto, 1984; at the Vatican, 1984; on the Feast of St Francis, 1984; in his Christmas message, 1984; addressing Columbian priests, 1986; and, when addressing an Italian lay movement, 1986.[2] Yet because of possible Marxist overtones,[3] in more official contexts, John Paul II appeared hesitant to use the actual terminology 'Preferential Option for the Poor'. In his social encyclical of 1981, *Laborem exercens*, the phrase is conspicuously absent. The relatively minor document—an Apostolic Exhortation—*Familiaris consortio*, which appeared less than three months later, used the terminology once. It reads,

> The Christian family is thus called upon to offer everyone a witness
> of generous and disinterested dedication to social matters, through
> a 'preferential option' for the poor and disadvantaged. Therefore, ad-
> vancing in its following of the Lord by special love for all the poor, it

---

1   Jean-Yves Calvez, "The Preferential Option for the Poor: Where Does it Come From for Us?," *Studies in the Spirituality of Jesuits* 21:2 (March 1989): 23.

2   Twomey, *The 'Preferential Option for the Poor' in Catholic Social Thought from John XXIII to John Paul II*, 251-55.

3   In *Fides et ratio* (§54), John Paul II notes that Marxist "opinions and methods" were the reason the CDF intervened in 1984 with its *Instruction on Certain Aspects of the Theology of Liberation*. Pope John Paul II, "Fides et ratio" http://www.vatican.va/holy_father/john_paul_ii/encyclicals/documents/hf_jp-ii_enc_15101998_fides-et-ratio_en.html (accessed 3 September 2012).

must have special concern for the hungry, the poor, the old, the sick, drug victims and those who have no family (§47).[4]

At this early stage of his pontificate, even though John Paul II links the Option to Christian discipleship and charity, there is no sustained reflection upon its meaning or even acknowledgement of its Latin American provenance.

2.2 THE DOCTRINAL INSTRUCTIONS FROM THE CONGREGATION FOR THE DOCTRINE OF THE FAITH (1984 AND 1986), AND THE FINAL REPORT OF THE EXTRAORDINARY SYNOD (1985)

The first instruction from the CDF was issued in 1984 and was titled *Instruction on Certain Aspects of the 'Theology of Liberation'*. It is a difficult document to appraise inasmuch as no specific liberation theologian are identified, and it is directed, in a rather abstract manner, at "certain forms of Liberation Theology which use, in an insufficiently critical manner, concepts borrowed from various currents of Marxist thought."[5] More fully, the instruction reads,

> The different theologies of liberation are situated between the 'Preferential Option for the Poor', forcefully reaffirmed without ambiguity after Medellín at the Conference of 'Puebla' on the one hand, and the temptation to reduce the Gospel to an earthly Gospel on the other. We should recall that the Preferential Option described at 'Puebla' is two-fold: for the Poor and 'for the Young'. It is significant that the Option for the Young has in general been passed over in total silence (§VI.5).

Marxist analysis was the chief concern. At root, the CDF questioned whether or not 'theologies of liberation' confuse the 'poor' of the scripture with the 'proletariat' of Marx,[6] and thus employed an unjustifiable dialectical social analysis.

---

4   Pope John Paul II, "Familiaris consortio" http://www.vatican.va/holy_father/john_paul_ii/apost_exhortations/documents/hf_jp-ii_exh_19811122_familiaris-consortio_en.html (accessed 4 September 2012).

5   See the Introduction of Congregation for the Doctrine of the Faith, "Instruction on Certain Aspects of the Theology of Liberation" http://www.vatican.va/roman_curia/congregations/cfaith/documents/rc_con_cfaith_doc_19840806_theology-liberation_en.html (accessed 4 September 2012).

6   See the Introduction, VI.5, and IX.10, in ibid.

The instruction, while not containing detailed deliberations on the Preferential Option for the Poor, does make reference to it. In the introduction to the document, the CDF notes that it does not intend the instruction to "be interpreted as a disavowal of all those who want to respond generously and with an authentic evangelical spirit to the 'Preferential Option for the Poor.'"[7] The CDF uses the Latin American terminology in full only twice, and both times it is placed in quotation marks. While the document is clear that there is such a reality as a genuine Christian Option for the Poor, it contains no sustained reflections on the nature of the authentic Option. However, it does argue that for some liberation theologians,

> [T]he class struggle is the driving force of history. History thus becomes a central notion. It will be affirmed that God Himself makes history. It will be added that there is only one history, one in which the distinction between the history of salvation and profane history is no longer necessary. To maintain the distinction would be to fall into 'dualism'. ... Along these lines, some go so far as to identify God Himself with history and to define faith as 'fidelity to history', which means adhering to a political policy which is suited to the growth of humanity, conceived as a purely temporal messianism. ... As a consequence, faith, hope, and charity are given a new content: they become 'fidelity to history', 'confidence in the future', and 'Option for the Poor.' This is tantamount to saying they have been emptied of their theological reality (§IX.3-5).

In the CDF's estimation, it appears that for unnamed 'certain theologians' the Option for the Poor is simply charity emptied of its theological content. It is no surprise that John Paul II was cautious about using the terminology considering that, for the CDF, the Option for the Poor could refer to orthodox stances, heterodox stances, and the gamut of perspectives in-between. But this caution also marks a point of development in the Magisterium's thinking—one that is first evident in this instruction—that is, the Option for the Poor is unambiguously linked to charity.

On 25 January, 1985, in the period between the publication of the two instructions, John Paul II announced that he would summon an Extraordinary Synod for the end of the year. The purpose of the Synod was to commemorate the Second Vatican Council and consider the place of the Council in the life of the Church. In general terms,

7   The instruction's introduction is unnumbered.

the Synod focused on the Church "externally—in its relations with secular society, and internally—in its efforts to put Vatican II into effect and also to deal with issues which had come to the surface during this time."[8] There were 165 participants: presidents of the world's (Catholic) Episcopal conferences, patriarchs and major archbishops of the Eastern Rites, heads of Vatican departments, papal appointees, auditors, and observers from other denominations.

Despite the difficulties the phrase 'Preferential Option for the Poor' had caused the Roman Magisterium in the period following Puebla, at the 1985 Extraordinary Synod the Catholic Church's Episcopacy showed no such hesitation. A subsection of the final report's chapter on the Church's Mission in the World is titled "Preferential Option for the Poor and Human Promotion."[9] It does not relate the Option to its heritage in CELAM documents, but it does—like CELAM—link the Preferential Option to the Second Vatican Council and the Gospels when it argues under the heading "Preferential Option for the Poor and Human Promotion," that the

> salvific mission of the Church in relation to the world must be understood as an integral whole. Though it is spiritual, the mission of the Church involves human promotion, even in its temporal aspects. ... In this mission there is certainly a clear distinction—but not a separation—between the natural and supernatural aspects. ... [I]t is thus necessary to put aside the false and useless opposition between, for example, the Church's spiritual mission and *diaconia* for the world.[10]

The bishops also suggest that a lack of liberty and spiritual goods can "in some way" also be considered forms of poverty.[11] The document is clear that all poverty is to be denounced.[12] But latent in that very phrasing a certain priority appears to be given to material poverty. There is not just reference to the Preferential Option for the Poor; but

---

8   Catholic Church: Extraordinary Synod of Bishops Rome 1985, *A Message to the People of God and the Final Report* (Washington D.C.: National Conference of Catholic Bishops, 1986), 2-3.

9   See, at II.D.6, ibid., 23-24.

10   Ibid., 24.

11   Ibid., 23.

12   Ibid., 24.

for the Synod there is also a non-exclusive priority given to material poverty over other forms of poverty.

In the conclusion of the section on the Church's mission, the bishops argue that, because the world is in continuous evolution, it is necessary to discern the signs of the times in order that the proclamation of the Gospel may be more clearly heard, and the Church's activity for the salvation of the world may be more efficacious.[13] To facilitate this end, the bishops argue, the Church ought to reconsider: (a) the Theology of the Cross and the Paschal Mystery in the preaching, the sacraments and life of the Church of our day; (b) the theory and practice of inculturation, as well as the dialogue with non-Christian religions and with non-believers; (c) the Preferential Option for the Poor; and, (d) the social doctrine of the Church as it relates to human promotion in ever new situations.[14] In terms of aiding the Church's activity in history, the bishops placed the Option for the Poor in theological company as august as the Theology of the Cross and the Paschal Mystery. And while the bishops neither cited Puebla, nor mentioned conversion or hermeneutics in relation to the Option for the Poor, they did place it at the heart of the mission of the Church as something distinct from—though related to—the social doctrine of the Church.

Three months after the Extraordinary Synod of 1985—in March, 1986—the Congregation for the Doctrine of the Faith released its second document aimed at clarifying issues surrounding Liberation Theology. Even the title, *Christian Freedom and Liberation*,[15] reflected a more positive approach. It was in fact scheduled for publication earlier than March, but John Paul II had insisted that the document be re-written. The pope made several criticisms of the draft, noting that it was too long, too abstract, too shallow in its use of scripture, and too critical of Base Ecclesial Communities.[16] Peter Hebblethwaite argued that the second document came more from the pen of John Paul II than it did from Cardinal Ratzinger. For Hebblethwaite, it

---

13   Ibid.

14   Ibid.

15   Congregation for the Doctrine of the Faith, "Instruction on Christian Freedom and Liberation" http://www.vatican.va/roman_curia/congregations/cfaith/documents/rc_con_cfaith_doc_19860322_freedom-liberation_en.html (accessed 4 September 2012).

16   Harvey Cox, *The Silencing of Leonardo Boff: The Vatican and the Future of World Christianity* (Oak Park, IL: Meyer-Stone Books, 1988), 114.

was, in this way, more an encyclical than an instruction.[17] Regardless
of the authorship of the document, it is certainly more conciliatory
towards Liberation Theology. In the chapter of the document on the
'Liberating Mission of the Church', a sub-section was titled: "A Love
of Preference for the Poor."[18] It treats: Jesus and Poverty, Jesus and the
Poor, Love of Preference for the Poor, and Basic Communities and
Other Christian Groups. It then concludes with a positive note on
contextual theological reflection.

With respect to the Option for the Poor, the second instruction
sought more distance from the Latin American terminology than
the Extraordinary Synod had thought necessary. The CDF remained
concerned about the Option for the Poor and feared that the Option
could be manipulated to represent an ontology of violence at odds
with a Christian understanding of reality. It argued:

> [t]he special Option for the Poor, far from being a sign of partic-
> ularism or sectarianism, manifests the universality of the Church's
> being and mission. This Option excludes no one. This is the reason
> why the Church cannot express this Option by means of reductive
> sociological and ideological categories which would make this pref-
> erence a partisan choice and a source of conflict (§68).[19]

With this concern in mind, the CDF had sought more traditional religious language to refer to the reality of the Option, rather than what it
saw as terminology with conflictualist sociological-political connota-
tions.[20] The phrasing it arrived at was 'special Option for the Poor' and

---

17   Peter Hebblethwaite, "Spiritual Points in Liberation Themes Basic to the
      Document: An Analysis," in *Liberation Theology & the Vatican Document:
      Perspectives from the Third World*, ed. Sonia R. Perdiguerra (Quezon City:
      Claretian Publications, 1987), 85.

18   Chapter IV.II, Congregation for the Doctrine of the Faith, "Instruction
      on Christian Freedom and Liberation".

19   Ibid.

20   In 1988 Josef Cardinal Ratzinger confirmed to Bishop Pedro
      Casaldáliga—who was then Bishop of São Félix do Araguaia in Brazil—
      that the move away from the possibility of a political understanding of the
      Option had been intentional. He informed the bishop directly, "we prefer
      to speak of a preferential love for the poor," because a "class-based" inter-
      pretation of the Option is charged with a meaning that "cannot be gotten
      away from." See Pedro Casaldáliga, *In Pursuit of the Kingdom/Writings*
      (Maryknoll, NY: Orbis Books, 1990), 231.

'love of preference for the poor' (§68). As in the first instruction, the CDF associated the Option with Christian love, that is, with charity, but this time it did so in unambiguously positive terms.

2.3 JOHN PAUL II'S OFFICIAL DEFINITION OF THE OPTION FOR THE POOR AND ITS RELATION TO PUEBLA AND MEDELLÍN

John Paul II's social encyclicals of 1987 and 1991—*Sollicitudo rei socialis* and *Centesimus annus* respectively—mark his definitive appropriation of the Preferential Option for the Poor. *Sollicitudo rei socialis* contains the first reference in an encyclical to the Option for the Poor. It mentions an 'option or love of preference for the poor' which judiciously combines the CDF's and the original Latin American phrasing.[21] More specifically, it argued: "This is an option, or a special form of primacy in the exercise of Christian charity, to which the whole tradition of the Church bears witness" (§42). John Paul II suggested that the Option for the Poor should be understood in terms of the practice of Christian love. He continued to move the Roman Magisterium's understanding of the Option for the Poor away from possible Marxist class-related readings. In *Centesimus annus* John Paul II confirms his position when he cites *Sollicitudo rei socialis* to define the nature of the Option for the Universal Church: the Preferential Option for the Poor is a "special form of primacy in the exercise of Christian charity" (§11).[22] This definition is quoted in the Church's official compendium of social doctrine,[23] and remains the official understanding of the Option for the Poor.

---

21   The first use, in full, is "option or love of preference" (§42). Pope John Paul II, "Sollicitudo rei socialis," http://www.vatican.va/holy_father/john_paul_ii/encyclicals/documents/hf_jp-ii_enc_30121987_sollicitudo-rei-socialis_en.html (accessed 3 September 2012).

22   Pope John Paul II, "Centesimus annus". John Paul II only seems to have approved of the phrase 'preferential option' in more official ecclesial contexts after Hans urs von Balthasar said it was a permanent part of the theological landscape. See Twomey, *The 'Preferential Option for the Poor' in Catholic Social Thought from John XXIII to John Paul II*, 299.

23   Pontifical Council for Justice and Peace, "Compendium of the Social Doctrine of the Church" http://www.vatican.va/roman_curia/pontifical_councils/justpeace/documents/rc_pc_justpeace_doc_20060526_compendio-dott-soc_en.html (accessed 3 September 2012).

John Paul II's usage and understanding of the Preferential Option for the Poor, whilst drawing on the heritage of the CELAM meetings at Medellín and Puebla, is distinct from the Latin American position. It is apparent from the above considerations that John Paul II prefers to speak of the Option for the Poor in terms of love, and does so in a manner that does not invoke the emphasis on conversion and hermeneutics given to the Option at Medellín and Puebla. This is not to say that the relevance of conversion to socio-political hermeneutics is unknown to John Paul II. For example, in the Post-Synodal Apostolic Exhortation *Ecclesia in America* he writes, "Hence, for the Christian people of America conversion to the Gospel means to revise 'all the different areas and aspects of life, especially those related to the social order and the pursuit of the common good' (§27)."[24] Despite this awareness—and the fact he mentions the Option for the Poor four times in the exhortation (§§18, 55, 58, 67)—nowhere in the exhortation or in his social encyclicals does he link the Option for the Poor to conversion. For John Paul II, the Option remains understood as a particular emphasis in the exercise of charity in the context of Christian social ethics. In this sense, although John Paul's and the Medellín-Puebla stance are congruent, they are not coextensive: these differing emphases represent a bifurcation in the doctrine of the Preferential Option for the Poor.[25]

---

24   Pope John Paul II, "Ecclesia in America" http://www.vatican.va/ holy_father/john_paul_ii/apost_exhortations/documents/hf_jp-ii_exh_22011999_ecclesia-in-america_en.html (accessed 4 September 2012).

25   While this chapter does not argue in favour of either interpretation of the Option for the Poor, there are possible limitations in the Roman Magisterium's stance. This contention can be bolstered by the manner in which social ethicist Kenneth Himes questions the Preferential Option for the Poor's placement in the *Compendium of the Social Doctrine of the Church* as a subsection of the universal destination of goods (§4.3.c). He writes, "A noteworthy aspect of Chapter Four's straightforward account of basic principles is that the Option for the Poor is treated as a subtheme or derivative principle of the universal destiny of goods. There is a logic to the placement, but it does not permit the full significance of the Option for the Poor to be explained. *There is an epistemological as well as moral dimension to the Option for the Poor.* ... To accept the Option for the Poor as one of the fundamental principles of Catholic social teaching is to embrace a particular *angle of vision* from which to *view reality* and engage in discernment. Placing the Option for the Poor under the rubric of the universal destiny

2.4 CONFIRMING THE OFFICIAL STANCE OF THE ROMAN MAGISTERIUM: BENEDICT XVI

Joseph Cardinal Ratzinger took the name Benedict XVI upon being elected as John Paul II's successor on 19 April, 2005. His first encyclical, *Deus caritas est*,[26] appeared in December of the same year. It was followed by two more encyclicals: *Spe salvi* in 2007 and *Caritas in veritate* in 2009.[27]

Pope Benedict is unambiguously committed to the welfare of the poor. And this commitment is evident in his encyclicals. For example, he writes in *Deus caritas est*:

> As the years went by and the Church spread further afield, the exercise of charity became established as one of her essential activities, along with the administration of the sacraments and the proclamation of the word: love for widows and orphans, prisoners, and the sick and needy of every kind, is as essential to her as the ministry of the sacraments and preaching of the Gospel. The Church cannot neglect the service of charity any more than she can neglect the Sacraments and the Word (§22).

Furthermore, a clear concern for the poor is evident throughout *Caritas in veritate* (§§15, 23, 26, 30, 32). One of its core emphases, and one that is made forcefully, is that the Church is responsible for charity

---

of goods misses a crucial point—namely that the Option for the Poor runs throughout the tradition of social teaching as a distinctive motif *that influences how Catholics understand the meaning of other basic principles."* Himes has very clearly indicated that, in his understanding, there is more to the Option for the Poor than its role in the moral calculus. It is, in some sense, pre-moral: it affects epistemology as well as ethics. Himes's point here hints at the strengths of the Medellín-Puebla stance. See Kenneth Himes, "To Inspire and Inform," *America*, June 6, 2005, 9-10. The emphases are added by the current author.

26 Pope Benedict XVI, "Deus caritas est" http://www.vatican.va/holy_father/benedict_xvi/encyclicals/documents/hf_ben-xvi_enc_20051225_deus-caritas-est_en.html (accessed 4 September 2012).

27 Pope Benedict XVI, "Spe salvi" http://www.vatican.va/holy_father/benedict_xvi/encyclicals/documents/hf_ben-xvi_enc_20071130_spe-salvi_en.html (accessed 20-June 2010). And Pope Benedict XVI, "Caritas in veritate" http://www.vatican.va/holy_father/benedict_xvi/encyclicals/documents/hf_ben-xvi_enc_20090629_caritas-in-veritate_en.html (accessed 3 September 2012).

and the State is responsible for justice (§§26-30).[28] It also contains a number of innovations with respect to Catholic Social Teaching and the welfare of the poor. Two significant matters can be cited: (a) ecological issues are brought into the scope of what Joseph Cardinal Bernadin famously called the Catholic Church's seamless garment of life (§51); and, (b) the principle of subsidiarity is applied in the call for global governance that meets the needs of a global economy (§67).

Despite the fact Benedict expresses a clear love for the poor in his encyclicals, they contain no explicit mention of the 'Preferential Option for the Poor' or a 'love of preference for the poor'. Even when Benedict focuses on the distinctive nature of the Church's charitable activity, he does not mention the Option for the Poor or its role in directing the exercise of Christian charity.[29] Likewise, his message for the celebration for the World Day of Peace in 2007, *The Human Person, the Heart of Peace*, uses traditional natural-law categories and human-rights language to speak of equality rather than making reference to the Option for the Poor (§§3, 6, 10, 12).[30]

Notwithstanding the fact that Benedict does not mention the Option for the Poor in his encyclicals, he does make reference to it elsewhere. His message for the celebration of the World Day of Peace in 2009, titled *Fighting Poverty to Build Peace*, recalls the Option in language reminiscent of John Paul's:

> These principles of social teaching tend to clarify the links between poverty and globalization and they help to guide action towards the building of peace. Among these principles, it is timely to recall in particular the 'preferential love for the poor', in the light of the primacy of charity, which is attested throughout Christian tradition, beginning with that of the early Church (§15).[31]

---

28   Pope Benedict XVI, "Deus caritas est".

29   See, at §31, Pope Benedict XVI, "Caritas in veritate".

30   Pope Benedict XVI, "Message of His Holiness Pope Benedict XVI for the Celebration of the World Day of Peace" http://www.vatican.va/holy_father/benedict_xvi/messages/peace/documents/hf_ben-xvi_mes_20061208_xl-world-day-peace_en.html (accessed 4 September 2012).

31   Pope Benedict XVI, "Message of His Holiness Pope Benedict XVI for the Celebration of the World Day of Peace: Fighting Poverty to Build Peace" http://www.vatican.va/holy_father/benedict_xvi/messages/peace/documents/hf_ben-xvi_mes_20081208_xlii-world-day-peace_en.html (accessed 4 September 2012).

Further, when addressing the Latin American bishops in 2007, Benedict argued "the Preferential Option for the Poor is implicit in the Christological faith in the God who became poor for us, so as to enrich us with his poverty (cf. 2 Cor 8:9)."[32]

Clearly, on the evidence, one cannot argue that Benedict does not believe in the Option for the Poor. Rather, it simply appears not to be an element of Christian thought that he seeks to put in the foreground. It is, therefore, fairest to conclude with respect to the Option for the Poor, Benedict continues in the tradition of John Paul II, without representing either a development or repudiation of that tradition.

3. CONFIRMING THE STANCE OF PUEBLA: LIBERATION THEOLOGY AND THE NATURE OF THE DOCTRINE OF THE PREFERENTIAL OPTION FOR THE POOR

Complementing the Roman Magisterium's understanding of the Preferential Option for the Poor is a second line of interpretation that is likewise rooted in the Medellín-Puebla formulation, but that also adheres to its 'conversion, hermeneutics, and praxis' understanding of the Option. James Nickoloff writes of this second line of thought, "the Option for the Poor involves more than the Church's social teaching ... at its core it concerns the Church's deepest understanding of who God is."[33] Moreover, it also includes analyzing reality from the perspective of the poor and acting for their well-being.[34] This approach to the Option is most evident in the works of major liberation theologians.

This section of the chapter employs the work of Gustavo Gutiérrez and Jon Sobrino to illustrate the existence of this second approach to the Option for the Poor in Liberation Theology. Gutiérrez and Sobrino are among the vanguard of liberation theologians, and they

32 Pope Benedict XVI, "Inaugural Session of the Fifth General Conference of the Bishops of Latin America and the Caribbean: Address of His Holiness Benedict XVI" http://www.vatican.va/holy_father/benedict_xvi/speeches/2007/may/documents/hf_ben-xvi_spe_20070513_conference-aparecida_en.html (accessed 3 September 2012).

33 *An Introductory Dictionary of Theology and Religious Studies*, s.v. "Option for the Poor."

34 Ibid. Donal Dorr also writes that the first step arising from the Option is analysis. See *The New Dictionary of Catholic Social Thought*, s.v. "Poor, Preferential Option for."

have presented detailed reflections focused on the nature of the Option for the Poor. The work of Gutiérrez and Sobrino is read in the key provided by the CELAM conferences of Medellín and Puebla: conversion, hermeneutics, and praxis. This section is by no means intended to be an exhaustive representation of Gutiérrez and Sobrino's stances on the Option. Rather, the aim is to illustrate that the three elements of the Medellín-Puebla approach to the Option for the Poor are all present in their work.

3.1 LIBERATION THEOLOGY, THE PREFERENTIAL OPTION FOR THE POOR, AND CONVERSION

In the Catholic Christian tradition, conversion is intimately linked to decision, and this is the manner in which Gutiérrez presents his understanding of the Option for the Poor. He argues that the Option is a constitutive element of being Christian and is required of all Christians. He writes, "The curious remark is sometimes made, 'The Option for the Poor is something which the non-poor have to make.' That is not true, for the poor also have to opt in favour of their brothers and sisters of race, social class, and culture. And so the Option for the Poor is a decision incumbent upon every Christian."[35] Gutiérrez, continuing to use the language of conversion, relates the Option for the Poor to the transformation of one's horizon. The Option for the Poor "implies leaving the road one is on" and entering the world of "the one excluded from dominant social sectors, communities, viewpoints, and ideas."[36] Although the Option takes one into the world of the poor, this is not a question of simple human compassion. Rather, one shares in the life of the poor because conversion to God means sharing in God's valuing of the universe, and God "prefers the forgotten, the oppressed, the poor, the forsaken."[37] When all is said and done, the

---

35   Gutiérrez, "Option for the Poor: Reviews and Challenges," 16.
36   Gutiérrez, "The Option for the Poor Arises from Faith in Christ," 318. This article contains the edited text of the speech he delivered at the CELAM meeting in 2007, held in Aparecida, Brazil. Interestingly, he considers the Option for the Poor under three headings that roughly correspond to the conversion, hermeneutics, and praxis triad: discipleship, hermeneutics, and proclamation. Moreover, in the conclusion he writes of the three elements as spiritual, theological, and evangelical.
37   Gutiérrez, "Option for the Poor: Reviews and Challenges," 16.

Option for the Poor means an option for the God of the Reign as proclaimed by Jesus.[38]

Alongside his understanding of the Option for the Poor as grounded in conversion to God, Gutiérrez also contends that conversion to God implies "conversion to the neighbor."[39] Such conversion means, "thinking, feeling, and living as Christ."[40] And further, it means "to commit oneself to the process of the liberation of the poor" and not only to do so generously but also "with an analysis of the situation and a strategy of action."[41] Conversion, for Gutiérrez, is not simply an internal transformation—though it certainly is that—but a transformation that reaches out to analysis and then action to transform history. Moreover, history plays a role in the transformation of the Christian: the "socio-economic, political, cultural and human environment,"[42] he argues, affects the whole process of conversion. So only through involvement with the neighbor in history will a Christian's conversion be complete.

Sobrino is explicit about the fact that the Option for the Poor needs to be understood—at its most basic level—in terms of conversion. It is not a point on which he reflects in depth. But it is one he makes with the utmost clarity. He writes, "The internal structure of this Option [for the Poor] is open to theoretical discussion. The position of Liberation Theology is that it has the structure of conversion, since it is made in distinct form, and historically in opposition to, other Options."[43] It is a decision and "when all is said and done, one cannot argue for or against it."[44] In suggesting this, he is not negating the ethical dimension of the Option for the Poor. He is simply stating that, from the perspective of Liberation Theology, the Option for the Poor

---

38   Gustavo Gutiérrez, "Option for the Poor," in *Mysterium Liberationis: Fundamental Concepts of Liberation Theology*, ed. Ignacio Ellacuría and Jon Sobrino (Maryknoll, NY: Orbis Books, 1993), 240.

39   Gutiérrez, *A Theology of Liberation: History, Politics, and Salvation*, 118.

40   Ibid.

41   Ibid.

42   Ibid.

43   Sobrino, "Central Position of the Reign of God in Liberation Theology," 375.

44   Ibid., 374.

is taken on a level that is more primary than that on which ethical reflection is conducted.[45] He writes more fully:

> The important thing is that the Option for the Poor is not pure evangelical or sociohistorical content, is not merely an ethical demand, and is not, of course, something that must be carried out because Church documents say that it must, so that, if these documents had not said so, Christians would be under no obligation to make such an Option. The Option for the Poor is something more primordial than this. It is an ultimate way of regarding the reality of the poor and of seeing in the liberation of the poor the necessary mode of correspondence to reality.[46]

For Sobrino, the Option for the Poor must be made with a "logical anteriority" to the "development of a theology of liberation."[47] The integrity of theology precisely as theology of liberation depends on the conversion of the theologian.

3.2 LIBERATION THEOLOGY, THE PREFERENTIAL OPTION FOR THE POOR, AND HERMENEUTICS

Gutiérrez claims, in a recent reflection on the Option for the Poor, that "if the following of Jesus is marked by the Preferential Option for the Poor, so is the understanding of faith that unfolds from these experiences and emergencies."[48] Gutiérrez refers to this second dimension of the Option for the Poor—the dimension that follows spiritual discipleship—as the "hermeneutics of hope" which arises from making the Option.[49] The condition of the poor, he argues, interrogates our faith and also provides new categories and principles that allow the Christian message to be deepened. The Option for the Poor operates within theological reflection, Gutierrez contends, citing Anselm's formula *fides quaerens intellectum*, in that it affects our understanding of the truths of faith.[50]

Sobrino is also clear that the Option for the Poor must be understood to have an hermeneutical element. He seems to phrase this in

---

45   Ibid., 375.
46   Ibid., 374-75.
47   Ibid., 375.
48   Gutiérrez, "The Option for the Poor Arises from Faith in Christ," 321.
49   Ibid.
50   Ibid., 322.

terms that are almost arbitrary when he says that, as an epistemological premise, the Option for the Poor is a wager.[51] He means by this that it is a premise that must be posited—a decision made, a judgment on balance of probabilities, a stance accepted—before any reading of the Gospel or history is undertaken. Once the Option has been made, one can be affected by the reality of the poor such that they become a *locus theologicus*.[52] Indeed, Sobrino suggests that the adoption of the Option for the Poor is the essential hermeneutic principle required for an adequate reading of the Gospel and of all historical reality. Sobrino also contends that it is the poor who give ultimacy to the mystery of God.[53] For Sobrino, the reality of God is made present in the poor, and the reality of history—of the Reign of God—breaks through in the poor.

When one reads Sobrino's work, one finds a clear sense that the Option for the Poor—its presence or absence—is a limit-condition on one's ability to accurately understand reality. He writes, " [It] remains clear that, in Liberation Theology and in all its varieties, the Option for the Poor—however one comes to it—is necessary for a reading of the Gospel, and furthermore, for an adequate reading of reality."[54] Without making the Option for the Poor—without being converted to God and thus to the poor—one will be incapable of interpreting reality accurately. Without conversion to the poor, one will simply truncate the data of the bible and of history. Or as Sobrino says elsewhere, "[p]rimary conversion, then, means letting truth be truth, seeing the world as it is, without oppressing it beforehand by dictating how it is to appear. In this sense, the Option for the Poor in Pauline language is necessary for a release from prison of the truth of the world, the world of the oppressed and the world of the oppressors."[55] For Sobrino, the Option for the Poor acts as the necessary hermeneutic premise for an understanding of reality, the Gospel, and the Reign of God itself.[56]

---

51 Sobrino, "Central Position of the Reign of God in Liberation Theology," 374.
52 Ibid., 375.
53 Sobrino, "Depth and Urgency of the Option for the Poor," 20.
54 Sobrino, "Central Position of the Reign of God in Liberation Theology," 374.
55 Ibid., 375.
56 Ibid., 376.

3.3 LIBERATION THEOLOGY, THE PREFERENTIAL OPTION FOR THE POOR, AND PRAXIS

For Gutiérrez, the Option for the Poor is ultimately actualized in the proclamation of the Gospel. The proclamation of the Gospel, Gutiérrez argues, is tied to the Reign of God and intimately linked to the promotion of justice. He cites the Roman Synod of 1971, Paul VI's *Evangelii nuntiandi*, and John Paul II's speeches as sources for the linking of evangelization and the promotion of justice. This linkage is representative of the call for a 'New Evangelization' made at Medellín and Puebla and is a call that John Paul II subsequently adopted.[57] The Option for the Poor is the "axis" of this New Evangelization,[58] an evangelization that does not dislocate temporal and spiritual realities from each other. This perspective finds footing in the final documents of Puebla, where the bishops argue "the best service to our fellows in evangelization" is one "which disposes them to fulfill themselves as children of God, liberates them from injustices, and fosters their integral advancement" (§1145).[59]

It is the Option for the Poor that leads Gutiérrez to argue that justice is not simply something pursued as part of a process of pre-evangelization; rather, justice is an essential part of the Reign of God, without exhausting the Reign's content. The Reign of God is not reducible to justice within history; nor is the Reign of God complete without justice in history. Moreover, inasmuch as the Reign is 'already' present, it is a gift, a grace. Inasmuch as the Reign is 'not yet' fully realized, it is also a task and a responsibility.[60] This is not to suggest that the Reign is realized by human activity. Rather, because history is oriented towards the Reign, we are to seek to co-create an approximation of the Reign until that time when it reaches its fullness beyond history. It is the Option for the Poor that starts, guides, and animates this process.

The Option for the Poor also conditions Sobrino's understanding of praxis. This is apparent when one considers his view of praxis as it relates to the mission of the Church and the Reign of God. With respect to the mission of the Church, Sobrino follows Jürgen

---

57   Gutiérrez, "Option for the Poor: Reviews and Challenges," 17.

58   Ibid.

59   Gustavo Gutiérrez, *The Power of the Poor in History: Selected Writings* (Maryknoll, NY: Orbis Books, 1983), 149.

60   Gutiérrez, "The Option for the Poor Arises from Faith in Christ," 323.

Moltmann. Sobrino argues "it is not the Church that 'has' a mission, but the reverse; Christ's mission creates itself a Church. The mission should not be understood from the perspective of the Church, but the other way around."[61] This understanding of the Church's mission permits Sobrino to assert that the Option for the Poor is a constitutive element in the Church's mission precisely because the Option for the Poor was Christ's option and thus shaped Christ's mission. In his words, "The Option for the Poor is thus decisive for the historical essence of the Church of Jesus."[62] Sobrino identifies four ways that the Option ought to be implemented by the Church in acting out its mission. First, the Option requires that the Church be dialectical in its historical analysis and that it stands firmly in opposition to all oppression. Secondly, the Church must be partial in its commitment to the poor and must place them at the center of all reality. Thirdly, the Church is also to engage in concrete historical situations even to the point—especially to the point—where this results in the oppression of the Church. And fourthly, the Option demands that the Church be humble in the way it relates to the poor, because there will always be a chasm between the non-poor who can take life for granted—the non-poor in the Church—and the poor who cannot take life for granted.[63]

The fact that Sobrino understands the Church's mission as a prolongation of Christ's mission brings the Reign of God to the fore as a theological element in his understanding of the Preferential Option for the Poor and praxis. That is to say, because the preaching and actualization of the Reign of God characterized Christ's mission, an understanding of the Reign of God in relation to the Option must also shape the Church's praxis in history. Sobrino writes,

> [I]t is the poor who will guide the fleshing out of what the Reign of God is today. Theoretically and historically, the concept of the Reign of God can be worked out in terms of other primacies than the poor. It can be developed from universal human needs, from the longing for freedom, from the desire for survival after death, from the utopia of continuous progress. This has actually been the point of departure for other theologies, and the differences among them in terms of their systematic concepts of the Reign of God are ultimately to be explained by the premises on which they read the

61   Sobrino, "Depth and Urgency of the Option for the Poor," 21.
62   Ibid.
63   Ibid., 31-32.

Gospel text and current historical reality. In terms of the Option for the Poor, the systematic concept of the Reign of God plies a precise course: the Reign of God is the Reign of the poor.[64]

Derived from conversion to the Option for the Poor, and the reading of reality that flows from this transformation, the praxis of the Reign of God is the praxis of the Option for the Poor. The praxis of the Reign of God is how the Option for the Poor is concretely made manifest.[65]

4. AN INDICATION OF BIFURCATION: CELAM IV AT SANTO DOMINGO (1992) IN COMPARISON WITH CELAM V AT APARECIDA (2007)

If one compares the final reports of the Latin American Episcopal Conference meetings of Santo Domingo, Dominican Republic in 1992, with those of Aparecida, Brazil in 2007, one can garner enough evidence to support the notion of a bifurcation in the doctrine of the Preferential Option for the Poor. Specifically, Santo Domingo, which was the first CELAM meeting after the tumultuous 1980s, can be seen to fall more in line with the Roman Magisterium's understanding of the Option for the Poor in that it is presented mostly in terms which relate it to ethical Christian activity. Aparecida, by contrast, appears to be more overtly in alignment with the stance reached at Puebla: conversion, hermeneutics, and praxis.

4.1 CELAM IV AT SANTO DOMINGO: A CAUTIOUS AFFIRMATION OF THE OPTION FOR THE POOR

In October 1992, CELAM held its fourth General Meeting at Santo Domingo, Dominican Republic. Some nine years earlier, in 1983, John Paul II had announced that the theme for the meeting would be the

---

64   Sobrino, "Central Position of the Reign of God in Liberation Theology," 375.

65   Ibid., 379. Vastly more could be said on the issue of the Option for the Poor and praxis in Liberation Theology—not the least of which is addressing the issue that praxis itself is treated in Liberation Theology as a hermeneutical principle—but such a presentation is beyond the ambit of this section.

"New Evangelization."[66] The CELAM IV meeting had in fact been delayed until 1992—there was no CELAM General Meeting in the 1980s—so that it could coincide with the 500th anniversary of the 'old evangelization', the arrival of Christopher Columbus. These nine years leading up to the conference involved a vast quantity of preparatory work. This included intra-Church discussions, meetings with laity, and empirical social-scientific research. This resulted in the drafting of a significant amount of supporting documentation.

Alfred Hennelly identifies three draft documents as the most significant of all preparatory work.[67] The first was titled *Consultative Document: New Evangelization, Human Development, and Christian Culture.* The Latin American bishops, however, rejected this document on the grounds that it did not incorporate the views of the national bishops' conferences. A second document, the *Second Report*,[68] was then drawn up. It provided a synthesis of the ideas of the national conferences. It was, however, rejected by the Vatican and some Latin American bishops. A final document, *Working Document*, was then composed and was subsequently approved by the Vatican. Remarkably, on the first day of the conference, despite years of preparation, the co-secretary general of the conference, then Bishop (later Cardinal) Jorge Medina Estévez, discarded the *Working Document.*[69]

---

66   Alfred T. Hennelly, "A Report from the Conference," in *Santo Domingo & Beyond: Documents & Commentaries from the Historic Meeting of the Latin American Bishops' Conference,* ed. Alfred T. Hennelly (Maryknoll, NY: Orbis Books, 1993), 25.

67   Ibid., 26.

68   Hennelly contends that the final document did not have the prophetic bite of those produced by the Medellín and Puebla conferences because the 'see—judge—act' methodology—which had been employed extensively in the formulation of the *Second Report*—was not used to formulate the final document. Ecclesiology, Christology, and the understanding of the relevance of CEBs are all affected by this methodological shift. Ibid., 31-35. One such reflection on ecclesiology reads, "It is a poor Church, in the process of conversion, which gives first place to the poor; in solidarity and communion with the impoverished masses of the continent. In situations of injustice and poverty, it brings its message to those who suffer the most. It is a Church that renews its vision from the viewpoint of the poor." Without the 'see—judge—act' methodology, this kind of reflection was not present in the *Final Document.* Ibid., 32.

69   Ibid., 26-27.

To solve the problem of a lack of working material, the bishops adopted as a framework the ideas present in John Paul II's opening address to the conference.[70] Whatever the cause of the organizational disarray at the meeting, the final document produced at Santo Domingo was generally considered unremarkable. Archbishop Marcos McGrath of Panama noted, "You'd find the general opinion that it is a good document. ... But if we'd had a few more days, it would have been much better."[71] Alluding to Jon Sobrino's description of Medellín as a leap forward and Puebla as a dainty step forward Hennelly suggests that Santo Domingo was a shaky step into the future.[72]

Despite the collapse of the Soviet Union one year prior to the meeting at Santo Domingo, the spectre of Marxism (understood by some as Communism) was never far away from the meeting. In his opening address, John Paul II said, "it is to be hoped that the fall of those regimes of so-called real socialism in Eastern Europe will lead people in this continent to realize that the value of such ideologies is ephemeral."[73] It is this fact that sets the scene for John Paul II to argue that the Preferential Option is "an option ... based essentially on God's word, and not on criteria provided by the human sciences or opposed ideologies, which often reduce the poor to abstract socio-political and economic categories. But it is a firm and irrevocable option."[74] In this vein, John Paul II continued, explaining the true origin of the Option for the Poor:

> There is no genuine human development, true liberation, or Preferential Option for the Poor unless it is based on the very

---

70   With such a build up, Peter Steinfels wrote that CELAM and the Vatican had displayed above all else a "Preferential Option for Dickering." Peter Steinfels, "CELAM & The Vatican: Preferential Option for Dickering," *Commonweal*, 20 November 1992, 5.

71   Ibid., 6.

72   Hennelly, "A Report from the Conference," 24.

73   Pope John Paul II, "Opening Address of the Holy Father," in *Santo Domingo & Beyond: Documents & Commentaries from the Historic Meeting of the Latin American Bishops' Conference*, ed. Alfred T. Hennelly (Maryknoll, NY: Orbis Books, 1993), 47.

74   Ibid., 50. At this point, John Paul is quoting his own address to the Roman Curia of December 21, 1984.

foundations of the dignity of the person and of the surroundings in which the person must develop, according to the Creator's design.[75]

For the Roman Magisterium, the means of combating erroneous understandings of the Option remain the same: Christology and Christian anthropology are at the root of any genuine Option for the Poor. Liberation theologians would concur with such an argument, but would then relate Christology and anthropology to the hermeneutics of history. Nevertheless, the suspicion that marked the Magisterium's attitude towards the Option for the Poor in the 1980s is again evident in John Paul's opening address. He again seeks to put distance between the Option for the Poor and socio-political analysis. This address, as noted, functioned as the foundation document for the meeting and thus shaped the final document.

The Option for the Poor receives explicit mention in nine sections of the final document (§§50, 92, 178, 179, 180, 200, 275, 296, 302).[76] The first reference to the Option establishes the context of its use at Santo Domingo: "the Church's social teaching, which is the basis for, and the stimulus to, the authentic Preferential Option for the Poor, must form part of any preaching and any catechesis" (§50). The Option for the Poor must be understood in terms of Christian Social Ethics. Apropos of this contention, four of the nine references to the Option for the Poor occur in Chapter II of the document, "Human Development" (§§178, 179, 180, 200). Under the heading "Impoverishment and Solidarity," the document argues that the basis for a Gospel-based non-exclusive Preferential Option for the Poor is Christ's activity in the synagogue, when he declares that he has come to bring good tidings to the poor (§178). Moreover, the Church, "which is called to be ever more faithful to its Preferential Option for the Poor," has worked to eradicate poverty and will continue to do so (§179). Further, the Church will assume with renewed commitment "Gospel-inspired and Preferential Option for the Poor, following the example and the words of the Lord Jesus, with full trust in God, austerity of life, and sharing in goods" (§180). And in addressing the

---

75 Ibid., 51.

76 Latin American Episcopal Conference, "Conclusions: New Evangelisation, Human Development, Christian Culture," in *Santo Domingo & Beyond: Documents & Commentaries from the Historic Meeting of the Latin American Bishops' Conference*, ed. Alfred T. Hennelly (Maryknoll, NY: Orbis Books, 1993), 153. The italics are in the original.

Church's role in establishing a 'New Economic Order', a pastoral direction is established that states the Church is to

> foster at various levels and in different sectors of the Church a social pastoral activity whose starting point is the Gospel's Preferential Option for the Poor, by being active through proclamation, denunciation, and witness and by encouraging cooperative undertakings in the context of a market economy (§200).

The document also links the Option for the Poor to Catholic education when it observes that the Preferential Option for the Poor includes the Preferential Option for the Poor to escape their poverty (§275). These considerations lead to the conclusions of the document, where, in terms of primary pastoral directions that the Latin American Church establishes, it states,

> We make ours the cry of the poor. In continuity with Medellín and Puebla, we assume with renewed ardor the Gospel Preferential Option for the Poor. This Option, which is neither exclusive nor excluding, will, in imitation of Jesus Christ, shed light on all our evangelization activity. ... With that light, we urge the development of a new economic, social, and political order in keeping with the dignity of each and every person, fostering justice and solidarity, and opening horizons of eternity for all of them (§296).

From this summary, it is clear that the Option for the Poor as presented in the documents of CELAM IV is not explicitly linked to conversion or hermeneutics, as it was at Medellín and Puebla. At Santo Domingo, the tight control the Vatican exercised over CELAM's meeting resulted in the Option for the Poor being expressed dominantly in terms of Christian Social Ethics to the exclusion of any explicit link to the fullness of Christian conversion and the hermeneutics of history.

4.2 CELAM V AT APARECIDA:
AN OVERT AFFIRMATION OF CELAM II, CELAM III, AND
MATURE LIBERATION THEOLOGY

At Aparecida, Brazil, CELAM met for its fifth General Meeting in 2007. It was the first CELAM meeting to be attended by Benedict XVI. Would he continue to make his mark, as pope rather than as prefect of the CDF, on the liberation thought of the continent? It quickly became evident that the legacy of Liberation Theology would be more apparent in the final document from Aparecida than it was at Santo Domingo.[77] This was obvious even during the meeting before any documents were finalized: John Allen commented on the significant place given to the Preferential Option for the Poor on the floor at the meeting, along with a positive place given to the concept of structural sin, Base Ecclesial Communities, and the 'see—judge—act' methodology.[78] From the perspective of those sympathetic to Liberation Theology, if Santo Domingo represented a shaky step forward, Aparecida appeared to be surefooted once more.

At CELAM V, "The bishops explicitly affirmed Liberation Theology's famous Option for the Poor, but tweaked it to become a 'preferential and *evangelical option*,' making clear this is no merely political or social commitment."[79] The question of how, if at all, the addition of 'evangelical' changes the Option is unclear. What is apparent is that this new phrasing is only employed twice in the final document, whereas the older formulation—Preferential Option for the Poor—is used thirteen times. In the document, the Option is obviously linked to charity, with five clear reflections on the topic (§§394, 395, 397, 409, 501). Moreover, a whole section within Part 8, "The Kingdom of God and Promoting Human Dignity," is devoted to the "Preferential Option for the Poor and Excluded." At Aparecida, the Preferential

---

77 The final document can be found online at: Latin American Episcopal Conference, "Documento Conclusivo" http://www.celam.org/aparecida. php (accessed 3 September 2012).

78 John Allen Jr, "CELAM Update: The Lasting Legacy of Liberation Theology" http://ncronline.org/node/11128 (accessed 4 September 2012).

79 John Allen Jr, "Sorting out the Results of the Latin American Bishops' Meeting" http://ncronline.org/node/11148 (accessed 4 September 2012). The italics are in the original.

Option for the Poor is again afforded the centrality that marked its treatment at Puebla.

Aparecida also marks the return of an overt ecclesial linking of the Option with conversion. The document reads,

> The Preferential Option for the Poor is one of the distinguishing features of our Latin American and Caribbean Church. Indeed, addressing our continent Pope John Paul II stated that 'for the Christian people of America conversion to the Gospel means to revise "all the different areas and aspects of life, especially those related to the social order and the pursuit of the common good."' (§391)

While the document from which they cite John Paul II—the Apostolic Exhortation *Ecclesia in America*—did not link the Option to conversion, at CELAM V, the bishops sought to do so. There appears to be a desire at Aparecida to once again make this link overt.

As regards hermeneutics, the matter is somewhat less clear, as there is no explicit statement of hermeneutical principles linked to the Option. Yet such a principle is not far beneath the surface when the document states,

> The disciples and missionaries of Christ must illuminate with the light of the Gospel all realms of social life. The Preferential Option for the Poor, rooted in the Gospel, requires pastoral attention devoted to the builders of society. If many contemporary structures produce poverty, it is partly due to the lack of fidelity to their Gospel commitments on the part of many Christians with special political, economic and cultural responsibilities (§501).

There is a clear awareness that the Option for the Poor demands a reanalysis of distorted structures within society that are the cause of poverty. And further,

> Through its social ministry the Church should welcome and journey with these excluded people in the appropriate environments. … In this task, concrete actions should be designed with pastoral creativity to influence governments to enact social and economic policies to deal with the varied needs of the population and lead toward sustainable development. With the aid of different ad hoc bodies and organizations the Church can engage in ongoing Christian interpretation and a pastoral approach to the reality of our continent, utilizing the rich legacy of the Church's social doctrine (§§402-403).

At Aparecida, the Church's social doctrine, which includes the Option for the Poor, is linked to the task of the Christian interpretation of history.[80]

Arguably, the Option for the Poor at Aparecida sits comfortably in the tradition of Medellín and Puebla. At Aparecida, it is again grounded in conversion, it is implicated in hermeneutics, and it operates continuously to direct the praxis of ministry and mission.

5. CONCLUSION

This chapter has sought to demonstrate the existence of a bifurcation in the evolutionary lineage of the doctrine of the Preferential Option for the Poor. The Roman Magisterium's official formulation of the Option locates it within official Catholic Social Teaching. It is, as John Paul II defined it in *Centesimus annus*, a "special form of primacy in the exercise of Christian charity" (§11).[81] The focus on conversion—the transformation to sharing in God's option, a participation in the life of the Reign—is absent in the official doctrine of the Option as developed by the Roman Magisterium since Puebla, as is the hermeneutical element of the Option. By contrast, for both Gutiérrez and Sobrino, Puebla's structure of conversion, hermeneutics, praxis remain. This chapter has also demonstrated that at Santo Domingo the Option for the Poor was presented in a manner which replicated John Paul II's official definition; whereas at Aparecida, CELAM again connected the Option for the Poor with its roots in Medellín and Puebla by reaffirming that the Option has the structure of conversion, and thus shapes hermeneutics and praxis.

---

80 Also related to hermeneutics—though not explicitly linked to the Option for the Poor—is the fact that the Young Christian Workers' 'see—judge—act' methodology, which did not appear in the final documents of Santo Domingo, returns at Aparecida. Although the Jocist method does not stipulate hermeneutical principles, it does identify a direction in which analysis and interpretation is to be conducted: from below upward. "In continuity with the previous general conferences of Latin American Bishops, this document utilizes the see-judge-act method. This method entails viewing God with the eyes of faith … so that in everyday life we may see the reality around us in the light of his providence, judge it according to Jesus Christ … and act from the Church … in spreading the Kingdom of God, which is sown on this earth and fully bears fruit in Heaven." (§5).

81 Pope John Paul II, "Centesimus annus".

This chapter argued in favor of neither the Roman Magisterium's doctrine of the Preferential Option for the Poor nor the understanding of the Option shared by Medellín-Puebla-Aparecida and Liberation Theology.[82] It has simply sought to identify the distinction so that an understanding of the Option for the Poor, using the work of Bernard Lonergan and Robert Doran, can be developed in Chapters 4 and 5.

---

82   The distinction between the two strands of thought can perhaps help explain the context that gave rise to Dom Hélder Câmara's quip, 'When I feed the poor, they call me a Saint. When I ask why are they poor, they call me a Communist.' Gutiérrez makes a similar observation, "A final remark on the topic of poverty: if you talk about the poor, people will probably regard you as sensitive and generous. But if you talk about the causes of poverty, they'll say to themselves, 'Is this a Christian speaking? Isn't such language really political?'" See Gutiérrez, "Option for the Poor: Reviews and Challenges," 15.

CHAPTER 3

LONERGAN STUDIES AND FOUNDATIONS FOR LIBERATION: THE CONVERTED SUBJECT

I. INTRODUCTION

This short chapter functions simply to introduce the elements of Bernard Lonergan and Robert Doran's work that are required to construct an understanding of the converted subject. Whatever the adequacy of the appellation 'transcendental Thomist', which is often applied to Lonergan, it correctly conveys two key aspects of his thought: he embraced—and arguably completed—the Kantian critical turn, and he also intensely valued Aquinas' achievement. It is this former focus, the explicit turn to the subject, which directly concerns this section of the chapter.

Apropos of this focus, this chapter: (1) summarizes Lonergan's theory of conscious intentionality and introduces his understanding of patterns of experience and realms of meaning; (2) presents Lonergan's understanding of the horizon of the subject; and, (3) outlines Lonergan and Doran's combined stance on religious, moral, intellectual and psychic conversion. The understanding of the converted subject outlined here in Chapter 3 is employed in the next chapters of this book to construct a theological understanding of the Preferential Option for the Poor from within the field of Lonergan Studies.

2. LONERGAN ON CONSCIOUS INTENTIONALITY:
THE SUBJECT AS CREATIVE

Lonergan's theory of conscious intentionality is the foundation of his critical realist philosophy. It is in *Insight*[1] that Lonergan first constructs a comprehensive account of human knowing and begins by noting that the human subject is a self-transcending reality.[2] This tendency to self-transcendence is an inbuilt impetus that animates the subject and is evident as one 'moves up' through four different 'levels' of conscious intentionality. It is characterized by the "detached, disinterested, unrestricted desire to know."[3] The four levels are differentiated by the intentional acts of the human subject, that is, the dynamically linked operations of experiencing, understanding, judging, and deciding.[4] This structure, Lonergan argues, is invariant. He refers to it as Transcendental Method or Generalized Empirical Method.[5]

---

1   Bernard J. F. Lonergan, *Insight: A Study of Human Understanding*, ed. Frederick E. Crowe and Robert M. Doran, Collected Works of Bernard Lonergan, vol. 3 (Toronto: University of Toronto Press, 1992).

2   Ibid., 1-31.

3   Ibid., 483.

4   Lonergan's criticism of any empiricist, rationalist or existentialist view of the human subject is that these positions effectively reduce human consciousness to a single operation, unrelated to and undistinguished from others. See Marc Smith, "Religious Language and Lonergan's Realms of Meaning," *Sophia: A Journal for Discussion in Philosophical Theology* 25:1 (1986): 20. This is the key to Lonergan's position: he has distinguished and related the full set of conscious operations of the human subject but has avoided the tendency to either conflate or separate them. See Bernard J. F. Lonergan, "Christology Today: Methodological Reflections," in *A Third Collection: Papers by Bernard J. F. Lonergan, S.J.*, ed. Frederick E. Crowe (New York: Paulist Press, 1985), 83. Not only is the human attentive, intelligent, reasonable, and responsible, but the world of meaning is mediated and "structured by intelligence, by reasonable judgment, by decision and action." Ibid., 79.

5   In *Method* the former terminology dominates. But 'Generalized Empirical Method' both harks back to *Insight* and was Lonergan's preference in the latter period of his life. 'Generalized Empirical Method' is employed in this book.

2.1 THE FIRST LEVEL OF GENERALIZED EMPIRICAL METHOD: EXPERIENCE

The first level of conscious intentionality is that of experience or presentation.[6] Empirical consciousness regards the data of both sensitive human experience and that of consciousness. That is to say, the data given to conscious intentionality at this empirical level includes both the data of sense (e.g., the five senses) and the data of consciousness (e.g., memories and self-presence).[7] Conscious intentionality is guided on this first level by the precept 'be attentive'. By attending to all relevant data, one is in a better position to know than if one fails to identify such data.

2.1.1 PATTERNS OF EXPERIENCE

The experience of the first level is not uniform, and one's stream of consciousness is directed by "conation, interest, attention, [and] purpose."[8] There are, then, different patterns of empirical consciousness. Among other patterns, the biological, the aesthetic, the practical, the intellectual, and the dramatic can be noted.[9] The biological pattern of experience has to do with the physiological functions of the person required for sustenance and survival. The aesthetic pattern has to do with the joys and pains of life that transcend the mere biological: aside from eating for sustenance like a soldier on combat patrol, one may appreciate *haute cuisine* as does a gourmet. The practical pattern of human experience has to do with the performance of day-to-day living in the world in terms of one's "daily tasks."[10] The intellectual pattern of experience functions as the "vitally adaptive collaborator of the spirit of inquiry"; it blocks from consciousness that which would disrupt the "passionless calm" required by the spirit of enquiry.[11] And lastly, the dramatic pattern of experience pertains to our day-to-day interactions with others inasmuch as we make our lives a work of art in the sense of "learning a role and developing in oneself the feelings appropriate to

---

6   Lonergan, *Insight: A Study of Human Understanding*, 30.

7   John Dadosky, *The Structure of Religious Knowing: Encountering the Sacred in Eliade and Lonergan* (Albany, NY: SUNY Press, 2004), 46.

8   Lonergan, *Insight: A Study of Human Understanding*, 205.

9   One can also note a mystical pattern of experience. Ibid., 410.

10   Ibid., 293.

11   Ibid., 210.

its performance."[12] It is via these different patterns of experience that data is proffered to the second level of conscious intentionality.

2.2 THE SECOND LEVEL OF GENERALIZED EMPIRICAL METHOD: UNDERSTANDING

The second level of conscious intentionality is the intellectual level. On this second level, intelligence operates to interrogate the data of experience. It is thus concerned with acts of understanding, that is, with insight into data and the formulation of concepts that express the intelligibility latent in any given set of data. When concepts are formulated from insights, they sit as formulations of answers to the kind of question operative at this level, the question 'What is it?' It is a question of the *formal meaning* of the data. Focused as it is upon intelligibility, the precept guiding activities at this second level of conscious intentionality is thus 'be intelligent.'[13]

2.2.1 REALMS OF MEANING AND DIFFERENTIATIONS OF CONSCIOUSNESS

Whilst on the topic of understanding, of questions of/pertaining to formal meaning, it is useful to note that Lonergan identifies four different 'realms of meaning':[14] the realm of common sense; the realm of theory; the realm of interiority; and the realm of transcendence. Lonergan argues that the individual who develops the ability to recognize and move freely between the four realms has achieved 'fully differentiated consciousness.'[15] He notes:

---

12   Ibid., 212.

13   Lonergan, *Method in Theology*, 13-16.

14   Ibid., 81.

15   Differentiations of consciousness are discussed here under the second level of consciousness because patterns of experience relate to experience in the same way as differentiations of consciousness relate to understanding. See Gerard Walmsley, *Lonergan on Philosophic Pluralism: The Polymorphism of Consciousness as the Key to Philosophy* (Toronto: University of Toronto Press, 2008), 209. Lonergan lists seven differentiations: the linguistic differentiation; the religious differentiation; the literary differentiation; the systematic differentiation; the scientific differentiation; the scholarly differentiation; and, the modern philosophic differentiation. Bernard J. F. Lonergan, "The World Mediated by Meaning," in *Philosophical and Theological Papers, 1965-1980*, Collected Works of Bernard Lonergan (Toronto: University of Toronto Press, 2004), 112-16. The religious

[i]n fully differentiated consciousness there are four realms of meaning. There is the realm of common sense with its meanings expressed in everyday or ordinary language. There is the realm of theory where language is technical, simply objective in reference, and so refers to the subject and his [or her] operations only as objects. There is the realm of interiority where language speaks indeed of the subject and his [or her] operations as objects but, nonetheless, rests upon a self-appropriation that has verified in personal experience the operator, the operations, and the processes referred to in the basic terms and relations of the language employed. Finally, there is the realm of transcendence in which the subject is related to divinity in the language of prayer and of prayerful silence.[16]

How ought one understand the notion of differentiated consciousness? It is perhaps best grasped by considering an example of what Lonergan calls troubled consciousness. Specifically, Lonergan illustrates the distinction and tensions between the realms of common sense and theory using a famous example from physics,[17] namely Sir Arthur Eddington's dilemma of the two tables.[18] Eddington writes, "I have settled down to the task of writing [lectures] and have drawn up my chairs to my two tables. Two tables! Yes; there are duplicates of every object about me—two tables, two chairs, two pens."[19] Eddington goes on to say that to the person of common sense the table is a 'thing': brown, solid and motionless. But to the physicist it is colorless; almost total emptiness except for the 'wavicles'[20] of which it is comprised. These 'wavicles', in contrast to the motionless table of common sense, are moving about the space the table occupies at high velocity. Which is the real table? To Eddington, following in the wake of Lockean thought, the scientific table is real and the table of common sense an illusion resulting from scientific ignorance. Lonergan is able to arrive at a different solution to Eddington's problem by employing the categories of common sense and theory, derived from a careful appropri-

---

(transcendent) and modern philosophic (interior) differentiations are of most relevance to this book.

16   Lonergan, *Method in Theology*, 257.
17   Ibid., 84.
18   Arthur Eddington, *The Nature of the Physical World* (Cambridge, UK: Cambridge University Press, 1928), xi–xv.
19   Ibid., xi.
20   Ibid., 201. A portmanteau from 'waves' and 'particles'.

ation of his interiority. Lonergan can affirm that the two tables are both equally real: the 'brown table' is the table understood within the realm of common sense (arising largely from practical and day-to-day patterns of experience); and, the 'table of "wavicles"' is the table as understood from within the realm of theory (arising from the intellectual patterning of experience).[21] That is, they are equally real, but simply understood by differing differentiations of consciousness. In being able to relate Eddington's predicament to differing realms of meaning, the relevance of the realm of interiority—which arises from the modern philosophical differentiation of consciousness—is demonstrated: "Mastery of this interior realm can provide one with the resources needed to address critical epistemological and metaphysical questions, and heal the tensions between the realms of common sense and theory."[22]

The final realm of meaning is the realm of transcendence. It relates to the transcendent, or religious, differentiation of consciousness. Lonergan writes of the religious differentiation of consciousness that it is

> [e]ndless in its variations, it commonly is marked by an intermittent withdrawal from everyday activities and concerns. It can be gregarious, but its more intense moments are often solitary and silent. ... So down the ages there have been people devoting their lives to a growth in holiness, and such ascetics and mystics develop a type of consciousness expressed by the peace and joy on the countenance of a statue of the seated Buddha.[23]

The realm of transcendence is thus the realm of religious experience in which one can detect "the emergence of gift as a differentiated realm."[24] It corresponds with the human desire for complete intelligibility, good

---

21   It should be noted that in a sense no patterning of experience excludes common sense: even the intellectual pattern requires it to 'get going'. Common sense is, of course, operative when experience is patterned in the practical manner. See Bernard J. F. Lonergan, *Understanding and Being: the Halifax Lectures on Insight*, ed. Elizabeth A. Morelli and Mark D. Morelli, Collected Works of Bernard Lonergan, vol. 5 (Toronto: University of Toronto Press, 1990), 307.

22   Neil Ormerod, "Augustine's *De Trinitate* and Lonergan's Realms of Meaning," *Theological Studies* 64:4 (2003): 781.

23   Lonergan, "The World Mediated by Meaning," 113.

24   Lonergan, *Method in Theology*, 266.

beyond all criticism and with the realm of human experience of loving and knowing God.[25]

Lonergan will thus write of differentiations of consciousness and the ability to distinguish the various realms of meaning.

> It is, of course, only in a rather highly developed consciousness that the distinction between the realms of meaning is to be carried out. Undifferentiated consciousness uses indiscriminately the procedures of common sense, and so its explanations, its self-knowledge, its religion are rudimentary. Classical consciousness is theoretical as well as common sense, but the theory is not sufficiently advanced for the sharp opposition between the two realms of meaning to be adequately grasped. Troubled consciousness emerges when an Eddington contrasts his two tables: the bulky, solid, colored desk at which he worked, and the manifold of colorless 'wavicles' so minute that the desk was mostly empty space. Differentiated consciousness appears when the critical exigence turns attention upon interiority, when self-appropriation is achieved, when the subject relates his different procedures to the several realms, relates the several realms to one another, and consciously shifts from one realm to another by consciously changing his procedures.[26]

This idea of distinct differentiations of consciousness is central to Lonergan's philosophical stance and the question of theological foundations. It reappears in the section of this chapter that addresses Doran's approach to theological foundations.[27]

---

25 Ormerod, "Augustine's *De Trinitate* and Lonergan's Realms of Meaning," 781.

26 Lonergan, *Method in Theology*, 84.

27 The realms of meaning are also the basis for Lonergan's understanding of three 'stages of meaning' in the unfolding of the polymorphism of consciousness in the Western tradition. He writes of these three stages: "In the first stage conscious and intentional operations follow the mode of common sense. In a second stage besides the mode of common sense there is also the mode of theory, where the theory is controlled by a logic. In a third stage the modes of common sense and theory remain, science asserts its autonomy from philosophy, and there occur philosophies that leave theory to science and take their stand on interiority." Ibid., 85. This chapter, indeed this book, represents an enquiry constructed in the third stage of meaning in which meaning is controlled by the differentiation of interiority.

2.3 THE THIRD LEVEL OF GENERALIZED EMPIRICAL METHOD: JUDGMENT

The third level of conscious intentionality builds upon the second. It can be noted that inasmuch as questions for intelligence yield insights formulated in concepts, they yield possible answers. But at the second level, the level of intelligence, they remain only possible answers. It remains for the third level of conscious intentionality, that of rational consciousness, to discern the truth of the possible positions raised by the second level of conscious intentionality. In this way, as the second level is concerned with intelligibility, the third level is concerned specifically with truth, reality and existence. The operative question at this level is, 'Is it so?' The third level of conscious intentionality is concerned with the act of judgment. The truth of a judgment is contingent upon the grasp of what Lonergan calls the 'virtually unconditioned'. If the conditions for judgment have been fulfilled—if there is enough evidence and if no further questions are forthcoming—then a judgment ought to ensue. Conversely, if there is insufficient evidence—if the conditions for judgment are not satisfied—then judgment should be withheld.[28] The precept guiding activities at this level is thus 'be reasonable': the process at this level requires weighing evidence to discern whether there is enough support for any given judgment.

This third level holds high significance in Lonergan's overall philosophical project. As Dadosky indicates, "the level of judgment is the foundation for Lonergan's epistemology in that he assumes that when one reaches a grasp of the virtually unconditioned one *knows*."[29] Moreover, three kinds of objectivity parallel the first three levels of conscious intentionality. As Lonergan writes:

> Human knowing is a compound of many operations of different kinds. It follows that the objectivity of human knowing is not some single uniform property but once more a compound of quite different properties found in quite different kinds of operation. There is an experiential objectivity in the givenness of the data of sense and of the data of consciousness. But such experiential objectivity is not the one and only ingredient in the objectivity of human knowing. The process of inquiry, investigation, reflection, coming to judge is governed throughout by the exigences of human intelligence and

---

28 Lonergan, *Insight: A Study of Human Understanding*, 305-06.

29 Dadosky, *The Structure of Religious Knowing: Encountering the Sacred in Eliade and Lonergan*, 47. The emphasis is Dadosky's own.

human reasonableness; it is these exigences that, in part, are formulated in logics and methodologies; and they are in their own way no less decisive than objectivity in the genesis and progress of human knowing. Finally, there is a third, terminal, or absolute type of objectivity, that comes to the fore when we judge, when we distinguish sharply between what we feel, what we imagine, what we think seems to be so and, on the other hand, what is so.[30]

It is in the grasp of the virtually unconditioned that absolute objectivity is reached. In that judgment, the reality of the object is affirmed as independent from the subject. It is a judgment of fact—of what is so—an affirmation of reality precisely as reality. In this way, the level of judgment is also the foundation for Lonergan's understanding of metaphysics: what is affirmed in judgment is existence.[31] But it is not the end of the questioning process, and this third level prepares the way for a fourth.

2.4 THE FOURTH LEVEL OF GENERALIZED EMPIRICAL METHOD: DECIDING

The fourth level of conscious intentionality concerns value. It is the existential or the ethical level of human conscious intentionality. The questions operative at this level are of the ilk, 'Is it valuable?' or 'Is it worthwhile?' or 'How shall I proceed?' It is the level of decision, of moral self-constitution, the level associated with judgments of value. In *Method* Lonergan assigns a central role for feelings on this fourth level of conscious intentionality: between judgments of fact of the third level and judgments of value on the fourth level sit the apprehensions of value that are revealed in feelings.[32] These are not the feelings associated with sensitive appetites, such as hunger, but rather the feelings that are associated with the drive towards moral self-transcendence.[33] Feelings play a constitutive role in moral discernment. And it is on the basis of chosen values—a process which itself affirms a scale of values inasmuch as one value is chosen over and above competing values—that a specific course of action is pursued. Focused as it is

30 Lonergan, "The Subject," 76.

31 Lonergan, *Insight: A Study of Human Understanding*, 381.

32 Lonergan, *Method in Theology*, 36-41.

33 Dadosky, *The Structure of Religious Knowing: Encountering the Sacred in Eliade and Lonergan*, 48.

upon value and decision, the precept Lonergan identifies as governing this level of conscious intentionality is 'be responsible.'

Lonergan summarizes his theory of conscious intentionality:

> What promotes the subject from experiential to intellectual consciousness is the desire to understand, the intention of intelligibility. What next promotes him from intellectual to rational consciousness, is a fuller unfolding of the same intention: for the desire to understand, once understanding is reached, becomes the desire to understand correctly; in other words, the intention of intelligibility, once an intelligible is reached, becomes the intention of the right intelligible, of the true and, through truth, of reality. Finally the intention of the intelligible, the true, the real, becomes also the intention of the good, the question of value, of what is worthwhile, when the already acting subject confronts his world and adverts to his own acting in it.[34]

It is this understanding of the subject that sits at the foundation of Lonergan's entire philosophical and theological enterprise.[35]

3. LONERGAN ON HORIZONS

The intentional operations of a subject are not performed in some kind of noetic or phenomenological vacuum. Rather, a subject operates and is oriented within a specific 'field of view', or, in Lonergan's terminology, an 'horizon'. He indicates his use of the term by analogy with a visible horizon:

> In its literal sense the word, horizon, denotes the bounding circle, the line at which earth and sky appear to meet. This line is the limit of one's field of vision. As one moves about, it recedes in front and closes in behind so that, for different standpoints, there are different horizons. Moreover, for each different standpoint and horizon, there are different divisions of the totality of visible objects. Beyond

---

34   Lonergan, "The Subject," 81.

35   It should be noted that the question of the precise number of levels of consciousness is a matter of ongoing discussion. Doran, relying on some of Lonergan's own comments, has argued for the possibility of a fifth level of consciousness. See Chapters 9 and 10 of Doran, *What Is Systematic Theology?* By contrast, for a stance that argues against the presence of a fifth level, see Michael Vertin, "Lonergan on Consciousness: Is There a Fifth Level?," *Method: Journal of Lonergan Studies* 12:1 (1994): 1-36.

the horizon lie the objects that, at least for the moment, cannot be seen. Within the horizon lie the objects that can now be seen.[36] Lonergan then argues that the extent of one's knowledge and range of interests are similarly bounded. As one's standpoint affects one's field of vision, likewise the "scope of one's knowledge and the range of one's interests vary with the period in which one lives, one's social background and milieu, one's education and personal development."[37] Lonergan contends that what is beyond one's horizon is "outside the range of one's knowledge and interests"; about such things one neither knows nor cares.[38] Conversely, what lies within one's horizon is in some sense—even if minimally so—an object of both knowledge and interest.

Horizons differ. Such differences can be complementary, genetic, or dialectical. Doctors, plumbers, and priests may largely live in different horizons, but they know of one another's worlds and acknowledge their complementary nature. These different horizons "in some measure include one another and, for the rest, they complement one another. Singly they are not self-sufficient, and together they represent the motivations and the knowledge needed for the functioning of a communal world. Such horizons are complementary."[39]

Genetic differences relate horizons to each other as part of a single process of development. "Each later stage presupposes earlier stages, partly to include them, and partly to transform them. Precisely because the stages are earlier and later, no two are simultaneous. They are parts, not of a single communal world, but of a single biography or of a single history."[40] Newtonian physics, for example, is presupposed by relativity theory. Relativity theory replaced Newtonian physics but includes the insights of Newtonian physics at the same time as it transcends it.

Dialectical differences exist when horizons conflict. What is held to be intelligible, true, good in one horizon is held to be unintelligible, false, evil in another. "Each may have some awareness of the other and so each in a manner may include the other. But such inclusion is also

---

36 Lonergan, *Method in Theology*, 235-36.
37 Ibid., 236.
38 Ibid.
39 Ibid.
40 Ibid.

negation and rejection."[41] Frederick Copleston and Bertrand Russell were aware of each other's philosophical stances in their famous debate on BBC radio, but—Copleston the theist and Russell the agnostic—patently disagreed on the nature of 'necessary being'.

Lonergan concludes his reflection on horizons by noting that they "are the structured resultant of past achievement and … the condition and the limitation of further development."[42] Learning is not simply adding new facts to old facts; rather new knowledge grows organically out of what a subject has already achieved. So it is that all of one's intentions, statements and deeds stand within contexts. It is to these contexts we appeal when

> we outline the reasons for our goals, when we clarify, amplify, qualify our statements, or when we explain our deeds. Within such contexts must be fitted each new item of knowledge and each new factor in our attitudes. What does not fit, will not be noticed or, if forced on our attention, it will seem irrelevant or unimportant.[43]

Horizons are thus the "sweep of our interests and of our knowledge; they are the fertile source of further knowledge and care; but they also are the boundaries that limit our capacities for assimilating more than we already have attained."[44]

4. LONERGAN AND DORAN ON CONVERSION: THE SUBJECT AS HEALED

Lonergan's understanding of conversion is underpinned by Joseph de Finance's differentiation of vertical and horizontal exercises of freedom.[45] These two differ in that a horizontal exercise of freedom occurs within an established horizon, whereas a vertical exercise of freedom consists in the set of judgments and decisions by which one moves from one horizon to another. While some exercises of vertical freedom may in fact deepen and broaden an extant horizon, other exercises of vertical freedom involve movement into a new horizon by means of an about-face. The new horizon "comes out of the old by repudiating characteristic features; it begins a new sequence that can keep reveal-

---

41   Ibid.
42   Ibid., 237.
43   Ibid.
44   Ibid.
45   Ibid., 40, 237.

ing ever greater depth and breadth and wealth. Such an about-face and new beginning is what is meant by a conversion."[46] So it is that conversion is to be understood with reference to the exercise of vertical liberty. James Marsh notes, "Conversion is, then, a function of the whole person, but most fundamentally of the so-called fourth level of freedom, building on, retaining, and going beyond the first three levels of experience, understanding, and judgment."[47] Such conversion, according to Lonergan, may be religious, moral, or intellectual. To these, Doran has added, with the approval of Lonergan, psychic conversion.[48] Lonergan identified the usual causal sequence of conversion as moving from religious to moral to intellectual.[49] This is the sequence in which the conversions are discussed in this chapter, with psychic conversion in the last place.[50]

These transformations of consciousness—conversions—are called for precisely because there are negative features operative within human consciousness that obstruct the operation of human attentiveness, intelligence, reasonableness, and responsibility. Lonergan refers to these impediments to the unrestricted desire to know under the general heading of bias. Bias represents a flight from complete understanding. It does not eradicate the desire to know, but limits the range of one's desire to know. It suppresses certain kinds of questions. Lonergan identifies four kinds of bias: dramatic bias (unconscious bias), individual bias (individual egoism), group bias (collective

---

46   Ibid., 237-38.

47   James L. Marsh, "Praxis and Ultimate Reality: Intellectual, Moral, and Religious Conversion as Radical Political Conversion," *Ultimate Reality and Meaning* 13:3 (1990): 225.

48   For religious, moral and intellectual conversion, see Lonergan, *Method in Theology*, 238. While Lonergan originally wrote of three kinds of conversion, he was later convinced of the existence of a fourth, *viz.*, psychic conversion as understood and developed by Doran. See John Dadosky, "Healing the Psychological Subject: Towards a Fourfold Notion of Conversion?," *Theoforum* 35:1 (2004): 78.

49   Lonergan, *Method in Theology*, 243.

50   Doran does not take a definitive stance as to where in the series of conversions psychic conversion occurs. Inasmuch as it is a reflectively based transformation involving self-appropriation, it occurs after intellectual conversion. It serves in that sense, and for explanatory purposes, to treat psychic conversion in that context. Doran, *Theology and the Dialectics of History*, 161.

egoism), and general bias (the bias of common sense hostile to theoretical understanding and long term solutions). While it is beyond the ambit of this chapter to consider these biases in depth, it serves well to flag them lest Lonergan's position appear too optimistic. Lonergan is acutely aware of the existence of bias and its corrosive effects within individuals and in history. It is precisely because of the existence and effect of these kinds of bias that conversion holds such a central role in Lonergan's work.[51] The hard work of rooting out bias is an essential component in the process of conversion.[52]

4.1 TRANSFORMATIONS OF HORIZON: RELIGIOUS, MORAL, INTELLECTUAL, AND PSYCHIC CONVERSION

Religious conversion, according to Lonergan—and quoting Paul Tillich—"is being grasped by ultimate concern."[53] The operative principle, the impetus for the transformation of the subject through religious conversion, lies beyond the individual. In the Christian tradition, Lonergan notes, the agent is identified as God, who floods our hearts with the gift of divine love through the Holy Spirit: it is operative grace in which God replaces the heart of stone with a heart of flesh.[54] God transforms the subject such that one's being becomes a being-in-love with God. Like all love, it is self-surrender. When one is in love, love is the "first principle" from which flows "one's desires and fears, one's joys and sorrows, one's discernment of values, one's decisions and deeds."[55] Moreover, when one is in love with God one's self-surrender is "a surrender, not as an act, but as a dynamic state that is prior to and principle of subsequent acts."[56] This dynamic state is "conscious without being known" and as such "it is an experience of mystery."[57] Moreover, "because it is being in love, the mystery is not merely attractive but fascinating; to it one belongs; by it one is possessed. Because it

---

51 Lonergan treats dramatic bias in *Insight: A Study of Human Understanding*, 191–203. And individual, group and general bias are treated at ibid., 218–42.
52 Lonergan, *Method in Theology*, 240.
53 Ibid.
54 Ibid., 241.
55 Ibid., 105.
56 Ibid., 240.
57 Ibid., 105.

is an unmeasured love, the mystery evokes awe."[58] Being-in-love is not detached from the world; rather, as consciousness on the fourth level,

> It is the type of consciousness that deliberates, makes judgments of value, decides, acts responsibly and freely. But it is this consciousness as brought to a fulfillment, as having undergone a conversion, as possessing a basis that may be broadened and deepened and heightened and enriched but not superseded, as ready to deliberate and judge and decide and act with the easy freedom of those that do all good because they are in love. So the gift of God's love occupies the ground and root of the fourth and highest level of man's intentional consciousness. It takes over the peak of the soul, the *apex animae*.[59]

So if religious conversion, in Christian language, is operative grace, then this grace becoming effective in subsequent acts, in 'one's discernment of values, one's decisions and deeds,' is cooperative grace. Such actions point towards the issue of moral conversion.

Moral conversion—according to Lonergan's position in *Method*—becomes apparent when one starts to move from hedonism,[60] from narcissism, from self-indulgence, from self-gratification, to a position where one begins to choose the truly valuable. That is to say, there comes a moment in the individual's moral formation when she discovers that choosing not only affects the objects chosen or rejected in the exercise of freedom; it also affects her very self-constitution. "Then is the time for the exercise of vertical freedom and then moral conversion consists in opting for the truly good, even for value against satisfaction when value and satisfaction conflict."[61] Moral conversion can thus be characterized by a change in the criterion to which a subject appeals in her decision-making: it "changes the criterion of one's decisions and choices from satisfactions to values."[62]

Intellectual conversion, for Lonergan, is rooted in the affirmation that human knowing follows a specific and normative pattern of

---

58   Ibid.

59   Ibid., 107.

60   Doran has related Lonergan's stance on moral conversion, as presented in *Method*, to St Ignatius Loyola's three 'times of election.' This highly cogent development of Lonergan's stance is acknowledged, but is not rehearsed here.

61   Lonergan, *Method in Theology*, 240.

62   Ibid.

operations. Rudimentary intellectual conversion may manifest itself simply as a commitment to truth. But in its fullest sense, it involves the acknowledgement that knowing is a composite performance of interrelated operations: experiencing, understanding, judging and believing. This is not the simple affirmation of a theory that may seem to correlate more or less with human cognition; rather it is an affirmation possible only after one has struggled with the process of self-appropriation and identified this normative structure within one's own consciousness. In this way, intellectual conversion eradicates an

> exceedingly stubborn and misleading myth concerning reality, objectivity, and human knowledge. The myth is that knowing is like looking, that objectivity is seeing what is there to be seen and not seeing what is not there, and that the real is what is out there now to be looked at.[63]

Intellectual conversion, then, moves the subject beyond an horizon that conceives of knowing as looking, and orients the subject towards the world mediated by meaning.

Psychic conversion is intimately connected with the realities studied by depth psychology. Using Sigmund Freud's terminology, psychic conversion has to do with the functioning of 'the censor' that sits at the borderline between consciousness and underlying neural manifolds. It is the censor that is responsible for the admission of images into consciousness. "When the censor operates constructively, it sorts through irrelevant data and allows us to receive the necessary images needed for insights. When the censor is repressive, it does not allow access to images that would allow needed insights."[64] In psychic conversion, the censor's functioning is transformed from a destructive to a constructive role. It is important to note that the censor primarily represses images and not feelings. And because images are concomitant with feelings, when an image is repressed, the feelings appropriate to that image can become detached from it and attach themselves to an incongruous image. It is in the process of achieving psychic conversion that such incongruous images are identified, and the victimization or

---

63   Ibid., 238.

64   Dadosky, "Healing the Psychological Subject: Towards a Fourfold Notion of Conversion?," 79. For a detailed discussion, see Doran, *Theology and the Dialectics of History*, 139-76.

psychological scarring at root of dramatic bias can begin to be traced.[65] If someone suffers an injustice at the hands of the legal system—say the courts permitted foreclosure on his business loans under dubious circumstances—he may become enraged at the presence of any symbol that he associates with state authority such as lawyers, police, politicians or even traffic lights. Such a wound would taint his conscious intentionality in the form of a dramatic bias that would compromise his ability to respond to genuine social values. It is psychic conversion that facilitates identifying the true source of such dramatic bias and provides the possibility of healing victimhood.

A brief summary of the four dimensions of integral conversion can now be presented: religious conversion refers to the transformation of one's horizon resulting from God's love flooding one's heart such that the sweep of one's concern embraces ultimate meaning; moral conversion is a change in one's criterion of the good from what is merely satisfying to what is truly valuable; intellectual conversion opens one up to a broader understanding of the real, in which knowing is no longer considered a form of looking but as that which is known through a composite performance of experiencing, understanding and judging; and, psychic conversion enables the censor to function constructively so that feelings and symbols enter consciousness in a manner that facilitates the subject successfully negotiating the tension of matter and spirit. In Doran's words, "Religious conversion ... affects ... a dimension of consciousness—at times Lonergan called it a fifth level—where we are pure openness to the reception of grace; moral conversion affects the fourth level; intellectual conversion affects the second and third levels; and psychic conversion affects the first level."[66] Total personal conversion includes all these dimensions, and all are in some sense required for an individual to appropriate the foundations

---

65   Dadosky, "Healing the Psychological Subject: Towards a Fourfold Notion of Conversion?," 79. For Doran, it is the dream that points to the dimension of the interior life that is most affected by psychic conversion. This is not to say that psychic conversion only pertains to dream interpretation, but, rather, because the censor is more relaxed during sleep, the data available to the subject in dreams is highly relevant to the process of full self-appropriation. During sleep, repressed images are freer to emerge. In this sense, dream interpretation—in the context of psychotherapy—can facilitate psychic conversion.

66   Doran, *Theology and the Dialectics of History*, 59.

constructed in *Theology and the Dialectics of History* and expanded upon in *What is Systematic Theology?*

5. CONCLUSION

This short chapter had a single purpose: to introduce Lonergan's thought in a manner relevant to a critical grounding of the Preferential Option for the Poor. The first section of the chapter began with a presentation of Lonergan's intentionality analysis. It then considered the horizons within which the subject operates. Lastly, it considered the conversions—religious, moral, intellectual, and Doran's notion of psychic conversion—by which one transcends prior horizons. This chapter has prepared the reader for what is to follow in the next three chapters. That is, Chapters 4 and 5 present an account of the contribution Lonergan's work on conversion makes to understanding the Preferential Option for the Poor. Religious and moral conversion are treated in Chapter 4 and intellectual and psychic conversion in Chapter 5. Then, the final chapter, Chapter 6, details Doran's specific grounding of the Preferential Option and links that understanding to the Church's mission.

CHAPTER 4

INTEGRAL CONVERSION AND THE PREFERENTIAL OPTION FOR THE POOR PART I: RELIGIOUS AND MORAL CONVERSION AS SPONTANEOUS

I. INTRODUCTION

C hapter 2 of this book indicated the foundational role played by conversion in Liberation Theology's understanding of the Preferential Option for the Poor. Gustavo Gutiérrez writes of the Option, it "is a decision incumbent upon every Christian" that "implies leaving the road one is on" and entering the world of "the one excluded from dominant social sectors, communities, viewpoints, and ideas."[1] Jon Sobrino also argues that "the position of Liberation Theology" is that the Option "has the structure of conversion, since it is made in distinct form, and historically in opposition to, other options."[2] Despite the centrality accorded to conversion by these liberation theologians in understanding the Option for the Poor, the precise issue of the 'structure of conversion' remains somewhat vague in their writings.

This chapter and the next seek to relate Lonergan and Doran's understanding of conversion, introduced in Chapter 3 of the present work, to the Option for the Poor, and to do so theologically.[3] The

---

1   Gutiérrez, "Option for the Poor: Reviews and Challenges," 16. And Gutiérrez, "The Option for the Poor Arises from Faith in Christ," 318.

2   Sobrino, "Central Position of the Reign of God in Liberation Theology," 375.

3   While it is not the aim of this book to proceed in a purely philosophical manner, it should be noted that James L. Marsh, who draws heavily on Lonergan's philosophy, argues that "there is a Preferential Option for the Poor that can be argued for philosophically as well as religiously." See James L. Marsh, *Praxis, Process, and Transcendence* (Albany, NY: SUNY Press, 1999), 213. See also, James L. Marsh, *Critique, Action, and Liberation*

chapter is not an exegesis performed upon any specific liberation theologian's approach to conversion and the Option for the Poor, still less upon Liberation Theology as a whole. Likewise, the precise nature of the interrelations of the conversions is not the focus of this chapter.[4] This chapter considers the conversions in their usual causative

---

(Albany, NY: SUNY Press, 1995), 174-76. The present work begins 'from above' in religious conversion.

4   Although Lonergan uses the notions of 'sublation' and 'causation' to express the unity and mutually reinforcing nature of the various kinds of conversions, the present work takes this unity as given. Lonergan employs the term sublation in the sense in which Karl Rahner employs it rather than the manner in which it is used by G.W.F. Hegel. Lonergan argues, "[W]hat sublates goes beyond what is sublated." That which sublates "introduces something new and distinct" and "puts everything on a new basis." But "far from interfering with the sublated or destroying it, on the contrary," what sublates needs the sublated, "includes it, preserves all its proper features and properties, and carries them forward to a fuller realization within a richer context." Lonergan contends that when the three conversions occur in the one consciousness, intellectual conversion is sublated by moral conversion, which in turn is sublated by religious conversion. Intellectual conversion, with its commitment to truth, is taken up by moral conversion whereby the subject is oriented not only to truth but to the wider world of value. "But this in no way interferes with or weakens his devotion to truth. He still needs truth, for he must apprehend reality and real potentiality before he can deliberately respond to value. The truth he needs is still the truth attained in accord with the exigences of rational consciousness. But now his pursuit of it is all the more secure because he has been armed against bias, and it is all the more meaningful and significant because it occurs within, and plays an essential role in, the far richer context of the pursuit of all values." In a similar manner, religious conversion can sublate moral conversion. "Questions for intelligence, for reflection, for deliberation reveal the *eros* of the human spirit, its capacity and its desire for self-transcendence." But it is not until that desire for self-transcendence is fulfilled, even if in an inchoate manner, that the subject's being is transformed and she becomes a subject in love. She is then "grasped, possessed, owned through a total and so an other-worldly love. Then there is a new basis for all valuing and all doing good. In no way are fruits of intellectual or moral conversion negated or diminished." Rather than diminishment, the "pursuit of the true and the good is included within and furthered by a cosmic context and purpose." Moreover, "there now accrues to [the subject] the power of love" which enables her "to accept the suffering involved in undoing the effects" of decline in history. Lonergan, *Method in Theology*, 241-42. In terms of causation, religious conversion often proves to be the impetus for both moral and

sequence as identified by Lonergan in terms of the graced relations within consciousness. And along the healing vector of consciousness, the usual sequence of healing begins with religious conversion and moves to moral conversion, from religious and moral conversion to intellectual conversion, "and from these three conversions ... to psychic conversion."[5] This trajectory provides the structure of the next

---

intellectual conversion. Lonergan writes, "Though religious conversion sublates moral, and moral conversion sublates intellectual, one is not to infer that intellectual comes first and then moral and finally religious. On the contrary, from a causal viewpoint, one would say that first there is God's gift of his love. Next, the eye of this love reveals values in their splendor, while the strength of this love brings about their realization, and that is moral conversion. Finally, among the values discerned by the eye of love is the value of believing the truths taught by the religious tradition, and in such tradition and belief are the seeds of intellectual conversion. For the word, spoken and heard, proceeds from and penetrates to all four levels of intentional consciousness. Its content is not just a content of experience but a content of experience and understanding and judging and deciding. The analogy of sight yields the cognitional myth. But fidelity to the word engages the whole man." Ibid., 243. So it is that the conversions do not 'compete' with one another but rather cooperate and reinforce each other. Elsewhere Lonergan has written: "Conversion is three-dimensional. It is intellectual inasmuch as it regards our orientation to the intelligible and the true. It is moral inasmuch as it regards our orientation to the good. It is religious inasmuch as it regards our orientation to God. The three dimensions are distinct, so that conversion can occur in one dimension without occurring in the other two, or in two dimensions without occurring in the other one. At the same time, the three dimensions are solidary. Conversion in one leads to conversion in the other dimensions, and relapse from one prepares for relapse from the others." Lonergan, "Unity and Plurality: The Coherence of Christian Truth," 70. And what Lonergan says here of the three conversions applies to the four conversions: psychic conversion may be present or absent in any combination with the other conversions. But it forms a unity with the other conversions. It cooperates with them and strengthens them when it is present; and relapse from psychic conversion prepares the way for relapse from the others. See Robert M. Doran, "Dramatic Artistry in the Third Stage of Meaning," in *Theological Foundations* (Milwaukee, WI: Marquette University Press, 1995), 250-52. And, more broadly, see Doran, *Theology and the Dialectics of History*, 42-63; 211-53.

5   Robert M. Doran, "What is the Gift of the Holy Spirit?" http://www.lonerganresource.com/pdf/contributors/20091029-Robert_Doran-What_Is_the_Gift_of_the_Holy_Spirit.pdf (accessed 19-May 2011). As noted in the last chapter, Doran does not take a definitive stance as to where

two chapters as they answer the question: how might one understand the Option for the Poor from Lonergan and Doran's perspective on the fourfold integral conversion of the subject? The focus remains on Lonergan's approach—on religious, moral, intellectual, and psychic conversion in turn—but each section will engage with Liberation Theology inasmuch as such engagement helps to illustrate the power of Lonergan's stance and its relevance to liberation concerns, specifically the Preferential Option for the Poor. Moreover, in the sections on moral conversion in this chapter, and on intellectual conversion, and psychic conversion in the next, the issue of bias and its effects on history are discussed, for it is conversion alone that can undo the effects of sin in history.

2. RELIGIOUS CONVERSION AND THE PREFERENTIAL OPTION FOR THE POOR: SANCTIFYING GRACE AS THE FONT OF ALL CONVERSION

The preceding chapter noted that, in Christian terms, Lonergan understands religious conversion as being prompted by God's offer of divine love. When that offer of love is accepted, when the subject decides to return God's love, religious conversion is effected and the subject's horizon is transformed. Grace becomes operative in human consciousness, and the religiously converted subject has become a being-in-love. Like all love, being in love with God involves self-surrender. But when one is in love with God, "it is such a surrender, not as an act, but as a dynamic state that is prior to and principle of subsequent acts."[6] Lonergan writes,

> It used to be said, *Nihil amatum nisi praecognitum*, knowledge precedes love. The truth of this tag is the fact that ordinarily operations on the fourth level of intentional consciousness presuppose and complement corresponding operations on the other three. There is a minor exception to this rule inasmuch as people do fall

---

in the series of conversions psychic conversion occurs. Inasmuch as it is a reflectively based transformation involving self-appropriation it certainly occurs after intellectual conversion. And in this sense, and for explanatory purposes, it serves well to treat it in that position. Doran, *Theology and the Dialectics of History*, 161.

6   Lonergan, *Method in Theology*, 240.

in love, and that falling in love is something disproportionate to its causes, conditions, occasions, antecedents. For falling in love is a new beginning, an exercise of vertical liberty in which one's world undergoes a new organization. But the major exception to the Latin tag is God's gift of his love flooding our hearts. Then we are in the dynamic state of being in love. But who it is we love, is neither given nor as yet understood. Our capacity for moral self-transcendence has found a fulfillment that brings deep joy and profound peace. Our love reveals to us values we had not appreciated, values of prayer and worship, or repentance and belief. But if we would know what is going on within us, if we would learn to integrate it with the rest of our living, we have to inquire, investigate, seek counsel. So it is that in religious matters love precedes knowledge and, as that love is God's gift, the very beginning of faith is due to God's grace.[7]

Thus, being in love with God—that is, being sanctified by grace—is a transformed way of being in the world.[8] Such a state of being in love becomes the "first principle" from which flow "one's desires and fears, one's joys and sorrows, one's discernment of values, one's decisions and deeds."[9] To consider this 'outward flow' is to move towards

7   Ibid., 122-23.

8   In Trinitarian terms, one can identify such a state-of-being as a created participation in the active spiration of the Holy Spirit by the Father and the Son. See Doran, *What Is Systematic Theology?*, 108.

9   Lonergan, *Method in Theology*, 105. Again, in Trinitarian terms, this can be identified in terms of passive spiration: the state of grace issues in consistent loving acts, a habit of charity that is a created participation in the passive spiration that is the Holy Spirit itself. It is important to note that, by virtue of religious conversion—that is, due to sanctifying grace—a subject's horizon is transformed by her elevation to participation in divine life. This transformation affects each of the levels of consciousness. As Doran notes, "At each of the levels of individual consciousness a subject elevated to participation in divine life through sanctifying grace has two formal objects: the natural/proportionate object of each level and a supernatural/disproportionate object. Thus in explicit belief, the elevation of central form and the consequent horizon known as the light of faith elevate judgment by allowing the subject to know what one could not know without the elevation of central form and the light of faith. Likewise, on the level of decision, the elevation of central form and the consequent horizon of evaluation allow the subject to evaluate with God's own values, which I am assuming are quintessentially expressed in the Sermon on the Mount." Doran, "What is the Gift of the Holy Spirit?". At this point, Doran is citing: Jeremy Blackwood, "Sanctifying Grace, Elevation, and the Fifth Level

the issue of moral conversion, as religious conversion is always a case of not just being in love, but of being in love and in the world. Indeed, as Walter Conn writes, "the test of Christian conversion can be nothing else than the empirical one of love for one's neighbor."[10] The point here, however, is the nature of religious conversion as first principle. So any understanding of the Preferential Option for the Poor that is based on Lonergan's position on integral conversion is ultimately understood as grounded in religious conversion: when considered along the healing vector in consciousness, all conversion begins with religious conversion

Liberation theologians also appear to consider the Option to be rooted in religious experience—in religious conversion—even if the Option's particular characteristics are more evident with respect to other forms of conversion.[11] Liberation theologians are acutely aware that Liberation Theology arises from liberation spirituality.[12] Sobrino notes that the "purely explicative, deductive doctrinal theology of the past" is so limited as to be "no longer equal to the impact of reality on history and the Church."[13] He quotes Hans Urs von Balthasar: "Let us not clip the wings of a generation that has had the sensitivity to discover the unacceptability of a divorce between theology and spirituality, contemplation and action, Church and world."[14] So it is that Sobrino will contend that "spiritual experience is rooted in an encounter with God," and that this "experience of being met by God cannot

---

of Consciousness: Further Developments within Lonergan Scholarship," in *West Coast Methods Institute* (Loyola Marymount University: 2009), 9.

10   Walter Conn, *Christian Conversion: A Developmental Interpretation of Autonomy and Surrender* (New York: Paulist Press, 1986), 205.

11   Liberation theologians are no doubt concerned that religious conversion is only a starting point, not an endpoint. The footnotes to the opening paragraph in the previous chapter make this most clear.

12   See, for example, Gustavo Gutiérrez, *We Drink from Our Own Wells: The Spiritual Journey of a People*, trans. Matthew J. O'Connell (Maryknoll, NY: Orbis Books, 1984); Jon Sobrino, *Spirituality of Liberation: Towards Political Holiness*, trans. Robert R. Barr (Maryknoll, NY: Orbis Books, 1985). Sobrino's work draws heavily upon Gutiérrez's.

13   Sobrino, *Spirituality of Liberation: Towards Political Holiness*, 47.

14   Ibid., 48. Sobrino is quoting Hans Urs von Balthasar, "Teología y espiritualidad," *Selecciones de Teología* 13:50 (1974): 142. The original quotation can be found at: Hans Urs von Balthasar, "Theologie und Spiritualität," *Gregorianum* 50 (1969): 585.

be replaced by anything else. It is of a fundamental, foundational nature."[15] This experience provides the spiritual process with "its fundamental direction," and upon it depends the "depth of liberation we undertake."[16] To genuinely love our siblings before God, we must first have an "experience of the God who first loved us."[17]

Gutiérrez also argues that the Option for the Poor is grounded in conversion to God. He contends "when all is said and done, the Option for the Poor means an option for the God of the Reign as proclaimed to us by Jesus."[18] He writes,

> the ultimate reason for commitment to the poor and oppressed does not lie in the social analysis that we employ, or in our human compassion, or in the direct experience we may have of poverty. All these are valid reasons and surely play an important role in our commitment. But as Christians, we base that commitment fundamentally on the God of our faith. It is a theocentric, prophetic option we make, one which strikes its roots deep in the gratuity of God's love and is demanded by that love.[19]

Gutiérrez further observes that at the core of the Option to the poor "is a spiritual experience of the mystery of God who is, according to Meister Eckhart, both 'unnamable' and the 'omni-namable' one."[20] The Option contains, "at its very heart ... a spiritual, mystical element, an experience of gratuitousness that gives it depth and fruitfulness."[21] For Gutiérrez, the Option stems from the fact that God first loved us. Certainly, because of this love, our lives should respond to this gratuitous love of God. And in this respect he will speak of the Option in terms of discipleship with Christ.[22] But this takes us beyond the issue of religious conversion to the issue of a moral conversion prompted by religious conversion. Here it suffices to note that Gutiérrez contends

---

15   Sobrino, *Spirituality of Liberation: Towards Political Holiness*, 56.

16   Ibid.

17   Ibid., 58.

18   Gutiérrez, "Option for the Poor," 240.

19   Ibid.

20   Gutiérrez, "The Option for the Poor Arises from Faith in Christ," 319.

21   Gustavo Gutiérrez, *The Density of the Present: Selected Writings* (Maryknoll, NY: Orbis Books, 1999), 167.

22   Gutiérrez, "The Option for the Poor Arises from Faith in Christ," 319-21.

the Option for the Poor at its most basic level is a "theocentric option"[23] grounded upon, and set in motion by, divine grace. So Gutiérrez will write, "The experience of gratuitiousness is not a form of evasion but rather the locus of life and the reality that envelops and permeates the endeavor to achieve historical efficacy."[24] And, "This efficacy will be sought with ever increasing fervor in the measure that it reveals to us the gratuitous love of God: God's preference for the poor."[25] And further, "we have to understand that a true and full encounter with our neighbor requires that we first experience the gratuitousness of God's love."[26] Or, to use Sobrino's words, it is spirituality that empowers and cleanses praxis.[27]

3. MORAL CONVERSION AND THE PREFERENTIAL OPTION FOR THE POOR: VALUING CREATION AS GOD VALUES CREATION—CHARITY AND THE PREFERENTIAL OPTION FOR THE POOR

The preceding chapter identified Lonergan's conception of moral conversion in terms of the criterion to which one appeals in decision-making: there is a shift in the criterion from an appeal to satisfaction to an appeal to value.[28] So it is that moral conversion addresses the issue of one's orientation to value. In this chapter, moral conversion is considered inasmuch as it is prompted by religious conversion. In this regard it can be noted that, with respect to the fourth level of conscious intentionality, the apprehension of values occurs in feelings,[29] and, moreover, such apprehension occurs in accordance with a normative scale

---

23   Gutiérrez, "Option for the Poor," 239.

24   Gutiérrez, *We Drink from Our Own Wells: The Spiritual Journey of a People*, 113.

25   Ibid.

26   Ibid.

27   Sobrino, "The Centrality of the Kingdom of God Announced by Jesus: Reflections Before Aparecida," 93.

28   Lonergan, *Method in Theology*, 240.

29   For this reason, the healing of affective energies that flow from religious conversion plays a constitutive role in moral conversion. Doran, *Theology and the Dialectics of History*, 249.

of values.[30] When this occurs, it is "God's gift of his love" that reveals true values "in their splendor."[31] And on Lonergan's analysis, moral conversion consists in "the strength of this love [bringing] about their realization."[32] Moral conversion acknowledges that praxis, praxis in service to the community, is imperative.[33] This section of the chapter first considers the role of moral conversion in relation to Lonergan's understanding of decline in history, and then moves to relate it directly to the Preferential Option for the Poor.

3.1 MORAL CONVERSION IN HISTORY:
EGOISMS AND THE SHORTER CYCLE OF DECLINE

Moral conversion helps overcome both egoism in a particular person and collective egoism, which Lonergan usually names individual and group bias respectively.[34] Individual bias is a form of egoism

---

30 The scale of values is also employed in the next chapter of this book where Doran's theologically sensitive theory of history is outlined. On the scale of values—which moves from vital values, to social values, to cultural values, to personal values, to religious values—Lonergan writes, "Vital values, such as health and strength, grace and vigor, normally are preferred to avoiding the work, privations, pains involved in acquiring, maintaining, restoring them. Social values, such as the good of order which conditions the vital values of the whole community, have to be preferred to the vital values of individual members of the community. Cultural values do not exist without the underpinning of vital and social values, but none the less they rank higher. Not on bread alone doth man live. Over and above mere living and operating, men have to find a meaning and value in their living and operating. It is the function of culture to discover, express, validate, criticize, correct, develop, improve such meaning and value. Personal value is the person in his self-transcendence, as loving and being loved, as originator of values in himself and in his milieu, as an inspiration and invitation to others to do likewise. Religious values, finally, are at the heart of the meaning and value of man's living and man's world." Lonergan, *Method in Theology*, 31-32.

31 Ibid., 243.

32 Ibid.

33 Marsh, *Praxis, Process, and Transcendence*, 218.

34 This is not to suggest a strict correlation of the conversions with specific biases, much less a relationship of specific biases to the individual levels of consciousness. The biases rarely, if ever, occur in isolation from each other. But as Doran writes, "as I understand the relations of the conversions to the biases, religious and moral conversion affect principally individual

that distorts an individual's intelligence and her affective and experiential orientations. It overrides the normal intersubjective bonds of community and involves a suppression of the questions required to solve the problems of communal living in the pursuit of the good of order. These questions are suppressed—the operation of intelligence is impaired—in a manner that serves an individual's personal gain. The egoist "devotes his energies to sizing up the social order, ferreting out its weak points and its loopholes, and discovering devices that give access to its rewards while evading its demands for proportionate contributions."[35] Group bias, by contrast, relies on the intersubjective bonds of community:[36] it suppresses the questions that, if answered, would move society towards solving the issue of universal communal living in a way that includes those outside one's tribe, class, nationality, or race. As Kenneth Melchin writes, in group bias, the drive towards mutuality within a particular social group overrides the operations of intelligence and responsibility.[37]

Within history, moral conversion offsets what Lonergan calls the 'shorter cycle of decline'. The shorter cycle manifests as a distortion in the unfolding of what Lonergan identifies as the dialectic of community.[38] The dialectic of community is constituted by a dialectic of

---

and group bias, while intellectual conversion is needed to overcome general bias." It is the fact that conversions 'principally' affect biases in this manner that they are considered in this chapter in such a fashion. Doran, "Dramatic Artistry in the Third Stage of Meaning," 250.

35   Lonergan, *Insight: A Study of Human Understanding*, 246.

36   Ibid., 247.

37   Kenneth R. Melchin, *History, Ethics and Emergent Probability: Ethics, Society, and History in the Work of Bernard Lonergan* (Lanham, MD: University Press of America, 1987), 219.

38   For Lonergan, dialectic refers to "a concrete unfolding of linked but opposed principles of change. Thus there will be a dialectic if (1) there is an aggregate of events of a determinate character, (2) the events may be traced to either or both of the two principles, (3) the principles are opposed yet bound together, and (4) they are modified by the changes that successively result from them." Lonergan, *Insight: A Study of Human Understanding*, 242. And further, "For dialectic is a pure form with general implications; it is applicable to any concrete unfolding of linked but opposed principles that are modified cumulatively by the unfolding; it can envisage at once the conscious and the non-conscious either in a single subject or in an aggregate and succession of subjects; it is adjustable to any course of events, from

contraries—a dialectic of complementarity—between human intersubjectivity and practical common sense. Human intersubjectivity is
the basis of human community and it bonds members of a clan, tribe,
nation, class, and divides them from others.[39] Social order is grounded
upon this intersubjectivity and social order arises from a dialectical
interaction between intersubjectivity and practical common sense,[40]
where such common sense gives rise to technology, the economy, and
polity.[41] The shorter cycle of decline arises from the distortions of
intelligence engendered by group bias. Whereas individual bias has
to resist natural intersubjective impulses, group bias is reinforced by

---

an ideal line of pure progress resulting from the harmonious working of
the opposed principles, to any degree of conflict, aberration, break-down,
and disintegration; it constitutes a principle of integration for specialized
studies that concentrate on this or that aspect of human living, and it can
integrate not only theoretical work but also factual reports; finally, by its
distinction between insight and bias, progress and decline, it contains in a
general form the combination of the empirical and the critical attitudes essential to human science." Ibid., 268-69. Doran suggests that there are two
kinds of dialectic: dialectics of contradictories and dialectics of contraries.
The dialectic of contradictories is evident in the relationship between what
Lonergan identifies as the two kinds of human knowing. This is Lonergan's
more prevalent usage of the term 'dialectic'. The two types of knowledge
are: the sensate knowledge humans have in common with all animals;
and, the rational and spiritual intelligence that are unique to humans. For
Lonergan, sensing is not full human knowing. One resolves this dialectic
by breaking it and affirming that one is a knower who understands correctly only by a composite performance of experiencing, understanding,
and judging. A dialectic of contraries is manifest in what Lonergan identifies as the tension between the two types of consciousness. In Doran's
terminology such a dialectic arises from this duality of consciousness, that
is, in the tension between intentionality and psyche. The psyche is the experienced flow of life, the sensitive representation of the underlying neural
demand functions. It is comprised of the flow of our sensations, memories,
images, emotions, conations, associations, bodily movements, spontaneous
intersubjective responses, and of the symbolic integrations of these that
are our dreams. But the intentional operations of understanding, judgment
and decision re-pattern, organize and arrange our experiences. See Doran,
Theology and the Dialectics of History, 46-47. The relationship of psyche and
intentionality are expanded upon in the final section of this chapter.

39   Lonergan, *Insight: A Study of Human Understanding*, 237.

40   Ibid., 243.

41   Ibid., 232-33.

them. And so group bias places the resources of practical intelligence at the service of a particular group and concurrently deforms the desire to know (by limiting its scope) and the resultant social order (produced by skewed practical intelligence). The shorter cycle of decline hinges on "ideas that are neglected by dominant groups only to be championed later by depressed groups."[42] The injustice resulting from group bias reveals the distortions inherent in the scope given to practical intelligence, and in this way, it creates its own conditions for reversal. That is, "practical ideas neglected or resisted by recalcitrant power sooner or later join with the frustrated sentiments of the oppressed to generate either social reform or revolution."[43] This process, the reversal of decline, the redemption of history, is hastened by the presence of the morally converted subject, who can discern that group bias operates at the service of disvalue more than value, and who thus acts to hasten the demise of the shorter cycle and guard against its reemergence in service of the new dominant group.

3.2 MORAL CONVERSION AND THE PREFERENTIAL OPTION FOR THE POOR

To explain the nature of the relationship of moral conversion to the Preferential Option for the Poor, four key points need to be made: (1) the healing and elevation of the subject, the consequence of sanctifying grace, results in the situation whereby the subject values the universe in a manner congruent with God's valuing of the universe: this is the habit of charity; (2) 'value' does not refer simply to moral and religious values, but rather refers to the integral scale of values; (3) God's valuing of the universe is, for the Christian, revealed in the mission and ministry of Jesus of Nazareth that culminates in the Paschal Mystery; and, (4) the Preferential Option for the Poor is understood in this context. These four points are expanded upon here in turn.

First, the transformation of the subject by which she begins to shift the manner in which she evaluates, results—on the existential level of conscious intentionality—in the subject evaluating on the basis of God's own values. Again, there is a shift in horizon. The moral conversion that ensues from religious conversion thus results in the subject being oriented in such a manner that she values creation precisely

---

42   Ibid., 252.

43   Doran, *Psychic Conversion and Theological Foundations: Toward a Reorientation of the Human Sciences*, 97.

as God values creation: along the lines of charity. In Patrick Byrne's words, "insofar as perfect charity is de facto a person's existential concern, that person patterns his or her experiencing and orients his or her conscious intentionality towards doing whatever is in service of the true value of the whole universe."[44] And also, "A fully converted person is someone who in fact is oriented toward God and the universe as God actually values it—in all its intelligibility, its tragic dialectical complexity, and its mysterious redemptive goodness."[45] Nothing, and no one, lies outside God's concern.

Secondly, Doran writes of the effect of the healing love of God, "the gift of healing love thus opens one to the appreciation and choice of values that previously one may have not been able to attend to."[46] Where one had previously operated in a manner that prioritized lower values over higher ones, when one begins to operate out of charity, one moves "toward conformity with the integral and normative scale of values" in which values are ranked, in ascending order, vital, social, cultural, personal, and religious.[47] Here it should be noted that this scale includes vital values, and social values such as economic and political systems. To be sure, such values are outranked by cultural, personal, and religious values. But the issue of the basic biological integrity of human subjects and the economic means of sustaining such integrity finds its way into the discussion at this point.

Thirdly, for the converted Christian, the precise nature of God's valuation of the universe is revealed in the mission and ministry of Jesus Christ. That is, because Christ, in his humanity, enjoyed the Beatific Vision throughout his life, he was able to come to know and express, in human terms and in human history, the value God ascribes to the universe and to every human being in the historical order.[48] That is to say, it is through the exercise of his human intelligence, rationality, and responsibility—rooted in the concrete historically conditioned experiences of first-century Roman-occupied Palestine—that Jesus "translated" what he knew by virtue of the Beatific Vision into "humanly

44 Patrick H. Byrne, "Ressentiment and the Preferential Option for the Poor," *Theological Studies* 54:2 (1993): 233.
45 Ibid.
46 Doran, *Theology and the Dialectics of History*, 248.
47 Ibid.; Lonergan, *Method in Theology*, 31-32.
48 Byrne, "Ressentiment and the Preferential Option for the Poor," 237.

meaningful terms."[49] This is what Lonergan considers unique about Christ's human life: precisely the redemptive element, the manner in which Christ "worked out the *means* of expressing, through his human deeds and sufferings, the divine meaning of history."[50] And in doing so, Christ set himself in relation to the whole universe and every human in a manner that reveals God's relationship to the whole creation.

The question then arises: what is this manner in which God loves the created order, and what particularly Christian ethic is conveyed in the mission and ministry of Jesus Christ the Nazarene? God, simply as God, is one unrestricted act of self-love, love of the *summum bonum*, by which "God loves all else."[51] God wills only the good.[52] This willing of the good, God's valuing of the universe, is revealed in Christ and Christ's mission, and it culminates with the Paschal Mystery. In this manner, God's willing of the good is expressed in human history by acts of redemptive goodness. Lonergan wrote of Christ's redemptive work in terms of the 'Law of the Cross'—that is, the returning of good for evil—and it is this he calls the "proper Christian ethic."[53] It is an ethic that applies to the Christian understanding of the whole of history and is particularly relevant to the Option for the Poor.

Fourthly, the Law of the Cross relates to the issue of the Option for the Poor. God's valuation of the poor is—for the Christian—likewise apparent in the mission and ministry of Jesus of Nazareth, who knows God immediately and intimately. The Law of the Cross

49 Ibid.

50 Ibid. The emphasis is Byrne's. Byrne continues, "The acts by which Christ put into action his practical insights expressed an identification with God—a oneness or 'concord' of Christ's will with God's will." Ibid.

51 Ibid., 228.

52 Charles C. Hefling, "A Perhaps Permanently Valid Achievement: Lonergan on Christ's Satisfaction," *Method: Journal of Lonergan Studies* 10:1 (1992): 56.

53 Lonergan, "The Transition from a Classicist World-View to Historical Mindedness," 9. This quotation is from a question asked by Lonergan, which Hefling points out is clearly being asked rhetorically. See Charles C. Hefling, "On the Possible Relevance of Lonergan's Thought to Some Feminist Questions in Christology," ed. Cynthia S. W. Crysdale (Toronto: University of Toronto Press, 1994), 219. For some of Lonergan's most sustained treatment of the 'Law of the Cross', see Book 17 of Bernard J. F. Lonergan, *De verbo incarnato*, 3rd ed. (Romae: Pontificia Universitatis Gregoriana, 1964), 552-93.

"stresses the seemingly intractable, unfinished agenda of the order of human history."[54] The cross, as a symbol, "stands for something Christ did, more than something he suffered. But his outward expression proceeded from an inward judgment of value passed on those misdeeds *as* sins against the God he loved. In that what he did was expressing this love, siding with the offended rather than the offenders, his deed was pleasing to God."[55] In siding with the victims and not the perpetrators of sin, Jesus demonstrated solidarity with all victims of sin. God's horizon is unlimited and each person has a "role in the final value God intends."[56] This effects a radical reorientation of personal relationships: those who were the least in the eyes of the Empire and exclusive religion are in fact brought to center-stage by Christ's crucifixion. Those who were excluded are excluded no more. Inasmuch as concrete history has deviated from the path of the true human good, God—as shown by the Son of God's crucifixion—sides with the victims and not the perpetrators of sin. "If the Law of the Cross means anything, it means that neither retaliation nor yet even-handed justice alone can reverse inauthenticity, the oppression, the violence of our day."[57] Charity alone can "wipe the slate clean."[58] Byrne points out that from a Judeo-Christian viewpoint, God consistently chooses people who are 'out of it': "From the favouring of Abel, the Hebrew slaves in Egypt, and the innocuous David, to the revelation of a nonmilitary Messiah from Galilee, God persistently reveals the fertility of the improbable."[59] These are the people normally unnoticed by the successful. "But to neglect what God does not neglect ... is to fail to share God's orientation." [60] "The danger that Lonergan warns against in the very last sentence of *De Verbo Incarnato*—that those who learn of the excellence of the cross will end up following not Christ but Pilate, by

---

54   Byrne, "Ressentiment and the Preferential Option for the Poor," 238.

55   Hefling, "On the Possible Relevance of Lonergan's Thought to Some Feminist Questions in Christology," 212. The emphasis is in the original.

56   Byrne, "Ressentiment and the Preferential Option for the Poor," 238.

57   Hefling, "On the Possible Relevance of Lonergan's Thought to Some Feminist Questions in Christology," 217.

58   Lonergan, "The Transition from a Classicist World-View to Historical Mindedness," 8.

59   Byrne, "Ressentiment and the Preferential Option for the Poor," 239.

60   Ibid.

laying the cross on others—can become a terrible reality."[61] And it is that reality to which liberation theologians respond: Christian nations laying the Cross of Poverty on their own people.

In this context, moral conversion implies a transformation of the subject such that within her new horizon she now values the universe as God does—in solidarity with victims—and also seeks to make redemptive love manifest in history.

3.3 LIBERATION THEOLOGY, MORAL CONVERSION, AND THE OPTION FOR THE POOR

Liberation theologians are acutely aware of the moral element of conversion when they discuss the Preferential Option for the Poor. This Option corresponds, in part, to what Gregory Baum has called the "activist dimension" of contemporary Christian discipleship.[62] Orthodoxy, as right teaching, is not enough; the Option mandates, and even prioritizes, orthopraxis. Two key foci are of concern in this respect: conversion to the neighbor and building the Reign of God in history. To again follow Gutiérrez, conversion is "a requirement for solidarity."[63] And 'complete' conversion is characterized by, in his words, a "conversion to the neighbor."[64] Conversion to God, to be complete, as the ancient Christian doctrine of the unity of love of God and love of neighbor asserts,[65] must also be a conversion to the neighbor.[66] It is the identity of Christ and the poor (Mt 25:40) that makes this

---

61   Hefling, "On the Possible Relevance of Lonergan's Thought to Some Feminist Questions in Christology," 215.

62   Baum, *Essays in Critical Theology*, 157. Gustavo Gutiérrez has often cited Baum's reading of Puebla in this respect and it appears to have become a permanent part of Gutiérrez's understanding of the Option. See Gutiérrez, "The Option for the Poor Arises from Faith in Christ," 318.

63   Gutiérrez, *We Drink from Our Own Wells: The Spiritual Journey of a People*, 101.

64   Gutiérrez, *A Theology of Liberation: History, Politics, and Salvation*, 118. For a detailed account of Augustine's understanding of the unity of love for God and neighbor, see Raymond Canning, *The Unity of Love for God and Neighbor in St. Augustine* (Heverlee-Leuven: Augustinian Historical Institute, 1993).

65   See, at §15, Pope Benedict XVI, "Deus caritas est".

66   Gutiérrez notes, in an attempt to emphasize both the religious and moral elements of conversion, that contemplation and solidarity are "two sides of a practice inspired by a global sense of human existence that is a source

unity—and God's preference for the poor—most starkly apparent to the Christian.[67] In Lonergan's terms, it refers to the healing of group bias to offset the shorter cycle of decline. Like all conversion, there is a transformation of horizon which ensues: conversion to the neighbor, as quoted above, "implies leaving the road one is on, as the parable of the Good Samaritan teaches, and entering the world of the one excluded from dominant social sectors, communities, viewpoints, and ideas."[68] To do so as a Christian is to walk, moved by the Spirit, in the footsteps of Christ. For Gutiérrez, *La sequela Christi*, "walking with Jesus the Messiah," is the ultimate meaning of the Preferential Option for the Poor.[69] So it is that "service of the poor is the privileged, though not exclusive, means for following Christ."[70]

Gutiérrez argues that conversion is not simply an interior matter of personal spirituality. Conversion "involves the entire person as a corporeal being … and therefore also has consequences for the web of social relationships of which the individual is a part."[71] Conversion is indeed, as Byrne noted, a genuine and positive shift in relationships among persons. Such conversion to the neighbor, solidarity in history, is something to which all Christians are called: "The curious remark is sometimes made, 'The Option for the Poor is something which the non-poor have to make.' That is not true, for the poor also have to opt in favour of their brothers and sisters of race, social class, and culture. And so the Option for the Poor is a decision incumbent upon every Christian."[72] Conversion to the neighbor, in this sense, is required of the whole Church.[73]

The transformation of horizon that results from conversion to the neighbor translates into "thinking, feeling, and living as Christ."[74] It

of hope and joy." Gutiérrez, "The Option for the Poor Arises from Faith in Christ," 320.

67 See, at §15, Pope Benedict XVI, "Deus caritas est".
68 Gutiérrez, "The Option for the Poor Arises from Faith in Christ," 318.
69 Ibid., 319.
70 Ibid.
71 Gutiérrez, *We Drink from Our Own Wells: The Spiritual Journey of a People*, 98.
72 Gutiérrez, "Option for the Poor: Reviews and Challenges," 16.
73 Gutiérrez, *We Drink from Our Own Wells: The Spiritual Journey of a People*, 101.
74 Gutiérrez, *A Theology of Liberation: History, Politics, and Salvation*, 118.

further means "to commit oneself to the process of the liberation of the poor."[75] For Gutiérrez, conversion to the neighbor is "not a question of a withdrawn or pious attitude."[76] A Christian's conversion process is affected "by the socio-economic, political, cultural, and human environment in which it occurs."[77] A commitment in bringing about a change in these structures, where they are hostile to the Reign of God, is a function of authentic conversion. The authentic Christian must repudiate hitherto accepted oppressive structures. That is, the Christian transforms the way she relates to others, the way she relates to the Lord, the way she relates to her cultural milieu, to her social class. Anything that obstructs a profound solidarity with the poor must be left behind. "Only thus, and not through purely interior and spiritual attitudes, will the 'new person' arise from the ashes of the 'old.'"[78] Conversion to the neighbor means activity in history. To know God is to do justice. One cannot be both elevated to a participation in the divine life and avoid concrete human history.[79] And in not avoiding action, Gutiérrez writes that it means "to commit oneself to the process of the liberation of the poor" and not only to do so generously, but to do so "with an analysis of the situation and a strategy of action."[80]

4. CONCLUSION

This chapter has demonstrated that Lonergan Studies, the Magisterium, and liberation theologians can all agree on the relevance of religious and moral conversion to the Option for the Poor. By sanctifying grace, the subject is converted to a life of charity in which—like God—she prefers, non-exclusively, the victims of history. Such a commitment becomes a mark of Christian discipleship and activity in the world. God remains the mover. And it is God's valuing of the universe that is normative. However, the question of analysis, as raised by Gutiérrez's final quotation above, moves the discussion in the direction of intellectual conversion. From Lonergan's perspective, one of the values discerned by charity is truth. And in this manner, the trajectory

---

75   Ibid.
76   Ibid.
77   Ibid.
78   Ibid.
79   Ibid.
80   Ibid.

of conversion presses onward to intellectual conversion. So it is that the next chapter begins to treat intellectual conversion and to situate psychic conversion within the structure one can develop on that basis. It will be shown that many of liberation theology's claims regarding the Option for the Poor in fact have to do with what Lonergan means by the process of full intellectual conversion.

CHAPTER 5

INTEGRAL CONVERSION AND THE PREFERENTIAL OPTION FOR THE POOR PART II: INTELLECTUAL AND PSYCHIC CONVERSION AS SELF-REFLEXIVE

I. INTRODUCTION

It may seem that, with the realities of religious and moral conversion already discussed, there is no more to say regarding conversion and the Preferential Option for the Poor. The Roman Magisterium's stance on the Option is indeed limited to these two elements of conversion: conversion to Christ results in a primacy in the exercise of charity, and this is what John Paul II used to define the Preferential Option. However, as was noted in Chapter 2, there is a tension between the Magisterium and liberation theologians on the relevance of the Option for the Poor in that for liberation theologians more than charity is at stake. The Option for the Poor, from the perspective of Liberation Theology, includes a hermeneutic element. That is, the Option for the Poor changes the way one does theology; because of the Option, some methodologies are preferred over others.

This chapter begins to unpack the structure of intellectual conversion as it relates to liberation theology and the Option for the Poor. It treats intellectual conversion's ability to overcome a bias that is hostile to intellectual-theoretical endeavors and, if not overcome in some way, has drastic negative consequences for history. It elaborates intellectual conversion's role in overcoming alienation and ideology. And it addresses the contribution intellectual conversion makes to the task of devising a theological method that meets the needs of liberation theology.

This chapter also presents an account of the nature of psychic conversion as it relates to intellectual conversion. In this sense, it 'frames' psychic conversion within a nuanced understanding of the subject. It then demonstrates how psychic conversion heals the damage of a dramatic bias that, in functioning to protect subjects from insights that relate to painful historical emotional-psychological wounds, actually distorts the operation of the human spirit and thus skews human action in history. Lastly, this chapter demonstrates the direct relationship between the process of psychic conversion and being converted to the Preferential Option for the Poor.

2. INTELLECTUAL CONVERSION AND THE PREFERENTIAL OPTION FOR THE POOR: PHILOSOPHIC CONVERSION AT THE SERVICE OF HERMENEUTICS AND METHOD

Lonergan's stance on intellectual conversion is significant, and it gives a precise structure and methodological direction to the concerns of many liberationists.[1] Terrence Tilley contends in his review of Doran's *Theology and the Dialectics of History*—when Tilley purports to be defending the stance of liberation theologians—"The significance of a theological position is to be judged, I would say, not in its methodological roots, but by its practical fruits."[2] Tilley's position can be contrasted with Juan Luis Segundo's contention: "The one and only thing that can maintain the liberative character of any theology is not its content but its methodology ... the latter ... guarantees the continuing bite of theology."[3] Lonergan scholar Richard Liddy seems to hold a position

---

1   It serves well to recall that truth is a value to which the morally converted respond. In this way, intellectual conversion is an 'extension', or rather, grows out of, moral conversion.

2   Terrence Tilley, "Review of *Theology and the Dialectics of History* by Robert Doran," *Journal of the American Academy of Religion* 62:1 (1994): 189.

3   Juan Luis Segundo, *The Liberation of Theology* (Maryknoll, NY: Orbis Books, 1976), 39-40. This point is made also by the likes of Gustavo Gutiérrez, Susan Brooks Thistlethwaite and Mary Potter Engle. Gustavo Gutiérrez writes, "The theology of liberation offers not so much a new theme for reflection as a new way to do theology." See Gutiérrez, *A Theology of Liberation: History, Politics, and Salvation*, 12. Susan Brooks Thistlethwaite and Mary Potter Engle contend, "liberation theologies are not about rearranging the furniture in the house of theology, or even about redecorating or remodeling the house. Rather, they are about rebuilding

more in concert with Segundo's than Tilley's when he argues, that, "in a world where alienation and ideology reign, intellectual conversion is extremely important for the social and cultural effectiveness of moral conversion."[4] Indeed, if religious and moral conversions provide the animating and motivating force behind the Option for the Poor, it is intellectual conversion that guides the Option and ensures its efficacy.

Four sections below combine to illustrate the contribution intellectual conversion makes to liberation concerns. First, the nature of intellectual conversion and its consequences for the subject's horizon are briefly rehearsed. Secondly, intellectual conversion is related to decline in history, specifically that decline engendered by general bias (the bias of common sense). Thirdly, intellectual conversion's role in overcoming alienation and identifying ideology is identified. The final section contains a consideration of significant issues in theological method as they relate to liberation thought. On the whole, it should be noted, this section focuses on methodological issues in the service of hermeneutics—particularly as understood in Liberation Theology—whilst the next chapter of this book explicitly treats Doran's hermeneutics of history and the Option for the Poor.

2.1 INTELLECTUAL CONVERSION: THE GENERALIZED EMPIRICAL METHOD AND ITS CONSEQUENCES

There is "an explicit variety of intellectual conversion"[5] and, as the previous chapter observed, rudimentary intellectual conversion may manifest itself simply as a commitment to truth. But in its fullest sense, it involves not only acknowledging that knowing is a composite performance of interrelated operations—experiencing, understanding, and judging—it also involves a commitment to the epistemology and metaphysics that follow from this acknowledgement. This chapter focuses upon the more complete form of intellectual conversion as

---

the foundation (method) and redesigning the floor plan (categories)." See Susan Brooks Thistlethwaite and Mary Potter Engle, eds., *Lift Every Voice: Constructing Christian Theologies from the Underside* (Maryknoll, NY: Orbis Books, 1998), 14.

4   Richard M. Liddy, *Transforming Light: Intellectual Conversion in the Early Lonergan* (Collegeville, MN: Liturgical Press, 1993), 199.

5   Doran, *What Is Systematic Theology?*, 100.

elaborated upon by Lonergan in *Insight*[6] and developed in *Method in Theology*.[7]

Doran argues that the subject, in coming to intellectual conversion, makes something like the following three affirmations. First,

> fully human knowing occurs in a world mediated and constituted by meaning and motivated by values, not in the world of immediacy. It is a cumulative compound of operations occurring on the three distinct levels of (a) reception of data, (b) understanding of data (insight) grounding the procession or emanation of an inner word of conceptualization (definition, hypothesis, supposition) and leading to formulations, and (c) reflective grasp of the sufficiency of the evidence, the fulfillment of conditions for affirming one's understanding and conceptual synthesis, and so of a 'virtually unconditioned' that grounds the procession or emanation of a second inner word, the yes or no of rational judgment.[8]

It helps to recall at this point that the converted subject as considered in this chapter, *viz.*, along the healing vector—as religiously and morally converted—already possesses an existential orientation to value. Via intellectual conversion, she can relate the notion of value to the notions of the true and intelligible and thus becomes cognizant of the single thrust of self-transcendence, that is, of the nature of Generalized Empirical Method (Transcendental Method).

Secondly, once one acknowledges the character of Generalized Empirical Method, there arises a profound consequence: correlative with the desire to know is its object, *viz.*, being. "Being is whatever can be intelligently grasped and reasonably affirmed."[9] Being, on this understanding, is intrinsically intelligible "and since apart from being there is nothing, being is the real."[10] Reality, on this understanding, is what one knows through the operations of Generalized Empirical Method. Moreover, on this understanding, being, the real, is structured

---

6   Although Lonergan refrained from using the term 'intellectual conversion' in *Insight*, the whole work is—as Frederick Crowe notes—from beginning to end an exercise in prompting radical intellectual conversion. See Frederick E. Crowe, *Lonergan* (Collegeville, MN: Liturgical Press, 1992), 68.

7   Lonergan, *Method in Theology*, passim.

8   Doran, *What Is Systematic Theology?*, 100-01.

9   Ibid., 101.

10 Ibid.

in a manner whereby it is isomorphic with the levels of conscious intentionality. Correlative with experiencing, understanding, and judging are potency, form, and act. For Lonergan, these metaphysical terms
denote the constituent elements of the real that are, in turn, attentively
experienced, intelligently understood, and reasonably affirmed.

Thirdly, Doran notes that there also follows from intellectual conversion a specific understanding of objectivity.[11] "There is the experiential objectivity of the simple givenness of the data, the normative objectivity of fidelity to the desire to know, and the absolute objectivity of
true judgment grounded in the grasp of the virtually unconditioned."[12]
As Crowe phrases it, "Objectivity is an achievement of subjectivity."[13]
Or in Lonergan's famous formulation, "objectivity is simply the consequence of authentic subjectivity, of genuine attention, genuine intelligence, genuine reasonableness, genuine responsibility."[14] The subject is
both empowered and made responsible by this fact.

All three of these affirmations identified by Doran play a role in the
considerations that follow.

2.2 INTELLECTUAL CONVERSION: GENERAL BIAS AND
THE LONGER CYCLE OF DECLINE

Intellectual conversion plays the major role in the reversal of what
Lonergan calls the longer cycle of decline. At the root of the longer
cycle is what Lonergan refers to as general bias. General bias has to
do with the common-sense mode of understanding in which one's
concern is with the relations of things to oneself.[15] In general bias,
the common-sense mode of understanding—the mode dominantly operative in patterns of experience such as the practical pattern in
which one performs the daily tasks of one's living[16]—is elevated to a

---

11   Ibid.
12   Ibid., 101-02.
13   Crowe, *Lonergan*, 68.
14   Lonergan, *Method in Theology*, 265.
15   Where theoretical understanding may note that a vehicle is travelling at
     160km/h, relating distance and time to calculate velocity, common sense
     may note that the same vehicle is moving 'quickly' or 'slowly', depending on
     what the vehicle is and where it is or what it is doing (e.g., an automobile
     in a school zone compared with one on a racetrack; an airplane landing
     compared with one in level flight).
16   Lonergan, *Insight: A Study of Human Understanding*, 293.

position of omnicompetence. "Its focus is short-term practicality; its preoccupation is whatever is immediately realizable with whatever means are immediately at hand."[17] General bias results in other modes of understanding and knowing being treated as largely irrelevant if not utterly invalid and worthless.

General bias has drastic consequences for history, particularly when it operates in conjunction with group bias. Lonergan refers to the damage done to history by general bias as the 'longer cycle of decline'. To quote Lonergan on the longer cycle:

> This general bias of common sense combines with group bias to account for certain features of the distorted dialectic of community. As has been noted, at each turn of the wheel of insight, proposal, action, new situation, and fresh insight, the tendency of group bias is to exclude some fruitful ideas and to mutilate others by compromise. Now fruitful ideas are of several kinds. They may lead to technical and material improvements, to adjustments of economic arrangements, or to modifications of political structure. As one might expect, technical and material improvements are less subject to the veto of dominant groups than are changes in economic and political institutions. Again, when we shift to the second phase of the distorted dialectic, the resonant demands of the unsuccessful are for material well-being; and when the clamour goes up for economic or political change, such change is apt to be viewed simply as a necessary means for attaining more palpably beneficial ends. Accordingly, there arises a distinction between the shorter cycle, due to group bias, and the longer cycle, originated by the general bias of common sense. The shorter cycle turns upon ideas that are neglected by dominant groups only to be championed later by depressed groups. The longer cycle is characterized by the neglect of ideas to which all groups are rendered indifferent by the general bias of common sense.[18]

The longer cycle results in the deterioration of the social situation,[19] because the social situation is nothing other than a function of the intelligibility put into its construction. And where general bias is opera-

---

17   M. Shawn Copeland, "A Genetic Study of the Idea of the Human Good in the Thought of Bernard Lonergan" (Doctor of Philosophy, Boston College, 1991), 122.

18   Lonergan, *Insight: A Study of Human Understanding*, 251-52.

19   Liddy, *Transforming Light: Intellectual Conversion in the Early Lonergan*, 202-03.

tive in the group guiding the construction of the social order, the social situation is nothing other than a function of increasingly fragmented understanding. Moreover, detached intelligence—which becomes increasingly irrelevant as the social situation deteriorates—withdraws into an ivory tower. The historical data generated by the bias of common sense are what Lonergan terms "false facts," that is, they are the "actual existence of what should not be. The false fact leads to a grasp, an insight, that is not so much an inverse insight as a perverse insight."[20] As Copeland expresses it, "the exigencies of intelligence and reason, of self-appropriation find themselves 'irrelevant to the world as it is.'"[21] That world constructed by general bias is "expedient, pragmatic, unscrupulous, materialistic; willfully and contentedly ignorant of theory and philosophy; disdainful of all that it cannot immediately dominate or understand."[22] And so, detached and disinterested intelligence surrenders. The major consequence of this is with respect to speculative thinking. It comes to be considered as irrelevant precisely because common sense is incapable of "analyzing itself" and therefore "incapable of making the discovery that it too is a specialized development of human knowledge," and thus is "incapable of coming to grasp that its peculiar danger is to extend its legitimate concern for the concrete and the immediately practical into disregard of larger issues and indifference to long-term results."[23] Under the guidance of general bias, intelligence is crippled. Only via an intellectual conversion can the normative nature of Generalized Empirical Method be realized. Only then can the full range of human understanding—rooted in the polymorphism of consciousness—be granted full validity. Only then can a comprehensive higher viewpoint that seeks to undo the damage done by general bias, which Lonergan calls cosmopolis, begin to emerge. As Doran puts it, "Lonergan's project of the self-appropriation

---

20 Lonergan, *Understanding and Being: the Halifax Lectures on Insight*, 236.

21 Copeland, "A Genetic Study of the Idea of the Human Good in the Thought of Bernard Lonergan", 125.

22 Lonergan, *Understanding and Being: the Halifax Lectures on Insight*, 236.

23 Lonergan, *Insight: A Study of Human Understanding*, 251.

of rational self-consciousness is in the interests of precisely such a development."[24]

It should also be noted that there is a sense in which liberation theologians can display tendencies indicative of an absence of full intellectual conversion precisely regarding general bias. As commendably committed as liberation theologians are to the socio-political dimension of Christian witness, there are occasions in which a trace of general bias is evident with respect to the role culture plays in their analysis. Doran's dialogue with Juan Luis Segundo in *Theology and the Dialectics of History* reveals a tendency in Segundo's work to undervalue the role of culture.[25] Segundo's approach is indicative of a general bias hostile to theoretical understanding and long-term solutions: he abandons sociological theory and seeks a political solution.[26] That is, immediate political praxis is prioritized over culture, the sets of meaning and values that ought to justify the ordering of any given polity. Not surprisingly, given the dire situation with which liberation theologians are confronted, there is an understandable focus on the here-and-now, and certainly in recent times Liberation Theology has been more cognizant of the role of culture.[27] But it serves to flag here that general bias is perhaps an issue that has affected Liberation Theology and to note that Doran's theory of history—outlined in the next chapter of this book—provides a more adequate understanding of the role of culture in transforming the present situation to something that more closely approximates the Kingdom of God.

2.3 INTELLECTUAL CONVERSION: METHOD THAT OVERCOMES ALIENATION AND IDENTIFIES IDEOLOGY

Returning to the issue of the Preferential Option for the Poor and its relationship to intellectual conversion, two points are developed below. First, a discussion of intellectual conversion's function as a source of normativity deeply rooted in history is presented. And secondly, intellectual conversion as a means of empowerment is elaborated upon.

---

24   Robert M. Doran, "Education for Cosmopolis," *Method: Journal of Lonergan Studies* 1:2 (1983): 141.

25   Doran, *Theology and the Dialectics of History*, 435-36.

26   Segundo, *The Liberation of Theology*, 59-60.

27   Elizondo, "Culture, the Option for the Poor, and Liberation," 157-68.

2.3.1 A NORMATIVE METHOD ROOTED IN HISTORY

The first point to make about Generalized Empirical Method is that it is not simply one of many possible methods. Lonergan writes, "In brief, conscious and intentional operations exist and anyone that cares to deny their existence is merely disqualifying himself as a non-responsible, non-reasonable, non-intelligent somnambulist."[28] To deny the existence of the operations, one must employ them, thereby verifying their existence and invalidating any denial. Generalized Empirical Method is a rock on which one can build.[29] It is *the* normative method that lies at the root of all other genuine methods. Regardless of the field of specialization,

> all special methods consist in making specific the transcendental precepts, Be attentive, Be intelligent, Be reasonable, Be responsible. But before they are ever formulated in concepts and expressed in words, those precepts have a prior existence and reality in the spontaneous, structured dynamism of human consciousness. Moreover, just as the transcendental precepts rest simply on a study of the operations themselves, so specific categorial precepts rest on a study of the mind operating in a given field.[30]

So it is that Lonergan argues that the "ultimate basis of both transcendental and categorial precepts" is a self-critical "advertence to the difference between attention and inattention, intelligence and stupidity, reasonableness and unreasonableness, responsibility and irresponsibility."[31]

Generalized Empirical Method, with its rootedness in data, has never been far from the heart of liberation concerns, even if it was never explicitly identified as such by any liberation theologian. For example, John XXIII was closer than he probably appreciated to applying the transcendental precepts in the field of social ethics when he, adopting Joseph Cardinal Cardijn's 'see—judge—act' method, wrote in *Mater et magistra*:

> There are three stages which should normally be followed in the reduction of social principles into practice. First, one reviews the concrete situation; secondly, one forms a judgment on it in the light of

---

28 Lonergan, *Method in Theology*, 17.
29 Ibid., 19.
30 Ibid., 20.
31 Ibid.

these same principles; thirdly, one decides what in the circumstances can and should be done to implement these principles. These are the three stages that are usually expressed in the three terms: look, judge, act. … It is important for our young people to grasp this method and to practice it. Knowledge acquired in this way does not remain merely abstract, but is seen as something that must be translated into action.[32]

In this excerpt, there is a clear awareness of the need for a 'bottom-up' methodology that begins with data—with experience—rather than starting with pre-formulated concepts, and only then moves to judgment and action. Moreover, there is also a latent awareness in John XXIII's formulation of the methodology of the act of understanding. That is, judgment is made after bringing the concrete situation and social principles together to lead one to judgment. What intellectual conversion adds to the method is precisely overt consideration of this intellective moment: 'see—judge—act' becomes, in a manner which moves away from the ocular myth of knowing, 'experience—understanding—judgment—decision'. By inserting the level of understanding into this method, one becomes cognizant of the relevance of an heuristic structure for both understanding and judgment.[33] The significance of this point becomes clear in the next chapter when Doran's theologically attuned theory of history is summarized and discussed with reference to the Church's mission: Doran has provided

32   See, at §§236-237, Pope John XXIII, "Mater et magistra" http://www.vatican.va/holy_father/john_xxiii/encyclicals/documents/hf_j-xxiii_enc_15051961_mater_en.html (accessed 14-February 2011).

33   An heuristic structure "is a conjunction both of data on the side of the object and of an operative criterion on the side of the subject." Lonergan, "Christology Today: Methodological Reflections," 87. Moreover, heuristic structures form an *a priori* in that they shape the content of what is to-be-known. Lonergan, *Insight: A Study of Human Understanding*, 128. This is evident when the nature of an heuristic structure is understood as: data, question, insight, and judgment. In this process one aims to, "Name the unknown; work out its properties; use the properties to direct, order, guide the enquiry." Ivo Coelho, *Hermeneutics and Method: The 'Universal Viewpoint' in Bernard Lonergan* (Toronto: University of Toronto Press, 2001), 33. Thus the content of the "anticipated act of understanding is designated heuristically. The properties of the anticipated and designated content constitute the clues intelligence employs to guide itself towards discovery." Lonergan, *Insight: A Study of Human Understanding*, 126.

a critically-grounded heuristic structure for appraising progress and decline within history.

None of this, however, ought to suggest that Cardijn's method, which was, after all, a practical methodological pointer derived from his experience of the task of re-evangelizing the working classes of Europe, is able to sustain the weight of phenomenological interrogation. Rather, Lonergan's stance on Generalized Empirical Method ought to be understood as confirming Cardijn's basic insight: the situation needs to be understood in light of the present circumstances. As Alfred Hennelly contended regarding the CELAM meeting at Santo Domingo, it was precisely because of the absence of the 'see—judge—act' methodology—which had been employed extensively in the formulation of the *Second Report*—that the final document did not have the prophetic bite of those produced by the Medellín and Puebla conferences.[34] And there are any number of methods in Liberation Theology that follow the same trajectory from data to action: the 'see—judge—act' of Cardijn and the Jocists (Young Christian Workers); the 'insertion—analyze—reflect—plan' of the pastoral circle;[35] Clodovis Boff's three moments of theology derived from Louis Althusser's 'three generalities';[36] and, Ignacio Ellacuría's "getting a grip on reality," "taking on the burden of reality," "taking responsibility for reality," and "letting ourselves be enlightened by reality" as appropriated by Jon Sobrino.[37] What intellectual conversion brings to this situa-

---

34 Ecclesiology, Christology, and the understanding of the relevance of CEBs are all affected by this methodological shift. Hennelly, "A Report from the Conference," 31-35.

35 Joe Holland and Peter Henriot, *Social Analysis: Linking Faith and Justice* (Maryknoll, NY: Orbis Books, 1983), 7-8.

36 The first generality begins with the data of general, abstract, and ideological notions that it encounters in a culture. The second generality is the instance that does the work; it is the cognition that turns the data into knowledge. The third generality is the product—the empirical concepts or scientific generality—of the second generality working on the first. Boff summarizes this epistemology, writing "theoretical practice produces third generalities by the operation of a second generality on a first generality." Boff, *Theology and Praxis: Epistemological Foundations*, 71-72.

37 Sobrino writes, "Ellacuría understood the formal structure of intelligence as 'grasping hold and facing reality,' which can be seen in three dimensions: 'taking hold of reality' (the intellective dimension, originally from [Xavier] Zubiri, to which he added 'bearing the burden of reality'

tion of conversion to history is a critical confirmation of the validity of beginning with the data of history.

2.3.2 EMPOWERING THE SUBJECT: IDENTIFYING THE VECTOR OF CREATIVITY

Identifying Generalized Empirical Method involves an acknowledgement of the foundational nature of the questioning subject. This, as noted above and in the previous chapter, is not done in a manner that is indifferent to history.[38] Objectivity derives from the subject's authenticity. Such an understanding of objectivity places responsibility firmly on the subject rather than on any given inherited tradition. The subject, to be authentic, must be attentive, intelligent, rational, and reasonable. The focus is on the subject precisely as a questioning subject: 'What is it?', 'Is it?', 'Is it worthwhile?'

In Lonergan's understanding, ideology and alienation are directly measured by reference to fidelity to Generalized Empirical Method. He writes,

> The term, alienation, is used in many different senses. But on the present analysis the basic form of alienation is man's disregard of the transcendental precepts, Be attentive, Be intelligent, Be reasonable, Be responsible. Again, the basic form of ideology is a doctrine that justifies such alienation. From these basic forms, all others can be derived. For the basic forms corrupt the social good. As self-transcendence promotes progress, so the refusal of self-transcendence turns progress into cumulative decline.[39]

(the ethical dimension) and 'taking responsibility for reality' (the praxic dimension). To these I have added ... letting ourselves be carried by reality (the dimension of grace)." Sobrino, "The Crucified People and the Civilization of Poverty: Ignacio Ellacuría's "Taking Hold of Reality"," 2. See also, Michael Lee, *Bearing the Weight of Salvation: The Soteriology of Ignacio Ellacuría* (New York: Crossroad, 2008), 42-50.

38 The previous chapter quoted, among other theologians, Ignacio Ellacuría who argued that subjectivity "is an impoverished sign of what God and man are in history. It has value insofar as it attempts to give an immanent base to God's presence among human beings; but it tends to conceive human transcendence in individual terms, and hence in itself does not lead to praxis in societal life and history." Ellacuría, *Freedom Made Flesh: The Mission of Christ and His Church*, 92.

39 Lonergan, *Method in Theology*, 55.

And so the focus on overcoming ideology and alienation is a focus on the subject in her capacity for self-transcendence. It is one's persistent questioning that, in turn, reveals one's capacity for self-transcendence. This is precisely the focus of Paulo Freire and Antonio Faundez in *Learning to Question: A Pedagogy of Liberation*. They certainly do not adopt Lonergan's precise noetic phenomenology,[40] but there is a clear realization that the pedagogy of asking questions is "essentially democratic and for that very reason anti-authoritarian, never spontaneistic or liberal conservative."[41] For them, when knowledge is presented as 'ready made', ideology is being smuggled into the classroom. In this way, pedagogy, power and ideology are intimately linked. Neither junta nor democratically elected government can tell us what is the case. Freire and Faundez focus on fidelity to innate curiosity as a means of challenging authoritarianism.[42] In fact, Freire and Faundez are aware of the dangers of a Hegelian conceptualism, the belief that "reality is nothing more than the development of the Idea by means of concepts,"[43] and they seek to overcome it, not with a "model," but a method involving "a series of principles which must be constantly reformulated."[44]

From the perspective of Lonergan Studies, the key distinction missing in Freire and Faundez's perspective is the one between intentional operations and specific categorial precepts. As quoted above,

> Just as the transcendental precepts rest simply on a study of the operations themselves, so specific categorial precepts rest on a study of the mind operating in a given field. The ultimate basis of both transcendental and categorial precepts will be advertence to the difference between attention and inattention, intelligence and

---

40   From the perspective of Lonergan Studies, the meaning of some of Freire and Faundez's terminology is a little obscure. For example, they write "it is basically a pedagogy in the practice of which there is no place for a division between feeling a fact and learning its *raison d'etre*." Paulo Freire and Antonio Faundez, *Learning to Question: A Pedagogy of Liberation* (Geneva: World Council of Churches, 1989), 45. Presumably this has something to do with the transition from believing something to be a true, to knowing it to be so first-hand.

41   Ibid.

42   Ibid., 35.

43   Ibid., 29.

44   Ibid., 30.

stupidity, reasonableness and unreasonableness, responsibility and irresponsibility.[45]

The operations themselves remain constant; the categorial precepts differ from field to field. Lonergan can agree with Freire and Faundez that political activity, including education, cannot be value-neutral.[46] But he can also identify a normative foundation that alone is capable of overcoming alienation and ideology. It is a foundation that empowers one to discern what is authentic in inherited tradition whilst concurrently stressing the foundational relevance of personal achievement.[47] Lonergan would agree when Friere questions a model of education that "inhibits creativity and domesticates (although it cannot completely destroy) the intentionality of consciousness by isolating consciousness from the world, thereby denying men their ontological and historical vocation of becoming more fully human."[48] The authentic human subject—healed and elevated by grace—generates the set of questions that introduces the possibility of progress and redemption in history. And as Doran writes, also in the context of discussing Friere, "to discover this liberative power of inquiry and criticism is to discover something that unites humans across cultures."[49] Not only does it unite, but also it does so without being prescriptive or culturally imperialistic.

2.4 THE METHOD IN THEOLOGY: FROM HISTORY, TO THE AUTHENTIC SUBJECT, TO ORTHOPRAXIS

To this point the explication of intellectual conversion's significance for liberationists has not directly engaged the issue of Lonergan's

---

45   Lonergan, *Method in Theology*, 20.

46   Freire and Faundez, *Learning to Question: A Pedagogy of Liberation*, 31.

47   For a detailed account of the 'way of achievement' from below-upwards and the 'way of gift' from above-downwards, as related to the field of education, see Frederick E. Crowe, *Old Things and New: A Strategy for Education* (Atlanta, GA: Scholars Press, 1985). It is ultimately the decision of the theologian—and one not taken lightly—which doctrines are to be affirmed and which are to be left behind. See, for example, the sections on Dialectics, Foundations, and Doctrines in Lonergan, *Method in Theology*, 235-333.

48   Paulo Freire, *Pedagogy of the Oppressed* (New York: Seabury Press, 1970), 71.

49   Doran, *Theology and the Dialectics of History*, 40.

theological method. This section of the chapter contains a direct engagement with Lonergan's application of Generalized Empirical Method to the task of theology and explains its relevance to Liberation Theology.

2.4.1 LONERGAN'S THEOLOGICAL METHOD

For Lonergan, theological method is derived from an application of the four levels of conscious intentionality to the twofold nature of the theological task:

> There is mediating theology, that is, a phase of theology that mediates from the past into the present, a phase of indirect discourse in which researchers, exegetes, and historians report on what others have said and done. This is theology as hearing, as *lectio divina*. And there is mediated theology, a phase in which theologians stand on their own two feet and say, not what others have said but what they wish to say on their own account and of their own responsibility. Mediated theology is direct theological discourse in the present and with an eye to the future. It is a phase, not of hearing but of saying, not of *lectio divina* but of questions and answers, and of questions and answers not about what others have said and done but about the realities affirmed in the faith of the Church.[50]

When one applies the operations of the four levels of conscious intentionality to the two phases of theology, the result is an eightfold division of the task of theology. The first phase of theology begins with the specialization of *Research*. It is concerned with the data and corresponds to the empirical level of conscious intentionality. It seeks simply to make available all data relevant to any given theological task. *Interpretation*, which corresponds to the intelligent level of conscious intentionality, seeks to understand the meaning of the data. *History* seeks what was going forward, particularly in terms of doctrinal development—it is concerned with true judgments of fact *Dialectic* seeks to reduce incompatible versions of history to their roots. Through dialectic, on the level of decision, one encounters the beliefs and values of an historian (or historians), and one is able to identify the source of incompatible accounts of history. The second phase begins, whilst still on the level of decision, with *Foundations*. Where dialectic simply noted the roots of difference, in *Foundations* one takes a stand and objectifies

---

50   Robert M. Doran, "System and History: The Challenge to Catholic Systematic Theology," *Theological Studies* 60:4 (1999): 661.

one's positions. One constructs a fundamental theology. Foundations pave the way for a theologian to frame what she holds to be true as a matter of fact, *Doctrines*. Next, it is in *Systematics* that one proceeds to develop an analogical understanding of the truths of faith. Bringing this sketch of Lonergan's conception of theological method to a close is the final specialization, that of *Communications*. In *Communications* the meaning constitutive of Christianity is mediated to contemporary pastoral, interdisciplinary, and inter-religious situations.[51] This eight-fold theological method can be represented pictorially:

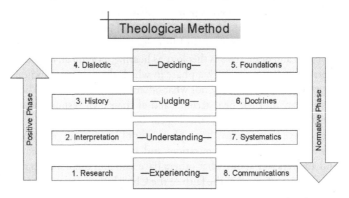

Figure 1: Bernard Lonergan's Theological Method.

This theological method is of key relevance to many liberation concerns that empower the Option for the Poor. Four such concerns are sketched here in turn.

2.4.2 INTEGRATING CRITICAL HISTORY INTO THEOLOGY

As noted in the section above, intellectual conversion is a conversion to history. Identifying and affirming the movement from experience, to understanding, to judgment and the contextualized role of decision embeds the subject in history. It is not surprising that the integration of critical history into theology was a key concern of Lonergan in his work. Within his theological method, it is the first three specializations that represent the role of critical history, moving, as they do, from empirical research into the data, through exegetical interpretations of these data, to historical reconstruction based on those interpretations.

---

51   Lonergan, *Method in Theology*, 125-368. And Doran, "System and History: The Challenge to Catholic Systematic Theology," 662.

What needs to be flagged at this point is not the significance of the first three specializations,[52] which, in any case is well known, but that critical history is sublated into the latter specializations of Lonergan's theological method.

2.4.3 IDENTIFYING AND COUNTERING IDEOLOGY: REFLECTIVELY-DIALECTICAL ORTHOPRAXIS

The Option for the Poor is an unequivocal option against oppression. Theological method must be able to take account of this fact. Sobrino writes, "The Option for the Poor must be carried out within a specific framework," namely, one that is dialectical.[53] Lonergan's method devotes an entire specialization to such a framework.

While the first three specializations clearly guard against ahistoricism, bringing history into theology is only half the battle. The time of 'the age of innocence'—when human authenticity could be assumed or taken for granted—has passed.[54] Indeed, the data employed in human studies may be a mixed product of authenticity and inauthenticity; or, the investigators themselves may be authentic or inauthentic.[55] This brings us to Lonergan's focus on dialectic. It may seem that a consideration of such a specialization—as a 'fourth-level specialization'—belongs in the previous section of this chapter that treated moral conversion. And there would be a logic to placing it there. It is considered here, however, because even if moral conversion introduces the imperative of praxis, it is intellectual conversion—considered in the third stage of meaning—that provides its critical grounding and guidance.[56] Intellectual conversion, when it occurs after religious and

---

52 For a comprehensive account of Lonergan's achievement in this respect see Frederick E. Crowe, "'All My Work has Been Introducing History into Catholic Theology,'" in *Lonergan Workshop 10*, ed. Frederick Lawrence (1994), 49-81.

53 Jon Sobrino, *No Salvation Outside the Poor: Prophetic-Utopian Essays* (Maryknoll, NY: Orbis Books, 2008), 31.

54 Lonergan, "Third Lecture: The Ongoing Genesis of Methods," 156.

55 Ibid., 157.

56 Doran distinguishes between primary and secondary processes in conversion in a helpful manner. He writes, "In the third stage of meaning, intellectual and psychic conversion refer both to the integrity of cognitional and psychic process (primary process) and to the *self-appropriation* of cognitional and psychic process (secondary process), but I contend that they affect secondary process most immediately; whereas religious and

moral conversion, adds this critical turn, and then religious and moral conversion can thereby be understood in relation to the normative pattern of operations within consciousness.

Dialectic seeks to uncover the source of differences and conflicts in historical studies. It is in dialectic that all alienation and ideology—whether stemming from an absence of religious, moral, intellectual or psychic conversion—are identified.[57] The theologian performing dialectical analysis seeks to identify what is a function of authenticity and also what is a function of inauthenticity. And authenticity is itself simply the presence of conversion in any given stage of meaning. Lonergan writes,

> The presence or absence of intellectual, of moral, of religious conversion gives rise to dialectically opposed horizons. While complementary or genetic differences can be bridged, dialectical differences involve mutual repudiation. Each considers repudiation of its opposites the one and only intelligent, reasonable, and responsible stand and, when sufficient sophistication is attained, each seeks a philosophy or a method that will buttress what are considered appropriate views on the intelligent, the reasonable, the responsible.[58]

So in dialectic one seeks to develop what is a function of conversion and reverse what appears to be incompatible with conversion. In this way it aims, Lonergan argues, at what Paul Ricoeur has labeled a hermeneutic of recovery and a hermeneutic of suspicion: suspicion regarding the inauthentic and recovery of the authentic.[59]

---

moral conversion (along with prephilosophic instances of cognitive integrity and constructive censorship regarding neural demands) affect primary process most immediately." See Doran, "Primary Process and the Spiritual Unconscious," 455.

57   There is a strong connection here with what Gutiérrez contends when he argues that "an authentic Christian conversion must lead to an unmasking of the social mechanisms that turn the worker and the peasant into marginalized persons." And further, "The will to conversion should lead to ... concrete analysis." Gutiérrez, *We Drink from Our Own Wells: The Spiritual Journey of a People*, 98.

58   Lonergan, *Method in Theology*, 247.

59   Lonergan, "Third Lecture: The Ongoing Genesis of Methods," 157. Jim Kanaris's brief discussion regarding dialectic and praxis is very helpful. See Jim Kanaris, "Bernard Lonergan's Philosophy of Religion" (Doctor of Philosophy, McGill University, 2000), 226-28.

Dialectic can be performed with respect to any species of value within the genus of the true scale. Lonergan's most significant demonstration of the technique of dialectic is with respect to the process of discerning the presence and absence of intellectual values in the historical period leading up to the emergence of the Council of Nicaea's affirmation of the consubstantiality of the Son of God with God the Father.[60] Lonergan determined that: Tertullian adhered to an understanding of reality as corporeal as per naïve realism; Origen adhered to an implicit idealism in which the real was the idea; and Athanasius made the breakthrough to a Christian realism.[61] Even when focusing on intellectual values, Dialectic functions as a praxical method. Lonergan begins with intellectual value commitments and then proceeds from these value commitments to engage in a hermeneutics of recovery and suspicion in his theoretical dialectical analysis. In this way, Dialectic functions as a value-critical method that complements the methods of critical history.[62]

Liberation theologians also operate in this manner when they discern a radically distorted social situation—for example, make the value judgment (in charity) that extreme poverty is contrary to God's valuing of people—and then engage in a hermeneutics of suspicion and recovery regarding Christian sources, interpretations of those sources, and written histories, that may support such a distorted social situation. This is not to say that such theologians explicitly employ Lonergan's understanding of dialectic. But they do move from explicit practical value judgment, made from within their concrete milieu, to a position where they foreground and develop specific doctrines on the basis of these judgments. For example, involvement in historical Jesus studies has been used by liberation theologians to counter those who seek the mystification of Christ's mission.[63] In the mission of Jesus

---

60   Bernard J. F. Lonergan, *The Triune God: Doctrines*, ed. Robert M. Doran and H. Daniel Monsour, trans. Michael G. Shields, Collected Works of Bernard Lonergan, vol. 11 (Toronto: University of Toronto Press, 2009), 29-255. And also, Lonergan, "The Origins of Christian Realism."

61   Lonergan, *The Triune God: Doctrines*, 29-255.

62   Lamb, *Solidarity with Victims*, 138.

63   See, for example, Jon Sobrino, *Jesus the Liberator: A Historical-Theological Reading of Jesus of Nazareth* (Maryknoll, NY: Orbis Books, 1993). John Meier has criticized Sobrino's Christology on historical grounds. But this critique of Meier's appears to be unclear on the relationship of Christology

of Nazareth, God, history, and socio-cultural critique are inextricably linked. It has resulted in liberation theologians emphasizing Christ's preaching and enacting of the Reign of God.[64] It is also such dialectical work that has resulted in Liberation Theology's foregrounding the symbol Reign of God as a means of ensuring a socio-political element within theological foundations.[65]

2.4.4 ENACTING THE REIGN: ORTHOPRAXIS AND THE HERMENEUTIC CIRCLE

There are two further methodological issues relating to intellectual conversion that need to be developed. First, the "reflexively critical orthopraxis" of Dialectic does not replace traditional orthopraxis. Secondly, Lonergan's method also meets the needs of the 'hermeneutic circle' that is so essential to Liberation Theology's methodology.

The role of praxis is central in Liberation Theology. Indeed, Gustavo Gutiérrez famously sought to redefine theology as 'critical reflection on praxis' rather than the classic formulation of St Anselm, 'faith seeking understanding.'[66] It must be noted that Lonergan's method shares at least the basics of this orientation towards a primacy of praxis. That is, there exists in Lonergan's understanding of method a priority of praxis over theory. Indeed, good theory is practical. But also, in Lamb's characterization, "Praxis is not only the goal, but also the foundation of theory."[67] This is to note that the foundations of theology reside in nothing other than the ongoing conversion of the theologian. So it is that in Lonergan's approach, according to Lamb, "No theory *qua* theory can sublate praxis, although praxis can sublate theory."[68] A further quotation from Lamb emphasizes Lonergan's perspective:

---

to Historical Jesus studies. John P. Meier, "The Bible as a Source for Theology," *CTSA Proceedings* 43:1 (1988): 3-7. Sobrino is moving beyond the positive phase of history and into the normative phase of theology.

64   Sobrino, *Jesus the Liberator: A Historical-Theological Reading of Jesus of Nazareth*, 67-134.

65   Sobrino, "Central Position of the Reign of God in Liberation Theology," 350-88.

66   Gutiérrez, *A Theology of Liberation: History, Politics, and Salvation*, 3-12.

67   Lamb, *Solidarity with Victims*, 82.

68   Ibid., 83.

The self-referent of theologians [in Lonergan's approach] is their awareness that only authentic religious, moral, intellectual, psychic, and social forms of praxis can ground an authentic doing of theology. The object-referent is their varying efforts at thematizing new ways of doing theology within an interdisciplinary collaboration which would promote a critical praxis correlation that aims at academic, ecclesial, and social transformations.[69]

A fuller structure for conceiving of, and relating, such efforts is presented in the next chapter. For now it must suffice to note that there is an approach to praxis in Lonergan's work whereby 'praxis is mediated to praxis' via the converted subject.

The rootedness of Lonergan's method in the data—both at the stage of Research and Communications—points directly towards Liberation Theology's understanding of the 'hermeneutic circle'. Juan Luis Segundo takes the idea of the hermeneutic circle from Rudolf Bultmann and reshapes it, giving it a liberative character. Segundo defines his understanding of the hermeneutic circle as the "continuing change in our interpretation of the Bible which is dictated by the continuing changes in our present-day reality, both individual and societal. ... Each new reality obliges us to interpret the word of God afresh, to change reality accordingly, and then to go back and reinterpret the word of God again, and so on."[70] Whereas Lonergan treats the hermeneutic circle when he considers the functional specialization, *Interpretation*,[71] Segundo intends the circle to move beyond issues solely of interpretation. So while Segundo's hermeneutic circle, by definition, addresses the issue of interpretation, it also includes the transformation of reality on the basis of ongoing interpretations of the Bible. In this respect we can note congruence between, not Lonergan's functional specialization Interpretation and Segundo's hermeneutic circle, but between the latter and Lonergan's fuller theological method. This becomes most apparent when Segundo writes of the four factors of the hermeneutic circle: (1) it begins with an experience of reality that leads one to ideological suspicion; (2) it moves to an application of this suspicion to the ideological superstructure; (3) this leads to the suspicion that prevailing exegesis is likewise tainted; and, (4) a

69   Ibid., 84.
70   Segundo, *The Liberation of Theology*, 8.
71   Lonergan, *Method in Theology*, 153-73.

'purified' hermeneutic emerges.[72] Arguably, Segundo is describing here an application of the specialization of Dialectic. One gets the impression that it is social values more than cognitional ones that function as the starting point for Segundo. Nonetheless, he is writing of the process of identifying those positions that are incompatible with an accurate interpretation of the Biblical texts. It is Dialectic that furnishes theology with the resources it requires to engage in a critique capable of unmasking ideology, not simply with respect to hermeneutics—to mistaken interpretations of the Bible—but also as regards errors in research and the foregrounding of particular historical events.[73]

2.4.5 A COOPERATIVE METHOD: SYSTEMATIC, UNIFYING, AND FOUNDATIONAL

In the conclusion of his *A Philosophy of Liberation*, Enrique Dussel calls for an "international division of philosophic labor."[74] Dussel acknowledges that in such a division of labour there will be differing themes but also a consistent method and essential categories.[75] This division would assign to diverse groups and countries distinct tasks and not demand a uniformity of themes.[76] This division, which is meant to serve the Option for the Poor, would assign to diverse groups and countries distinct tasks and not demand a uniformity of themes. Generalized Empirical Method can aid in such a division, most obviously with respect to its systematic function, its unifying function, and its foundational function.[77]

The systematic and unifying functions of Generalized Empirical Method arise from the fact that, inasmuch as such method is objectified, a set of basic terms and relations that have their source in human consciousness can be derived. They not only provide a ground for epistemology and a structure which anticipates all reality proportionate to

---

72   Segundo, *The Liberation of Theology*, 9.

73   Dialectics provides a means of distinguishing between faith and ideology, a task that is central to Segundo's project. Ibid., 97-124.

74   Enrique Dussel, *Philosophy of Liberation* (Maryknoll, NY: Orbis Books, 1985), 195.

75   Ibid.

76   Ibid., 196.

77   For a step-by-step outline of the key functions of Generalized Empirical Method (Transcendental Method), see Lonergan, *Method in Theology*, 20-25.

human cognitional process, but such terms and relations function in a manner that is potentially unifying. Lonergan writes,

> Through the self-knowledge, the self-appropriation, the self-possession that result from making explicit the basic normative pattern of the recurrent and related operations of human cognitional process, it becomes possible to envisage a future in which all workers in all fields can find in transcendental method common norms, foundations, systematics, and common critical, dialectical, and heuristic procedures.[78]

Although it offers this common basis, Generalized Empirical Method does not do so in a manner that imposes categories or theories alien to any given culture. Nor is it to be believed simply on the basis of authority or as one theory among many. Rather, Generalized Empirical Method is open to verification by any subject on the basis of the data of her own consciousness. Its systematic and unifying functions are thus also radically egalitarian.

Lastly, the foundational function of Generalized Empirical Method is to be noted. Doran's *Theology and the Dialectics of History* is an exercise in the functional specialization that Lonergan calls foundations. As such, it is rooted in the converted subject. All four conversions contribute to Doran's understanding of the subject, and thus serve a role in providing the terms and relations from which he constructs his theory of history. The basic terms and relations

> articulate human interiority in the dimensions of both nature and grace, and the objects known or valued in the operations and states thus objectified will be expressed in categories derived from the interior and religious differentiations. Ultimately, again, for every term and relation there will exist, proximately or remotely, a corresponding element in intentional (or, as the case may be, nonintentional) consciousness.[79]

While it remains for the potential and openness of Doran's work to be demonstrated in Chapter 6, at this point it serves to note that—like Liberation Theology's understanding of the Option for the Poor—Doran builds his project on the objectification of the integral conversion of the subject as rooted in, and oriented towards, history.

---

78 Ibid., 24.
79 Doran, *What Is Systematic Theology?*, 100.

3. PSYCHIC CONVERSION AND THE PREFERENTIAL OPTION FOR THE POOR: HEALING THE UNIVERSAL VICTIMHOOD OF HUMANITY FOR THE SAKE OF THE VICTIMS OF HISTORY

Doran has introduced into Lonergan Studies an understanding of the psyche that complements Lonergan's own intentionality analysis. Psychic conversion, Doran's key contribution to the understanding of integral conversion, is intimately connected with the realities studied by depth psychology. This contribution, it is argued below, is significant in developing an integral understanding of the Preferential Option for the Poor. This section of the chapter seeks to: (a) briefly rehearse the nature of psychic conversion and its transformation of a subject's horizon by introducing the concepts of the derived and basic dialectics of the subject; (b) relate psychic conversion to dramatic bias and the cycles of decline in history; and, (c) explain the relevance that psychic conversion holds for an understanding of the Preferential Option for the Poor.

3.1 NOTES ON PSYCHIC CONVERSION: THE DERIVED AND BASIC DIALECTICS OF THE SUBJECT

To understand psychic conversion, some reflections are first needed on the nature of the psyche and its relationship to intentionality. This section seeks to achieve both these tasks in turn. The first section discusses the dialectic between intentionality and psyche, and the second addresses the issue of psychic conversion and the foundational dialectic of the subject.

3.1.1 THE DERIVED DIALECTIC OF THE SUBJECT: INTENTIONALITY AND PSYCHE

Within consciousness there are two sets of data: the intentional-spiritual elements and psychic elements. The intentional operations were discussed in the last chapter at some length. Doran, however, writes of the psychic set of data:

> It lies in the sensitive flow of consciousness itself, the polyphony, or, as the case may be the cacophony, of our sensation, memories, images, emotions, conations, associations, bodily movements, and spontaneous intersubjective responses, and of the symbolic integrations of these that occur in, indeed are, our dreams. These data

constitute the sensitively experienced movement of life, the pulsing flow of life, the psychic representation of an underlying manifold of neural function that reach a higher organization in sensitive consciousness.[80]

So it is that the term, 'psyche', for Doran refers to "the complex flow of empirical consciousness, whether sublated by successively higher levels or not."[81] Doran gives an example of his meaning by noting that "if the reader were only seeing the black marks on white paper, and feeling whatever inner sensations his or her organic and sensitive rhythms were producing, but were neither understanding nor trying to understand anything being read, there would be consciousness only at the level of the psyche."[82] The psyche stands in relation to intentionality. This relationship is constituted, like the dialectic of community, by a dialectic of contraries. The complementary nature of this relationship is evident when Doran writes:

> The psychic stream undergoes changes with the performance of the operations of the spirit. One feels differently after one has understood from the way one felt before the emergence of insight. So, too, one's dispositional immediacy is different after one has arrived at a judgment consequent on the grasp of sufficient evidence from one's 'self-taste' prior to such reflective understanding. Again, one's psychic experience is different upon the making of a decision from what it was when one was trying to decide on a course of action in a given situation. The psyche *is* endowed with a finality, as [Carl Gustav] Jung recognized, but that finality is to be understood as an upwardly directed dynamism toward participation in the operations of inquiry and understanding, reflection and judgment, deliberation and decision, and in the dynamic state of being in love in the family, in the community, and with God. The psyche is a potential participant in the clarity of insight, the assurance of judgment, the peace of a good conscience, the joy and dynamism of love. This potential is reflected in the psyche's own sensitive experience and will be manifest in our dreams. The psyche not only serves the spirit, in that we need its images if we are to understand anything, but it also

---

80   Doran, *Theology and the Dialectics of History*, 46.
81   Ibid.
82   Ibid.

participates in the spirit's very own life of understanding and world constitution and self-constitution.[83]

So the integral dialectic of the subject is maintained by holding a healthy psyche and authentic conscious intentionality together in creative tension. Both poles are affirmed, and both intentionality and psyche work together in the forging of self and world as works of dramatic art.[84]

The psyche is disrupted in playing its role in the forging of self and world as works of art by the presence of what Jung called negative complexes.[85] Complexes are the structural units of the psyche as a whole,[86] and all psychic energy is distributed into complexes. Some complexes aid in the search for direction and meaning in life; others impede the functioning of the intentional operations. The influence of the negative complexes is apparent when one recognizes that "there can be felt resistance to insight, manifest in the repressive exercise of the censorship; there can be a flight from understanding, a desire not to judge, a resistance to decision, and a habitual lovelessness."[87] Without affective participation in the process of self-transcendence, the operations of conscious intentionality are impaired. That is to say, "if our intentional operations have a constitutive influence on the quality of our psychic life, it is also the case that the quality of our psychic life has a great deal to do with the ease and alacrity with which intentional operations are performed."[88] The healing of the psyche involves freeing the psychic energy bound up in disordered complexes. When that energy is freed from being bound in negative complexes, it becomes able

---

83   Robert M. Doran, "Jung and Catholic Theology," in *Theological Foundations* (Milwaukee, WI: Marquette University Press, 1995), 155.

84   Ibid., 137.

85   Doran quotes Jung on the issue of complexes. Doran writes, "Jung described a complex as 'the *image* of a certain psychic situation which is strongly accentuated emotionally and is, moreover, incompatible with the habitual attitude of consciousness. This image has a powerful inner coherence, it has its own wholeness and, in addition, a relatively high degree of autonomy, so that it is subject to the control of the conscious mind to only a limited extent, and therefore behaves like an animated foreign body in the sphere of consciousness.'" See ibid., 157.

86   Ibid.

87   Ibid., 156.

88   Ibid.

to help rather than hinder the performance of the intentional operations. In this sense, damage to the psyche is an impediment to spiritual self-transcendence; healing the psyche becomes a requirement for an authentic spiritual life. This points us 'beneath' the dialectic of psyche and intentionality to a 'deeper', more fundamental dialectic, and the issue of psychic conversion.

3.1.2 THE BASIC DIALECTIC OF THE SUBJECT AND ITS HEALING IN PSYCHIC CONVERSION

This basic or foundational dialectic of the subject is a dialectic of contraries between the bodiliness of neural demands and dramatically patterned consciousness as it exercises censorship over the neural demands. The dramatic pattern of experience, it helps to recall, is the pattern in which one seeks to make one's life a work of art in the sense of "learning a role and developing in oneself the feelings appropriate to its performance."[89] What is at stake in this pattern of experience is, arguably,[90] the formation of the moral character of the subject.[91] That is to say, "The dramatic pattern is the pattern of experience operative in fourth-level operations, in existential, interpersonal, and historical agency, in praxis."[92] So it is that the presence or absence of psychic conversion directly affects the principal pattern of human experience and thus the existential complexion of the human being and the construction of human history.

It is 'the censor' that sits at this borderline of consciousness and the underlying neural manifolds demanding representation in consciousness. Indeed, it is the censor that is responsible for the admission of images into consciousness. "When the censor operates constructively, it sorts through irrelevant data and allows us to receive the necessary images needed for insights. When the censor is repressive, it

---

89 Lonergan, *Insight: A Study of Human Understanding*, 212.

90 The question of a possible distinction—and the nature of such a distinction—between the moral and the dramatic pattern of experience is not considered here. For such discussion, see Walmsley, *Lonergan on Philosophic Pluralism: The Polymorphism of Consciousness as the Key to Philosophy*, 160-68.

91 Copeland, "A Genetic Study of the Idea of the Human Good in the Thought of Bernard Lonergan", 103.

92 Doran, *Theology and the Dialectics of History*, 72.

does not allow access to images that would allow needed insights."[93] Further, when the censor functions negatively, "demands for affects are unhinged from their appropriate potential imaginal counterparts and cathected with incongruous cognitive elements."[94] It is psychic conversion that shifts the censor's functioning from a repressive to a constructive role. In psychic conversion, the images for needed insights, subsequent judgments, and decisions, are admitted to consciousness, along with the appropriate concomitant feelings that function to reinforce the intentional operations. In this way, the integrity of this primary dialectic of the subject is a requirement for the integrity of the derived dialectic of the subject: psychic conversion is needed for the psyche to be able to collaborate with conscious intentionality.

3.2 DRAMATIC BIAS AND THE CYCLES OF DECLINE

Damage to the psyche has significant consequences for the issue of decline in history. Lonergan refers to the specific bias that pertains to the wounding of the psyche as dramatic bias. Dramatic bias is a function of the existence of negative complexes. It affects the dramatic subject, that is, the subject operating in the dramatic pattern of experience. In a case where the censor operates in a manner tainted by dramatic bias— where the dramatic patterning of experience is affected by bias—the neural demand functions fail to find appropriate representation in the psyche. Dramatic bias thus affects the subject operating in the dramatic pattern of experience, and, as noted above, this is the pattern, "operative in fourth-level operations, in existential, interpersonal, and historical agency, in praxis."[95] In this manner dramatic bias has a drastic impact upon one's existential life and in history.

If individual, group, and general bias all impinge upon the operation of intelligence and reasonability, dramatic bias's roots are 'deeper' in the subject. Dramatic bias, which results from the victimization of the psyche, arises from a fear of insights relating to the original wound. It distorts the subject's attempts to live with elegance and dignity in the presence of other humans. The bias inhibits the collaboration of imagination and intelligence in the task of supplying to consciousness the

---

93 Dadosky, "Healing the Psychological Subject: Towards a Fourfold Notion of Conversion?," 79. For a detailed discussion, see Doran, *Theology and the Dialectics of History*, 139-76.

94 Doran, *Theology and the Dialectics of History*, 73.

95 Ibid., 72.

materials—images with their appropriate affects—one would employ in structuring one's life as an existential work of art.[96] But dramatic bias establishes a blind spot, or a scotoma.[97] As dramatic bias becomes "established, it prevents the proper development of affective attitudes; as an aberration of the psychic center, it is repressive and inhibits conscious performance or behaviour."[98] Said otherwise, dramatic bias "blunts healthy psychological affective development, debilitates effective behaviour, and weakens the development of common sense."[99]

There is not a third cycle of decline that relates specifically to dramatic bias. What needs to be noted, given the nature of dramatic bias—its foundational nature at the level of experience—is that it compounds all other biases. Indeed,

> Because dramatic bias is or can be joined to any of the three biases of practical common sense or to any combination of them, it is effectively corrected only by the sustained operations of conscious intentionality in its triply converted state, where a scheme of recurrence is established that sets up a defensive circle to prevent the systematic interference of any form of biased intentionality.[100]

Dramatic bias does not establish a distinct cycle of decline, rather, it drastically exacerbates both the shorter and longer cycles of decline.

What should be noted with respect to overt liberation concerns, which were firmly oriented to meeting the distortions of the shorter cycle of decline, is that group bias—ultimately responsible for the shorter cycle—has a significant affective component. In group bias, the intersubjective component of the dialectic of community reinforces a functioning of practical intelligence that is distorted in such a manner as to exclude insights that would challenge the position of the dominant group. As Doran phrases it, psychic complexes are heavily predominant in the functioning of group bias.[101] That is, psychic disorder reinforces group bias. And therefore the healing of such complexes in psychic conversion also helps arrest the shorter cycle of decline. In

---

96   Doran, "Dramatic Artistry in the Third Stage of Meaning," 238-39.

97   Lonergan, *Insight: A Study of Human Understanding*, 215.

98   Copeland, "A Genetic Study of the Idea of the Human Good in the Thought of Bernard Lonergan," 108.

99   Ibid.

100   Doran, "Dramatic Artistry in the Third Stage of Meaning," 250-51.

101   Doran, *Theology and the Dialectics of History*, 232.

psychic conversion, the intersubjective distortions at the root of group bias are exposed and they thus become more likely—or at least now possible—to be overcome. When psychic conversion is coupled with religious and moral conversion, the intersubjectivity that is a component pole in the dialectic of community is empowered to move beyond group limitations as it heads, in the limit, to embrace not simply the human species but also all of creation as bound together by its relationship to the creator. This is perhaps, at least in part, what Gutiérrez means when he says that conversion is "a requirement for solidarity"[102] and always a "conversion to the neighbor."[103]

3.3 PSYCHIC CONVERSION AND THE PREFERENTIAL OPTION FOR THE POOR

Returning to psychic conversion and the Option for the Poor, it is apparent that this dimension of conversion is easily missed. One needs significant familiarity with one's own conscious intentionality to fully identify the nature of psychic conversion. But that is not to say that it holds no significance for understanding the Preferential Option for the Poor. Rather, it holds great significance: psychic conversion, when critically appropriated, speaks to the issue of the universal victimhood of humanity, whether one's psyche is the victim of misused freedom or of history.

It is arguably the case that the most significant manner in which psychic conversion functions as an element of the Option for the Poor has to do with the issue of victimhood. Primarily, the issue of the universal victimhood of humanity becomes evident in the close study of the sensitive psyche in its vulnerability. Specifically, the negative complexes within the psyche—those that "prevent one from participating in the creative adventure of pursuing and finding direction in the movement of life"—are "*victimized* compositions of energy."[104] These compositions may arise from the misuse of one's freedom.[105] But likewise, they

---

102   Gutiérrez, *We Drink from Our Own Wells: The Spiritual Journey of a People*, 101.

103   Gutiérrez, *A Theology of Liberation: History, Politics, and Salvation*, 118.

104   Doran, *Theology and the Dialectics of History*, 233.

105   Michael T. McLaughlin, *Knowledge, Consciousness and Religious Conversion in Lonergan and Aurobindo* (Rome: EPUG, 2003), 140.

may equally—perhaps more commonly—arise from disorder in society.[106] Indeed, as Lonergan contends the dialectic of community holds
a priority over the dialectic of the subject.[107] Or, as Doran phrases
it, "It is the community that sets the stage for the subject's dramatic
pattern of experience."[108] And the "more dominant the psychic factor
in the bias, the more is the source of the bias and of its destructive consequences to be located" outside the subject in history.[109] The point,
however, is that regardless of where blame lies—with history or misused freedom—it does not lie with the psyche: the disordered complex itself indicates the victimhood of the psyche. The compositions
and distributions of psychic energy begin to be set early on in one's
life without one's willful involvement: in the context of one's familial
relationships, by one's location in the class structure, by the broader machinations of world history. This point is also made by Ignacio
Martín-Baró, a social psychologist and one of the Jesuit Martyrs of El
Salvador, who writes that trauma has a dialectical character in that it
"must be understood in terms of the relationship between the individual and society."[110] In this relationship, society holds a priority such
that the traumatogenic structures, or social conditions that give rise to
trauma, must be treated along with the psychological problems of any
given individual, or trauma will simply be exponentially multiplied.[111]
In the situation here referred to by Doran and Martín-Baró, the psyche is clearly not responsible for its own damaged state. This is readily
apparent when one considers bias. As Doran writes,

> there is an increasing dominance of psychic as opposed to inten-
> tional features involved in the genesis and functioning of the bias as
> one moves from general through egoistic and group bias to dramat-
> ic bias. Dramatic bias is the consequence of complexes [of psychic
> energy] beyond the immediate reach of immediate self-determina-
> tion. The functioning of psychic complexes is also quite predomi-
> nant in group bias, less so in egoistic or individual bias, and least of

106 'Society', here, refers to the dialectic of community and also the dialectic of culture that will be introduced in the next chapter.
107 Lonergan, *Insight: A Study of Human Understanding*, 243.
108 Doran, *What Is Systematic Theology?*, 126.
109 Doran, *Theology and the Dialectics of History*, 234.
110 Ignacio Martín-Baró, *Writings for a Liberation Psychology* (Cambridge,
MA: HUP, 1994), 124-25.
111 Ibid.

all in general bias, which is a function more of moral and intellectual than of psychic maldevelopment, more of pneumopathology than of psychopathology.[112]

In theological terms, what is being referred to in this process of victimization, the production of victimized complexes, is a function of 'the sin of the world', that is, "a dimension of what the scholastics called *peccatum originale originatum*, the result of the permeation of the human world by a basic refusal."[113]

In psychic conversion, these complexes can be healed and the psychic tainting of one's orientation can likewise be overcome. It is, of course, divine love—the healing, downward vector in human consciousness—that, at root, effects this recovery. As has been mentioned above, along the healing vector, religious conversion, operative grace, first affects the fourth level of conscious intentionality and particularly the "affective dimension of consciousness at that fourth level as it is manifest in the primordial apprehension of values."[114] But the affective freedom engendered by religious conversion, and so central to moral conversion, is also required for "the normative objectivity that constitutes spontaneously operative *intellectual* authenticity."[115] This is so because insight and truth are values to which a consciousness healed by love can respond. But in a case where a psyche is damaged, seeking, let alone facing, the truth is enormously difficult precisely because of the pain involved in doing so.[116] As Doran notes, it is at this point that the healing vector begins "to affect the third and second levels of conscious performance in the dramatic pattern of experience."[117] One begins to desire the truth about oneself, despite the pain involved, and once one does so effectively, repressive censorship begins to be transformed into constructive censorship.[118] Intelligence is thus freed to collaborate with psyche in admitting to experience images with their concomitant affects. That is to say, the healing vector touches upon the empirical

---

112   Doran, *Theology and the Dialectics of History*, 232.
113   Ibid., 238.
114   Ibid., 248.
115   Ibid., 249.
116   Ibid., 250.
117   Ibid.
118   Ibid.

level of conscious intentionality and liberates the creative vector within consciousness.

The key element of this process of relevance to us now is the issue of the painful nature of psychic self-appropriation and where this leads in terms of hermeneutics. In this process, what becomes apparent is the victimized nature of the psyche. Appropriated psychic conversion calls attention to the universal victimhood of humanity. All are perpetrators of sin. But all are also victims. Being attentive to the damage done to psyche,

> if one is really serious about it, will serve to establish one in solidarity with those whose participation in the dialectic of history seems to mark them as the victims of sin of the world; for negotiation of one's own psychic darkness will teach one that there are dimensions of the history of all of us that are not responsible for their own at times tragic disorder.[119]

Or, as Doran phrases it elsewhere, and to quote him at length:

> Psychic conversion has the fuller significance, then, of enabling us to appropriate the story of our ongoing dramatic engagement as beings-in-the-world, as subjects now become responsible for the constitution of ourselves and of history. The conversion of the repressive censorship to a constructive censorship is the key to the self-appropriation of our dramatic artistry, to an existential self-appropriation of ourselves as world-constitutive agents in the dialectic of history. Such self-knowledge is not existential in the narrow sense of individualized and privatized internal self-communication isolated from the other historical dialectics. For those dialectics set the conditions for the dialectic of intentionality and psyche constitutive of an individual's development. Even more, because psychic conversion enables us to attend to the dimensions of our own being that have been victimized by the sin of the world, it establishes a point of solidarity with the most victimized peoples of history that can facilitate our assumption of the pattern of the suffering servant in cooperating with God's salvific intention to establish the reign of God through the implementation of the integral dialectics that would constitute the alternative situation to be evoked by a contemporary systematic theology. As the situation of the victimized elements of our own being is hermeneutically privileged in the interpretation of our own stories, so the situation of the poor is

---

119   Doran, *What Is Systematic Theology?*, 124.

hermeneutically privileged in the interpretation of history. Contact with either one facilitates a truthful acknowledgment of the other.[120] This perhaps should be even more the case when the damage to our psyche is identified as being done by the dialectic of community (or as is introduced in the next chapter of this book, the dialectic of culture). We are all victims of history. Some are simply affected economically-politically more so than others.

4. CONCLUSION

The last two chapters have sought to establish the relevance of the Lonergan-Doran perspective on integral conversion for an understanding of the Option for the Poor. They did not show only that Lonergan Studies is not inimical to the Option for the Poor, they also demonstrated that Lonergan and Doran's work in fact serve liberation concerns. In Chapter 2 it was shown that seminal liberation theologians—viz., Gutiérrez and Sobrino—claim that the Option has the structure of conversion, hermeneutics and praxis. Without seeking to demonstrate a strict correlation with the liberationist perspective this chapter has indicated that all three elements are present in any understanding of the Option for the Poor grounded in Lonergan Studies: fourfold conversion implies both hermeneutics (particularly in intellectual conversion) and praxis (particularly in moral conversion) in service of loving liberation of the poor (set in motion by religious conversion and facilitated by psychic conversion).

Having established the core of the manner in which the Option for the Poor relates to integral conversion, the question can now be asked: does Lonergan Studies have anything further to contribute? The argument of the present work is a resounding 'yes'. To support this assertion, Chapter 6 builds upon the prior achievements of Chapters 4 and 5. It centers upon the comprehensive theory of history that Doran constructs in *Theology and the Dialectics of History*. It demonstrates that this theory—built on the foundations of the converted subject— not only provides a sophisticated transcendental grounding of the Option for the Poor, but that it does so in a manner that meets the key concerns of many liberation theologians.

---

120   Doran, *Theology and the Dialectics of History*, 252.

CHAPTER 6

ROBERT DORAN'S ACHIEVEMENT, THE PREFERENTIAL OPTION FOR THE POOR, AND LIBERATION THEOLOGY: CONVERSION TO THE KINGDOM OF GOD AND THE MISSION OF THE CHURCH

I. INTRODUCTION

The previous chapter argued that an understanding of conversion derived from Lonergan and Doran's work provides a comprehensive grounding for the Option for the Poor. Lonergan Studies not only grounds the Magisterium's approach to the Option in terms of religious conversion and subsequent moral conversion to charity, but also grounds the Option in a manner that includes Liberation Theology's broader concern for hermeneutics and method. Moreover, Lonergan Studies can move beyond Liberation Theology's traditional concerns to consideration of psychic conversion's relevance to the Option for the Poor, particularly as it relates to the universal victimhood of humanity. It is, of course, beyond the ambit of this final chapter to demonstrate that the full significance the previous chapter's argumentation holds for the whole discipline of theology or even any of its sub-disciplines. This chapter does demonstrate, however, that the Option for the Poor is critically grounded by the theologically sensitive theory of history contained in Doran's *Theology and the Dialectics of History*.[1] Further, in this chapter it is demonstrated that Doran's theory of history is able to meet many of Liberation Theology's explicit needs with respect to theological foundations.

This chapter has three sections. The first contains a summary of Doran's theologically attuned theory of history, which, it is also demonstrated, provides a highly cogent schema for understanding not

---

[1] Ibid.

only society but also the Christian concept of the Kingdom of God. The second section introduces Liberation Theology's understanding of the doctrine of the Kingdom of God by focusing first on the mission of the Church, and secondly upon Jon Sobrino's reflections on the "Central Position of the Reign of God in Liberation Theology."[2] The final section of the chapter seeks to demonstrate the fact that Doran's theology of history can fulfill the needs of Liberation Theology with respect to a systematic theology of the Reign of God whilst simultaneously avoiding some of the pitfalls—be they merely perceived or actually extant—that have dogged Liberation Theology.

2. DORAN'S *THEOLOGY AND THE DIALECTICS OF HISTORY* AND THE CONVERTED SUBJECT IN HISTORY: CATEGORIES FOR THE KINGDOM OF GOD

This section of the chapter introduces Doran's theologically attuned theory of history that he envisages as theological foundations. To do so, it draws primarily on his *Theology and the Dialectics of History* and *What Is Systematic Theology?* To focus on matters germane to the issue of the Option for the Poor, this section then explains the nature of 'society' within Doran's theoretical account of history.

Doran intends his *Theology and the Dialectics of History* to facilitate the theologian's task of constructing "the meanings constitutive of that praxis of the Reign of God through which the human world itself is changed."[3] His view of theology is grounded upon "a theory of history elaborated with a theological end in view" which is thereby able to "specify just what the Reign of God in this world would be."[4] That is,

---

2   Sobrino, "Central Position of the Reign of God in Liberation Theology," 350-88. And also, see Sobrino, "The Centrality of the Kingdom of God Announced by Jesus: Reflections Before Aparecida," 77-98.

3   Doran, *Theology and the Dialectics of History*, 5.

4   Ibid., 12. It is appropriate to flag the similarity between this stance and that of Liberation Theology. Jon Sobrino argues that the Reign of God is the unifying and foundational concept of Liberation Theology; he notes that for Ignacio Ellacuría the Reign of God is *the* object of theology. The Reign was chosen by liberation theologians—over and against other realities such as the resurrection—because it posits an indissoluble link between God and history. Sobrino argues, "An evangelical determination of the Reign of God is surely of the highest importance for our faith. But

he develops an heuristic structure for the understanding of progress, decline, and redemption within the historical process. Three key elements need to be rehearsed to understand his project: the scale of values; the vectors of creating and healing; and the dialectics of history. These three elements are sketched here before Doran's understanding of society is outlined.

2.1 THE SCALE OF VALUES

The unifying element of Doran's project is the scale of values.[5] Following Lonergan, he notes that it is our feelings that respond to values. But in the same manner that feelings need to be discerned, so all values are not equal and appropriate choices among them require discernment. The integrally converted subject responds to values in a specific order of preference. Five levels of value can be distinguished: vital, social, cultural, personal, and religious values.[6] It is worth quoting Lonergan on this scale:

> Vital values, such as health and strength, grace and vigour, normally are preferred to avoiding the work, privations, pains involved in acquiring, maintaining, restoring them. Social values, such as the good of order which conditions the vital values of the whole

---

in itself it does not furnish a systematic concept of the Reign for today. Liberation Theology, which unlike other theologies maintains the central character of the Reign, considers that the systematic concept of the Reign should be based on and should synthesize what is essential to the evangelical concept." Sobrino, "Central Position of the Reign of God in Liberation Theology," 371.

5 The scale functions as the unifying concept of Doran's heuristic structure for the understanding of historical process because values are 'final causes'. As Andrew Beards writes, "human actions, and thus collective and collaborative human actions, occur because of final causes in the sense of ends, or values willed and/or chosen." See Andrew Beards, *Method in Metaphysics: Lonergan and the Future of Analytical Philosophy* (Toronto: University of Toronto Press, 2008), 307. It is the choosing of value that ensures progress and redemption within history. And the choosing of disvalue (sometimes the lower value) which precipitates decline.

6 Kenneth Melchin follows Doran's approach to the scale of values in that for him it is also a question of isomorphism between the knower's consciousness and the known. See his approach in Kenneth R. Melchin, "Democracy, Sublation, and the Scale of Values," in *The Importance of Insight: Essays in Honour of Michael Vertin* ed. John J. Liptay and David S. Liptay (Toronto: University of Toronto Press, 2007), 183-96.

community, have to be preferred to the vital values of individual members of the community. Cultural values do not exist without the underpinning of vital and social values, but none the less they rank higher. Not on bread alone doth man live. Over and above mere living and operating, men have to find a meaning and value in their living and operating. It is the function of culture to discover, express, validate, criticize, correct, develop, improve such meaning and value. Personal value is the person in his self-transcendence, as loving and being loved, as originator of values in himself and in his milieu, as an inspiration and invitation to others to do likewise. Religious values, finally, are at the heart of the meaning and value of man's living and man's world.[7]

Vital values are those goods essential to the quality of physical life, such as food, health, and shelter. Social values are concerned with the good of order, the distribution of power and communal identity. Cultural values provide the meaning of life, and they can be mediated through story, myth, philosophy, science, art, or many other systems of meaning. Personal values deal with issues of individual integrity and self-transcendence. But the mover of all things, God, initiates and sustains personal integrity by the gift of grace at the level of religious value. These five interrelated levels of values sit as the foundation of Doran's project.

2.2 THE VECTORS OF CREATING AND HEALING

The second element of Doran's project is comprised of the vectors of creating and healing: a two-fold movement within consciousness. He describes the first vector, the 'upward' vector of creating, when he writes of the movement that begins before consciousness and unfolds through the levels of consciousness—through sensitivity, intelligence, rationality, and responsibility—to find its fulfillment at the apex of human consciousness.[8] Yet there is also a complementary movement downward. Lonergan writes:

> There is development from below upwards, from experience to understanding, from growing understanding to balanced judgment, from balanced judgment to fruitful courses of action, and from fruitful courses of action to new situations that call for further

---

7   Lonergan, *Method in Theology*, 31-32.
8   Doran, *Theology and the Dialectics of History*, 31. See also Lonergan, "Natural Right and Historical Mindedness," 174-75.

understanding, profounder judgment, richer courses of action. But there also is development from above downwards. There is the transformation of falling in love: the domestic love of the family; the human love of one's tribe, one's country, mankind; the divine love that orientates man in his cosmos and expresses itself in worship.[9]

This second healing vector is rooted in love, ultimately in the religious conversion that underlies all conversions, and it complements the achievements of the human spirit. Lonergan believes that development from above downwards conditions our development from below upwards. Ideally—*viz.*, when the human subject is in love with God—the vectors are concurrently operative and the corrosive effect of bias upon human achievement is overcome by divine grace. A transformation rooted in being-in-love then guides the creative process of the human subject. It will be seen below that it is these creating and healing vectors that Doran employs to account for the movement from level to level of the integral scale of values.

2.3 THE DIALECTICS OF HISTORY: PERSONAL, CULTURAL, SOCIAL

As noted in the previous chapter, Doran suggests that two forms of dialectic can be identified by the appropriation of one's interiority. These dialectics are based on distinct kinds of opposition: opposition by way of contradictories giving rise to 'dialectics of contradictories' and opposition by way of contraries giving rise to 'dialectics of contraries'.[10] Dialectics of contradictories take the form of an opposition of exclusion. In dialectics of contradictories the opposed principles are mutually exclusive—a case of either/or—and such a dialectic can only be resolved by the choice of one pole over the other: true and false is an example of such a dialectic.[11] Dialectics of contraries, by contrast, are dialectics in which there exists a creative tension between the two poles. A dialectic of contraries represents a tension between opposed principles that is reconcilable in a higher synthesis. Both poles are preserved and strengthened to maintain a creative tension. So it is that a dialectic of contraries has two poles: one is a principle of transcendence (Doran calls it the operator), and the other is a principle of

9   Lonergan, "Healing and Creating in History," 106.

10   Doran, *What Is Systematic Theology?*, 185. See also Lonergan, *Insight: A Study of Human Understanding*, 11-24.

11   Doran, *Theology and the Dialectics of History*, 64-92.

limitation (Doran calls it the integrator). In a dialectic of contraries, the operator transforms the integrator and they work together in an inclusive manner.

Doran identifies dialectics functioning as the principle of integrity at the level of personal value. By analogy, he suggests that a dialectic is operative at each of the levels of cultural and social value. As noted in the previous chapter, the integrity of the human person is a function of the successful navigation of the dialectics of the subject: the basic dialectic between bodiliness (integrator) and spirit (operator); and, the derived dialectic between the psyche (integrator) and conscious intentionality (operator). It was also noted in Chapter 4 that the integrity of the dialectic of community at the social level of value resides in the successful functioning of a dialectic between spontaneous intersubjectivity (integrator) and practical intelligence (operator). The integrity of the dialectic of culture was not mentioned in detail in the previous chapter, and it serves now to introduce it more fully.

2.3.1 THE DIALECTIC OF CULTURE

Drawing on Eric Voegelin's work, Doran posits that the dialectic of culture involves a dialectic between cosmological culture (integrator) and anthropological culture (operator).[12] Doran writes that cosmological truth "is the discovery that direction in the movement of life lies in a harmony between human decisions and actions, on the one hand, and the rhythms and processes of nature, on the other hand, that is, in a synchronicity between culture and nature."[13] He contrasts this with anthropological truth, which he understands as "[establishing] by a more specialized reflection that the ultimate measure of human integrity is a reality beyond the cosmos, and that the direction is found in the movement of life as the human spirit and psyche are attuned to the drawing or inclination initiated by this world-transcendent measure orienting the soul to itself."[14]

Doran writes, when specifically considering cosmological culture:

> Cosmological symbolizations of the experience of life as a movement with a direction that can be found or missed find the paradigm of order in the cosmic rhythms. This order is analogously

---

12   Doran, *What Is Systematic Theology?*, 172-74.
13   Doran, *Theology and the Dialectics of History*, 216.
14   Ibid.

realized in the society, and social order determines individual rectitude. Cosmological insight thus moves from the cosmos, through the society, to the individual. ... Cosmological constitutive meaning has its roots in the affective biologically based sympathy of the organism with the rhythms and process of non-human nature.[15]

Such symbolizations are apparent in the cultures of the many indigenous peoples throughout the world. Indeed, it is characterized, in the extreme, by what Raimundo Panikkar—who also draws on Voegelin—refers to as the ecumenic moment of time-awareness in which,[16] "Nature, Man and the divine are still amorphously mixed and only vaguely differentiated."[17] The ecumenic moment describes a culture in which cosmological symbolizations dominate. In Panikkar's analysis, it was the dominant moment of culture until the invention and the spread of writing.[18] In ecumenic or nonhistorical consciousness, time is anthropocosmic; the distinction between humanity and nature is not yet made, or if it is, it is only vaguely made.[19] Human beings still share the world with the gods. Because the gods have not been banished or made transcendent, nature is mysterious and divine.[20] The idea of a "collective enterprise different from what nature does or separated from the rhythms of the cosmos makes no sense to pre-historical Man."[21] Life is an active struggle lived in the now, not postponed until the future. Resources are used for the moment and not acquired as a means for political domination in the future.[22] All

---

15 Doran, "The Analogy of Dialectic and the Systematics of History," 54-55.

16 Whereas, for Doran, 'anthropological culture' and 'cosmological culture' name ideal types, it should be noted that Panikkar appears to have pre-history and more concrete historical periods in mind. It appears that he has applied such types to differing epochs, when he speaks of the ecumenic, economic, and catholic moments.

17 Raimundo Panikkar, *The Cosmotheandric Experience: Emerging Religious Consciousness* (Maryknoll, NY: Orbis Books, 1993), 54. Panikkar uses the term 'Man' to refer to the androgynous human being and his usage is preserved in direct quotations but not repeated elsewhere.

18 Ibid., 93.

19 Ibid., 95.

20 Ibid.

21 Ibid., 96.

22 Ibid., 96-98.

reality struggles together; there is no clear delineation among God, nature, and humanity. By contrast, in anthropological culture, the "measure of integrity is recognized as world-transcendent and as providing the standard first for the individual whose ordered attunement to the world-transcendent measure is itself the measure of the integrity of the society. Anthropological insight moves from God through the individual to the society."[23] It first becomes evident in the intellectual history of the West with the emergence of the Ancient Greek philosophical tradition. In more recent times, as Ormerod notes, anthropological culture rose to prominence during the Enlightenment, when reason became the ground of meaning and value (with or without God as an ultimate ground).[24] Panikkar refers to a culture in which anthropological meanings dominate as the economic moment of human time-awareness. It is characterized by the rational-scientific "thrust toward the future ... [because] our destiny is (in) the future."[25] In the economic moment, rationality emerges as the supreme criterion by which all is judged. Reason comes to be identified with the spirit,[26] yet even spiritual fulfillment is something for the future. Within the economic moment, God is no longer immanent. Union with God, so understood, is not possible during an earthly lifetime. Hope must always be directed toward a future beyond this life and this earth. The deliverance of humanity from mundane surrounds is only possible when humanity can become fully transcendent. The economic moment holds that it is only when humanity is fully transcendent that it can be united with a God that is not only transcendent, but that is also absent from creation.[27]

---

23   Doran, "The Analogy of Dialectic and the Systematics of History," 55.

24   Neil Ormerod and Shane Clifton, *Globalization and the Mission of the Church* (New York: T&T Clark, 2009), 33.

25   Panikkar, *The Cosmotheandric Experience: Emerging Religious Consciousness*, 100.

26   Ibid., 35.

27   Gnosticism can be recognized as an archetypical form of the economic moment in that it preaches salvation through knowledge because it has "resigned itself to saving only the soul, the spiritual part of Man and the cosmos. To do so it must condemn matter and even exclude the World completely." Ibid., 73. Indeed, for Gnosticism, there will be no New Heaven and no New Earth.

It needs to be noted that it is neither cosmological nor anthropological culture, whether taken jointly or severally, that actually maintains the tension of the dialectic of culture. Rather, such creative tension at the level of culture is, proximately, a function of soteriological culture in which divine agency enters into history and reveals divine meanings and values.[28] That is,

> [s]oteriological truth witnesses to the action of [the] world-transcendent measure in the concrete experiences of individuals and communities, establishing friendship between God and human beings and reconciling human beings in community with one another, thus establishing history as a form of existence by redeeming human persons and communities from the distortions of the dialectics constitutive of historical process, and attuning existence to the promptings that are indications of the will of God, as God establishes us in love through grace or places us on the true path to life and keeps us there by God's own self-communication to us in revelatory experience and grace.[29]

Soteriological culture can be characterized by what Panikkar refers to as the catholic—with a lower-case 'c'—moment of time-awareness. The catholic moment of human time-awareness "maintain[s] the distinctions of the second moment without forfeiting the unity of the first."[30] It is at a higher turn of the spiral, to use Panikkar's terminology, where humanity does not regress to the first moment, but reawakens to the awareness of the pervading presence of unity and cosmological rhythms. The catholic moment stands as a middle-term between the ecumenic and economic moments. Panikkar calls the experience of reality as differentiated but unbroken "the cosmotheandric intuition,"[31] that is, the realization that "reality cannot be reduced to a single principle," and that reality itself has a fundamentally tripartite structure—freedom/transcendence, consciousness, and matter/energy.[32] In this sense, it is the catholic moment that holds together the integrator (ecumenic moment) and the operator (economic moment). The catholic

---

28 Doran, *Theology and the Dialectics of History*, 216. Also, Ormerod and Clifton, *Globalization and the Mission of the Church*, 35.

29 Doran, *Theology and the Dialectics of History*, 216.

30 Panikkar, *The Cosmotheandric Experience: Emerging Religious Consciousness*, 54.

31 Ibid., 62.

32 Ibid., 121.

moment, in a sense, establishes a tension between the extremities of the ecumenic and economic moments such that the truth present in each moment is not forfeited, but is rather brought into creative tension with the other. The catholic moment, therefore—which Panikkar refers to as "mystical awareness,"—relies on the insights of the ecumenic and economic moments.[33] Cosmological unity and anthropological particularity are held in tension by the catholic moment such that it offers an holistic form of cultural awareness.[34]

2.4 PROGRESS, DECLINE, AND REDEMPTION: 'SOCIETY' WITHIN DORAN'S THEOLOGICAL FOUNDATIONS

Doran assembles these three key elements—the scale of values, the vectors of creating and healing, and dialectic—to conceive of history as a complex network of dialectics of subjects, cultures, and communities.[35] Said otherwise, these elements provide an heuristic structure that enables the understanding of historical process and also society. For Doran, 'society' is a generic term.[36] With more precision, he claims that a society is comprised of five distinct but interrelated elements: intersubjective spontaneity, technological institutions, the economic system, the political order, and culture.[37] Culture has two dimensions, the everyday infrastructural level that informs a given way of life, and

---

33   Ibid., 133.

34   The following quote goes some way towards capturing Doran's stance on the nature of cosmological-soteriological-anthropological culture: "Exclusively cosmological constitutive meaning betrays the fact that the distinctly intentional dimensions of human consciousness have either not yet been discovered or, having been discovered, have subsequently been forgotten. Exclusively anthropological constitutive meaning betrays the fact that the sensitive psychic dimensions of human consciousness have been relegated to oblivion as the disengagement of spirit from psyche succumbs to the hubris that instrumentalizes the capacities of cognition and decision in the service of power. Both cosmological and anthropological constitutive meaning stand in need of the soteriological higher synthesis that would integrate one with the other; and this is so because the psyche without direction from the spirit and the spirit without a base in the psyche are the two features of the constant and permanent structure of the human that stand in need of redemption." Doran, *Theology and the Dialectics of History*, 510.

35   Ibid., 144.

36   Ibid., 359.

37   Ibid., 361.

the reflexive superstructural level that arises from scientific, philosophic, scholarly and theological objectifications. Doran sets forth the interrelationship of these components in six points.[38]

First, spontaneous intersubjectivity—the communal sense that bonds family, friends, and nation—functions on its own as one of the elements of society in the dialectic of community. Secondly, practical intelligence, which is the other constitutive principle of the dialectic of community, gives rise to three constitutive elements of society, viz., technological institutions, the economic order, and the political-legal echelon of society. Thirdly, in a society operating along an optimum line of progress, these three elements must be kept in dialectical tension with spontaneous intersubjectivity. Fourthly, the integrity—and inversely the distortion—of the dialectic of community is a function, proximately of the infrastructural level of culture, and more remotely, of the reflexive superstructural level of culture. Fifthly, spontaneous intersubjectivity, technological institutions, economic systems, political-legal institutions, and everyday culture constitute the infrastructure of a healthy society. Moreover, the reflexive level of culture constitutes society's superstructure; and culture at *both* levels is a limit-condition upon the possible existence of an integral dialectic of community. Sixthly, there is needed at the superstructural level an orientation that takes responsibility for the dialectic of community. This orientation addresses the integrity of cultural values at both the superstructural and infrastructural levels (Lonergan refers to this specialisation of intelligence as cosmopolis).[39] In terms of progress and decline as measured by this understanding, Doran offers a helpful summary:

> From above, then, religious values condition the possibility of personal integrity; personal integrity conditions the possibility of authentic cultural values; at the reflexive level of culture, such integrity will promote an authentic superstructural collaboration that assumes responsibility for the integrity not only of scientific and scholarly disciplines, but even of everyday culture; cultural integrity at both levels conditions the possibility of a just social order; and a just social order conditions the possibility of the equitable distribution of vital goods. Conversely, problems in the effective and recurrent distribution of vital goods can be met only by a reversal

---

38   This is the more concise presentation taken from Doran, *What Is Systematic Theology?*, 174-75.

39   Doran, *Theology and the Dialectics of History*, 361.

of distortions in the social order; the proportions of the needed reversal are set by the scope and range of the real or potential maldistribution; the social change demands a transformation at the everyday level of culture proportionate to the dimensions of the social problem; this transformation frequently depends on reflexive theoretical and scientific developments at the superstructural level; new cultural values at both levels call for proportionate changes at the level of personal integrity; and these depend for their emergence, sustenance, and consistency on the religious development of the person.[40]

Society is proceeding along a line of pure progress inasmuch as the dialectics at the levels of culture and society function as dialectics of contraries. So for Doran, social schemes that are responsible for the just distribution of vital goods can in fact result in an unjust distribution of vital goods. In such a case, new technological institutions, economic systems, and political-legal structures are required to promote the just distribution of vital goods; or, at the other pole of the dialectic of community, new intersubjective habits or stances may need to be cultivated so that distortions such as racism or classism can be transcended at the visceral level. New social schemes are possible only if new cultural values emerge to motivate and sustain the existence of these new values. And the new cultural values informing the transformed social structures are a function of individuals' conversions and their originating values.

It may help to represent this theology of history pictorially:

---

40   Ibid., 96-97.

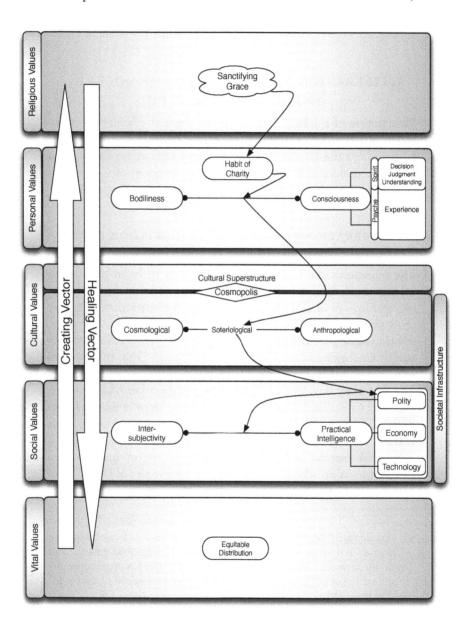

Figure 2: Doran's Theology of History.

From this integrated theology of history, the focus now turns to Liberation Theology and its understanding of the Kingdom of God.

3. LIBERATION THEOLOGY AND THE DOCTRINE OF THE KINGDOM OF GOD

This section of the book has two parts: the first contains a presentation of Liberation Theology's understanding of the mission of the Church; and the second contains an illustration of how Liberation Theology understands the doctrine of the Kingdom of God, which emerges as central in Liberation Theology's understanding of the mission of the Church.

3.1 LIBERATION THEOLOGY AND THE MISSION OF THE CHURCH: BUILDING FOR THE KINGDOM OF GOD

The mission of the Church, of course, needs to be in some sense collinear with Christ's mission, lest the former be posited as working against—or at least heading in directions other than—the latter, a situation that is surely theologically absurd. Along these lines, Sobrino has argued that the Church does not so much 'have' a mission as that Christ's mission gave birth to the Church. That is, "The mission should not be understood from the perspective of the Church, but the other way around."[41] How does Liberation Theology understand Christ's mission? In concert with modern biblical scholarship, Liberation Theology asserts that the Kingdom of God stands at the center of Christ's mission. Theologian John Fuellenbach notes, "Almost all exegetes and scholars are in agreement on this point: the center of Jesus' preaching and teaching is the Kingdom of God."[42] And despite criticisms leveled at Liberation Theology by Catholic bib-

---

41   Sobrino, "Depth and Urgency of the Option for the Poor," 21.

42   Fuellenbach argues "the word *Kingdom* occurs 160 times in the Christian scriptures, with 120 occurrences in the synoptic gospels" and that "the formula *Kingdom of God* or *Kingdom of Heaven* occurs over one hundred times in the gospels in the following distribution: Matthew, fifty-five times; Mark, fourteen times; Luke, thirty-nine times. On the lips of Jesus we find the phrase ninety times." He continues, "The word *Church* is used only twice: Matthew 16:18 and 18:17. This fact led to A. Loisy's often quoted polemical comment: 'Jesus preached the Kingdom of God and what came out was the Church.'" John Fuellenbach, *The Kingdom of God:*

lical scholar John Meier,[43] it appears that—on the issue of the mission of Christ, at least—Liberation Theology's reading of scripture is not dissimilar from that of Anglican biblical scholar N. T. Wright. Wright argues that the content of Jesus's prophetic proclamation "was the 'Kingdom' of Israel's God."[44] Following Wright's logic, one must concur like Liberation Theology that the Church's mission must have something—indeed, quite a lot—to do with the Kingdom of God. Wright proceeds to note that in no way does the Paschal Mystery eclipse the relevance of the Kingdom of God: Jesus' death is not about anything other than "the Kingdom work to which he devoted his short public career."[45] It is to the Kingdom of God one must look in order to grasp the nature of the Church's mission.

In terms of the mission of the Church, Ignacio Ellacuría writes, "The greatest possible realization of the Kingdom of God in history [the very thing that Jesus came to announce and bring about] is what the true followers of Jesus must pursue."[46] This is not intended in a Pelagian sense. And, again, Liberation Theology is not without biblical warrant to make this claim. This stance can be seen to accord with that of Wright, who outlines his understanding of the relationship between Christ's mission and the Church's mission by noting that the "Kingdom inaugurating public work of Jesus" is precisely what the Church—as the community of Jesus' followers—"have

---

the Message of Jesus Today (Maryknoll, NY: Orbis Books, 1995), 4. See also Alfred Loisy, L'evangile et l'eglise (Paris: Picard, 1902), iii.

43 As noted in the previous chapter of this book, John Meier has criticized Sobrino's Christology on historical grounds. He also takes aim at Segundo's use of the Historical Jesus. See Meier, "The Bible as a Source for Theology," 3-14.

44 N. T. Wright, Jesus and the Victory of God (Minneapolis: Fortress Press, 1996), 11.

45 N. T. Wright, Surprised by Hope: Rethinking Heaven, the Resurrection, and the Mission of the Church (New York: HarperOne, 2008), 204. See also, Wright, Jesus and the Victory of God, 540-611.

46 As quoted by Sobrino, "The Centrality of the Kingdom of God Announced by Jesus: Reflections Before Aparecida," 91. He is citing Ignacio Ellacuría, "Aporte de la teología de la liberación a las religiones abrahámicas en la superación del individualismo y del positivismo," Revista Latinoamericana de Teología (San Salvador) 10 (1987): 3-28.

been commissioned and equipped to put into practice."[47] That is, "the Church that is renewed by the message of Jesus' resurrection must be the Church that goes to work [in the world of space, time, and matter] and claims it in advance as the place of God's Kingdom, of Jesus' lordship, of the power of the Spirit."[48] Resurrection, ascension and gift of the Spirit do not detract from this earth; rather, they make us agents of the transformation of the earth.[49] Wright is not suggesting that, "[we] 'build the Kingdom' all by ourselves," but, in a manner reminiscent of Liberation Theology's 'eschatological proviso,'[50] he argues, "we do build *for* the Kingdom."[51] Everything that Christians accomplish, when they work under the guidance of the Spirit that has been given to them, will be enhanced and transformed at Christ's final appearance.[52] But the Kingdom remains God's work.

Latent in this stance on the mission of the Church and the Kingdom of God is a specific soteriology and eschatology.[53] Quite simply, Liberation Theology understands that "there are not two histories, one profane and one sacred, 'juxtaposed' or 'closely linked.' Rather, there is only one human destiny, irreversibly assumed by Christ, the

---

47   Wright, *Surprised by Hope: Rethinking Heaven, the Resurrection, and the Mission of the Church*, 204.

48   Ibid., 265.

49   Ibid., 201.

50   'Eschatological proviso' is Johannes Baptist Metz's terminology. He uses it to prevent any strict identification of the fullness of the Kingdom, the Kingdom in its totality, with what can be achieved in history. Johannes Baptist Metz, *Theology of the World* (London: Burns & Oates, 1969), 111. Gutiérrez is somewhat critical of Metz on this point in that he is concerned not to encourage a withdrawal from complete political commitment. But Gutiérrez does not go so far as to equate what can be achieved in history by human deeds with the Kingdom. He argues that "the political is grafted onto the eternal" and thus keeps the two realms distinct without suggesting conflation or separation. Gutiérrez, *A Theology of Liberation: History, Politics, and Salvation*, 135. See also, Peter Hebblethwaite, *The Christian Hope* (Oxford: OUP, 2010), 161-62.

51   Wright, *Surprised by Hope: Rethinking Heaven, the Resurrection, and the Mission of the Church*, 143. The emphasis is Wright's own.

52   Ibid.

53   Any given soteriology, of course, also assumes (or explicitly takes) a stance on the relationship of sin to grace and the place of nature (if any) in that relationship.

Lord of history."[54] The human community, for Liberation Theology, is saved and fulfilled in history. The grace-sin conflict, the coming of the Kingdom and the expectation of the Parousia are all historical, earthly, social, and material realities.[55] That is to say, "the complete encounter with the Lord will mark an end to history but it will take place in history."[56] In the terminology that gave the movement its name, humanity is liberated within history. Thus, for Liberation Theology:

> To work, to transform this world, is to become a man and to build the human community; it is also to save. Likewise, to struggle against misery and exploitation and to build a just society is already to be part of the saving action, which is moving towards its complete fulfillment. All this means that building the temporal city is not simply a stage of 'humanization' or 'pre-evangelization' as was held in theology until a few years ago. Rather it is to become part of a saving process which embraces the whole of humanity and all human history. Any theological reflection on human work and social praxis ought to be rooted in this fundamental affirmation.[57]

And so, "The Church's mission is ... to proclaim an integral liberation because nothing is left untouched by the saving work of Christ."[58] This position stands firmly in opposition to more Platonic ones, such as that presented by Pope Benedict XVI when he writes—drawing on Origen—of a "mystical interpretation" of the Kingdom whereby "man's interiority [is] the essential location of the Kingdom of God."[59] In Benedict's understanding, Jesus' message of the Kingdom has few,

---

54   Gutiérrez, A Theology of Liberation: History, Politics, and Salvation, 86.

55   Ibid., 96-97.

56   Ibid., 97.

57   Ibid., 91.

58   Gutiérrez, The Truth Shall Make You Free: Confrontations, 142. See also Sobrino, "Central Position of the Reign of God in Liberation Theology," 356.

59   Pope Benedict XVI, Jesus of Nazareth: From the Baptism in the Jordan to the Transfiguration, trans. Adrian J. Walker (London: Bloomsbury, 2007), 49. The relevant reflection from Origen's On Prayer, "XXV.1 Your Kingdom Come," can be found at Origen, An Exhortation to Martyrdom; Prayer; First Principles: Book IV; Prologue to the Commentary On the Song of Songs; Homily XXVII on Numbers trans. Rowan A. Greer (Mahwah, NJ: Paulist Press, 1979), 131-34.

if any, socio-political ramifications.[60] For Liberation Theology, the Kingdom certainly involves the change of hearts. But changed hearts also change history by building an approximation to the Reign of God therein. Moreover, such transformed history—which, to employ Lonergan-Doran's categories, are comprised of healed dialectics of culture and community—can facilitate the change of other hearts. In Liberation Theology building in anticipation of the Kingdom is itself part of the salvific process.[61]

---

60 Pope Benedict XVI, *Jesus of Nazareth: From the Baptism in the Jordan to the Transfiguration*, 50. This appears to be the most correct reading of Benedict's intentions. He does note on the same page that the Kingdom "grows and radiates outward" from the inner space that is man's inner being. But there is nothing to suggest that he means this in a sense that has political ramifications.

61 It is in this context that Wright's understanding of salvation ought to be noted, for it seems to ground Liberation Theology's approach to soteriology solidly in historical studies. Drawing on a lifetime's work in biblical studies, Wright concludes, "salvation ... is not 'going to heaven' but 'being raised to life in God's new heaven and new earth.'" However, he continues, as soon as salvation is conceived in such a manner, "we realize that the New Testament is full of hints, indications, and downright assertions that this salvation isn't just something we have to wait for in the long-distance future. We can enjoy it here and now (always partially, of course, since we all still have to die), genuinely anticipating in the present what is to come in the future." "We were saved', as Paul would have it in Romans 8:24; but we are saved "'in hope' because we still look forward to the ultimate future salvation of which he speaks in (for instance) Romans 5:9-10." The point Wright makes here is that when "God saves people in this life, by working through his Spirit to bring them to faith and by leading them to follow Jesus in discipleship, prayer, holiness, hope, and love, such people are designed ... to be a sign and foretaste of what God wants to do for the entire cosmos." Wright, *Surprised by Hope: Rethinking Heaven, the Resurrection, and the Mission of the Church*, 198. The Kingdom of God, Wright concludes, "is thus to be put into practice in the world, resulting in salvation in both the present and the future, a salvation that is both *for* humans and, *through* saved humans, for the wider world." This, he contends, is the basis for the mission of the Church. Ibid., 205. To repeat, for Wright, Jesus' "Kingdom inaugurating public work" is precisely what the Church—as the community of Jesus' followers—"have been commissioned and equipped to put into practice." Ibid., 204. Such an understanding does not bracket the political or social dimensions of the Gospel or the Kingdom. Ibid., 203.

3.2 LIBERATION THEOLOGY AND THE DOCTRINE OF THE KINGDOM OF GOD

From the reflections above on the nature of the mission of the Church, it is clear that the doctrine of the Kingdom of God is of paramount significance in Liberation Theology. In a chapter of the authoritative *Mysterium Liberationis*—"Central Position of the Reign of God in Liberation Theology"[62]—Jon Sobrino outlines the foundational nature of the doctrine. There are three sections to his chapter of which the first and third concern the present focus: (a) "Liberation Theology as a Theology of the Reign of God"; and, (b) "Systematic Concept of the Reign of God."[63]

3.2.1 LIBERATION THEOLOGY AS A THEOLOGY OF THE REIGN OF GOD

Sobrino begins his description of Liberation Theology as a theology of the Reign of God by asking one question: "What faith reality, what *eschaton*, most adequately corresponds to a theology that assigns historical primacy to the liberation of the poor?"[64] He answers by positing that for Liberation Theology the most apt faith reality is that of the Reign of God. Indeed, he cites Ellacuría on the Reign of God, noting that it "is the very object of Christian dogmatic, moral, and pastoral theology: the greatest possible realization of the Reign of

---

62   Sobrino, "Central Position of the Reign of God in Liberation Theology," 350-88.

63   In the second section, "Determination of the Reign of God in the Gospel," Sobrino seeks to construct a biblical understanding of the nature of the Reign of God. Its contents lie beyond the focus of this book, but it should be noted that Sobrino is cognizant of the importance of rooting any understanding of the Reign of God in the data of the Gospel. See ibid., 357-71. This biblical-evangelical conception of the Reign of God is of the highest importance, but it "does not furnish a systematic concept of the Reign for today." Ibid., 371. The systematic conception that Sobrino proceeds to describe is the focus of this section of this book. For further reflections on Sobrino's understanding of the Kingdom of God in scripture, see Sobrino, "The Centrality of the Kingdom of God Announced by Jesus: Reflections Before Aparecida," 77-80. Moreover, the reflections above from Wright ought to suggest that liberation theologians are not too wide of the mark in their biblical understanding.

64   Sobrino, "Central Position of the Reign of God in Liberation Theology," 351.

God in history is what the authentic followers of Jesus are to pursue."[65] Sobrino explains the reasons why the Reign of God holds such centrality for Liberation Theology. He argues that the Reign of God: (1) does justice to Liberation Theology's nature as a theology of history; (2) holds great potential for systemization and unification; and, (3) accommodates Liberation Theology's focus on the irruption of the poor.

First, Liberation Theology seeks to locate Christian salvation precisely where it occurs: in history. Sobrino argues that Liberation Theology is a theology of history; it is prophetic in that it exposes and denounces all sin; it is praxic in that it understands itself as acting in and transforming history; and, it is popular in that it sees in the collective poor the addressee and subject of theology. It is for these reasons that Liberation Theology adopts the Reign of God rather than the Resurrection as its symbol of the *eschaton*. The Resurrection "can and does feed an individualism without a people, a hope without a praxis, an enthusiasm without a following of Jesus—in sum, a transcendence without history."[66] The Reign of God, by contrast, is not subject to these same pitfalls: it is communal; it insists on praxis; and, it is centered on Christ's mission. Moreover, the Reign of God derives its evangelical content from the fact of the Resurrection: it is the Resurrection event that confirms the centrality and scope of the Kingdom message.

Secondly, the Reign of God furnishes Liberation Theology with a systematically cogent means of organizing the whole of theology. It is worth quoting, as Sobrino does, a lengthy passage of Ellacuría's on this topic:

> What this conception of faith from a point of departure in the Reign of God does is posit an indissoluble conjunction between God and history. ... The Reign of God is immune to a whole series of perilous distortions. It is impervious to a dualism of (earthly) Reign and (heavenly) God, such that those who devote themselves to God would be doing something transcendent, spiritual, and supernatural. It rejects an identification of the Reign of God with the Church, especially with the institutional Church, which would imply both

---

65   Ibid., 352. Sobrino is here again citing Ellacuría, "Aporte de la teología de la liberación a las religiones abrahámicas en la superación del individualismo y del positivismo."

66   Sobrino, "Central Position of the Reign of God in Liberation Theology," 354.

an escape from the world into the Church, and an impoverishment of the Christian message and mission that would culminate in a worldly Church—a secularization of the Church by way of a confirmation of its institutional aspect to secularistic values of domination and wealth, and by subordinating it to something greater than it by far, the Reign of God. It rejects a manipulation of God, a taking of the name of God in vain in support of injustice, by insisting that the name and reality are properly invoked in the historical signs of justice, fraternity, freedom, a Preferential Option for the Poor, love, mercy and so on, and that without these it is in vain to speak of a salvific presence of God in history.

The Reign of God in history as a Reign of God among human beings exposes the historical wickedness of the world, and thereby the reign of sin, that negation of the Reign of God. Over and above a certain natural sin (original sin) and a personal sin (individual sin), the proclamation of the Reign and the difficulty of seeing it implanted evinces the presence of a 'sin of the world', which is fundamentally historical and structural, communitarian and objective, at once the fruit and cause of many other personal and collective sins, and its propagation and consolidation as the ongoing negation of the Reign of God. Not that structures commit sin, as liberation theologians are sometimes accused of saying; but structures manifest and actualize the power of sin, thereby causing sin, by making it exceedingly difficult for men and women to lead the life that is rightfully theirs as the daughters and sons of God.

This sinful power is utterly real. It is intrinsically sin, and the fruit of sin, and here we may recall the traditional explanations of original sin; but further, it causes sin by presenting obstacles to the dynamism of the Reign of God among human beings, to the presence of the life-giving Spirit amidst the principalities and powers of death. Thus, without being deprived of its essential immanence, the evil of the world acquires a transcendent dimension. ... The destruction of human life, or its impoverishment, is anything but a purely moral problem; it is also, absolutely and unqualifiedly, a theological problem—the problem of sin in action, and the problem of life denied in human existence.[67]

---

67 Ibid., 355. Again, he is citing Ellacuría, "Aporte de la teología de la liberación a las religiones abrahámicas en la superación del individualismo y del positivismo."

Sobrino notes that the fundamental point made by Ellacuría in this passage is that the Kingdom of God unifies transcendence and history without separation or confusion.[68] An understanding of the Kingdom of God can thus unify theological doctrines—Trinitarian, Christological, Ecclesiological—whilst concurrently providing theology with a means of understanding what is opposed to the Reign. In this manner the real dialectic, the ultimate duality with which theology must contend, is not history and transcendence, but rather "the irreconcilable binomial of Reign and anti-Reign, the history of grace and sin."[69]

Thirdly, the Reign of God facilitates the uptake of the irruption of the poor into theology. Liberation Theology begins with a pre-theological moment. That is, it begins with the immersion of the theologian in the data of history before any theology is done. That reality is precisely one of mass, unjust poverty in which there concurrently exists a hope for liberation. It is the reality of the cry of the poor as they thirst for liberation. "Elsewhere, where theology has been unable to discover the irruption of the poor—either because the latter has been less perceptible or because of a lack of interest in discovering it—the course taken has been in the direction not of the Reign of God, but of the resurrection."[70] But in the Third World, Sobrino contends, given the choice between the two *eschatons*—between the Resurrection and the Reign of God—the liberation of the poor requires the adoption of the latter as its organizing principle.

3.2.2 SYSTEMATIC CONCEPT OF THE REIGN OF GOD

After arguing for the centrality of the Reign of God, Sobrino proceeds to identify three premises that are required to ensure the adequacy of any given systematic concept of the Reign of God. The basic premise is the Preferential Option for the Poor. That is, the Option for the Poor is made before a theologian develops an understanding of the Reign of God.[71] In this way, the Kingdom of God is not set in opposition to the Option for the Poor, but rather, "in terms of the Option for the Poor, the systematic concept of the Reign of God plies a precise course: the

---

68   Sobrino, "Central Position of the Reign of God in Liberation Theology," 355.

69   Ibid., 356.

70   Ibid., 357.

71   Ibid., 375.

Reign of God is the Reign of the poor."[72] Once the Option has been adopted, one can be affected by the reality of the poor such that they become a *locus theologicus*.[73] Indeed, Sobrino posits that the embrace of the Option for the Poor is the essential basic hermeneutic principle required for an adequate reading of the gospel and of all historical reality. From the Option for the Poor, and with respect to the Reign of God, two further hermeneutic premises flow. First, the Reign of God must be able to take seriously the hope held by the poor. That is, the Reign of God must be able to provide a promise of life in the face of the anti-Reign.[74] It is, in this sense, a dialectical hermeneutic. The second principle is that it is in practice that the Reign is revealed. That is to say, after one has acted in service of the Reign, one is in a position to understand more about the Reign than one did before such action was performed. The Option for the Poor, therefore, results in one adopting a perspective that is congruent with the hope of the poor for life and also a commitment to praxis such that the Reign will be ever more fully understood.

The three premises frame what Sobrino calls a systematic concept of the Reign of God. At the root of his systematic conception is the striking observation—striking to a citizen of the first-world, at least—that for the poor "to live right now would be as much of a miracle as to live after death."[75] Liberation Theology thus insists on life as the historical content of the Reign. The Reign of God is "a historical reality (a just life for the poor) and a reality with and intrinsic tendency to be more (ultimately utopia)."[76] Although life is the non-negotiable foundation of the Reign, life—as a concept—is always open to more. Liberation Theology is in no sense reductionist. Liberation theologians insist on life because it is polyvalent and multidirectional. Life, if people are fortunate enough to have it, is always open to becoming ever-fuller life. To illustrate this point, Sobrino seeks to develop a 'phenomenology of the 'more' in bread'. He claims that bread is food. But it is also activity and toil, it needs to be shared within a community and for other groups, it becomes sacramental in the festival of maize where poetry

---

72   Ibid.
73   Ibid.
74   Ibid., 376-77.
75   Ibid., 376.
76   Ibid., 380.

and singing occur as bread opens out to art and culture, and it needs to be supported by a spirit of community.[77] The Reign leads to more, and there are no *a priori* limits on this ever-fuller life—but it begins with bread. The material life is the germ of a fuller life, and this is precisely why Liberation Theology speaks of integral liberation: social, cultural, and spiritual liberation are only possible if life exists.[78] So while Liberation Theology is acutely aware that utopia (*ou topos*/no place) is never realized in history, it insists that in some *topoi* (places) the will of God is better realized than it is in others.[79]

4. THE KINGDOM OF GOD, THE PREFERENTIAL OPTION FOR THE POOR, AND THE MISSION OF THE CHURCH: DORAN'S *THEOLOGY AND THE DIALECTICS OF HISTORY* AS LIBERATION THEOLOGY

Doran's theoretical account of history, and of society within history, is able to transcendentally ground an understanding of the Preferential Option for the Poor which mirrors the understanding of the Option as it is arrived at by the Latin American bishops at Puebla. The bishops understood the Option as rooted in conversion, and resulting in proportionate hermeneutics and praxis. This section of the chapter demonstrates that Doran's theory of history: (1) functions as theological foundations that can account for history as unified, and that, in turn, can facilitate the systematization of the whole of theology; and, (2) functions hermeneutically in a manner proportionate to the irruption of the poor. In this way, Doran's theory of history is: dialectical, praxis oriented, and incorporates an understanding of 'life as the content of the Reign'. Moreover, this section of the chapter concurrently illustrates that Doran's theory of history can meet some of the charges leveled at Liberation Theology whilst still functioning in a profoundly liberative manner.

---

77   Ibid., 380-81.
78   Ibid., 381.
79   Ibid., 382.

4.1 FROM THE UNITY OF THE SUBJECT TO THE UNITY OF HISTORY AND THE UNITY OF THEOLOGY

Doran grounds his theory of history—and the Preferential Option for the Poor—in a critical-realist transcendental anthropology. This is to say, he builds his theological foundations on the reality of the converted subject, and in this manner he grounds his heuristic structure of history and the unity of theology. This section of the chapter seeks to illustrate that, from the basis of the unity of the subject, Doran is able to accommodate Liberation Theology's understanding of the unity of history and theology in such a manner that it also affords the Option for the Poor a capability for maximum potential as an element of theological foundations.

The first point to be noted is that the basic terms and relations employed in *Theology and the Dialectics of History*

> articulate human interiority in the dimensions of both nature and grace, and the objects known or valued in the operations and states thus objectified will be expressed in categories derived from the interior and religious differentiations. Ultimately, again, for every term and relation there will exist, proximately or remotely, a corresponding element in intentional (or, as the case may be, nonintentional) consciousness.[80]

So, for Lonergan, theological foundations are not to be found in a set of propositions, from which one deduces conclusions that are implicit in the premises; rather, foundations inhere in the converted subject. Lonergan understands theology to be a "direct function, without remainder" of a theologian's state of conversion, that is, a function of his "religious, moral, intellectual and aesthetic integrity."[81] In Lonergan's words, "foundational reality ... is conversion."[82] Explicit theological foundations, therefore, consist in a theologian's reflexive thematization of her state of conversion.[83] It is through the process of objectifying conversion that the categories employed in a critically grounded theology are derived.

There are two kinds of theological categories: general theological categories and special theological categories. General theological

---

80   Doran, *What Is Systematic Theology?*, 100.
81   Doran, *Theology and the Dialectics of History*, 149.
82   Lonergan, *Method in Theology*, 267.
83   Ibid., 269-71.

categories are those categories that theology shares with other disciplines. In Lonergan's understanding, in the third stage of meaning, they are derived from interiorly differentiated consciousness. They are derived from a differentiation—a specialization or development—of consciousness that determines its basic terms and relations "by adverting to our conscious operations and to the dynamic structure that relates them to one another."[84] The ground of general theological categories is "the attending, inquiring, reflecting, deliberating subject along with the operations that result from attending, inquiring, reflecting, deliberating and with the structure within which the operations occur."[85] Said otherwise, the ground of general theological categories is arrived at when one applies Generalized Empirical Method to the data of consciousness, thereby identifying the normative pattern of operations—experience, understanding, judgment, decision—as an invariant process immanent within the subject. Moreover, the interior differentiation of consciousness places "abstractly apprehended cognitional activity within the concrete and sublating context of human feeling and of moral deliberation, evaluation, and decision."[86] In this manner, the interior differentiation of consciousness has its base in intellectual conversion and objectifies moral conversion, bringing it into its critically grounded purview.[87] From this invariant basis, one can build a set of terms and relations—critically grounded terms and relations that anyone can, in principle, identify in her own consciousness—that function as general theological categories.[88]

In a similar manner, special theological categories are derived from religiously differentiated consciousness.[89] Religiously differentiated consciousness is largely a question of being familiar with the gift of God's love because this offer "gives human living an orientation to what is transcendent in lovableness."[90] It has, in this way, its base in religious conversion. That is, it is religious conversion that religiously

---

84   Ibid., 274.

85   Ibid., 285-86.

86   Ibid., 275.

87   Ibid., 274.

88   Ibid., 285-88.

89   Ibid., 288-91.

90   Ibid., 278. And Doran, *What Is Systematic Theology?*, 95.

differentiated consciousness objectifies and which provides theological foundations with its specifically religious categories.[91]

Returning now to the issue of the unity of history, one of Gutiérrez's key insights, and also a point central to Liberation Theology, is that "history is one."[92] He argues, to quote more fully a passage cited above,

> [T]here are not two histories, one profane and one sacred "juxtaposed" or "closely linked." Rather there is only one human destiny, irreversibly assumed by Christ, the Lord of history. His redemptive work embraces all the dimension of existence and brings them to their fullness. The history of salvation is the very heart of human history.[93]

Precisely because there are not two histories, one sacred and one profane, running parallel, one cannot speak of spiritual liberation without also speaking of liberation from poverty and oppression. Spiritual liberation and other forms of liberation can be distinguished, they are certainly not to be conflated, but they cannot be separated. Gutiérrez also laments the fact that theology has not yet fashioned the categories that would allow theologians to express this unified approach to history. That is, he feels that theologians work under the fear of falling back into old dualities or being accused of not sufficiently safeguarding divine gratuitousness.[94]

Gutiérrez's fears are perhaps well justified when one considers the position of fellow liberation theologian Clodovis Boff. Boff has drawn a distinction between 'first theology' and 'second theology'. The former, like special theological categories, addresses specifically 'religious' realities—"the classic themes of God, creation, Christ, grace, sin, eschatology, the virtues, the commandments, and so on."[95] The latter, like general theological categories, "will have 'secular' realities for its subject matter: for example, culture, sexuality, or history—including, here, political history."[96] It is on the basis of this distinction—and invoking the Preferential Option for the Poor—that Boff argued to allow conflictualist social theory a priority of access to the data of the social

---

91   Doran, *What Is Systematic Theology?*, 95.
92   Gutiérrez, *A Theology of Liberation: History, Politics, and Salvation*, 86.
93   Ibid.
94   Ibid.
95   Boff, *Theology and Praxis: Epistemological Foundations*, xxviii.
96   Ibid.

situation.[97] The conclusions reached by dialectical sociology in its analysis of, in Boff's case, Latin American society, become the starting point for theologies of liberation that are a species of second theology. The data proffered by social sciences are *operated upon* by the theological concepts of the Bible and tradition (the concepts of first theology). From Doran's perspective—and from Gutiérrez's—Boff is breaking what is a single project, the understanding of history, into two projects: first sociological, then secondarily theological. Inasmuch as liberation theologians felt constrained to choose between the extant, developed sociological theories, functionalist and dialectical, they certainly made the right decision. Moreover, they sought to modify dependency theory so that it was 'adequately' Christian. But Doran has argued at some length that the 'one real world' needs to be understood in a manner that does not separate the situation and tradition. Precisely inasmuch as it is systematic, theology is not "a correlation of the categories appropriate to the tradition with the categories adequate to the situation."[98] Rather, understanding the social situation, as Ormerod notes, requires categories of sin and grace—special categories—so that social data are not truncated, because sin and grace, in part, constitute the data of social reality.[99] Therefore, employing Doran's *Theology and the Dialectics of History* provides—at a foundational level, at least—the required methodological unity to account for Liberation Theology's insistence that history and liberation are one.

Lastly, under the topic of the unity of theology, it should be noted that Doran's theory of history is an exercise in the functional specialization of Foundations.[100] And as noted in the previous chapter of this book, theological foundations, in Lonergan's understanding, function as the framework within which all doctrinal theology, systematic theology, and practical theology are to be understood. In this sense, it is to be noted that Doran's work can meet Liberation Theology's expressed desire for an understanding of the Kingdom of God that can unify theological doctrines: Doran's theory of history is the foundation of the normative phase of theology, and as such it is the foundation of

97   Ibid., 59. Also, see Gutiérrez, *A Theology of Liberation: History, Politics, and Salvation*, 86.

98   Doran, *Theology and the Dialectics of History*, 453.

99   Neil Ormerod, "A Dialectic Engagement with the Social Sciences in an Ecclesiological Context," *Theological Studies* 66:4 (2005): 832.

100   Doran, *Theology and the Dialectics of History*, 7.

dogmatic, systematic, and practical theology.[101] It should also be noted that the grounding that Doran provides for the Preferential Option for the Poor within theological foundations means that the Option, in his understanding, is not simply one doctrine among many. As a constitutive element of theological foundations, the Option for the Poor will be active in the remaining three specializations of the normative phase of theology. The Option for the Poor will thus affect the theology produced by a theologian regardless of whether it is Trinitarian theology, Christology, Ecclesiology, or any other theological subject-matter.

4.2 THE PREFERENTIAL OPTION FOR THE POOR AND THE MISSION OF THE CHURCH: THE UPPER BLADE OF HISTORY AND HERMENEUTICS

Liberation Theology's understanding of the Kingdom of God provides it with elements of an heuristic tool of dialectical critique. Understood as the Kingdom of life for the poor, the Kingdom of God stands in dialectical relationship to what Sobrino calls the anti-Kingdom. It is the understanding of the Kingdom of God that Liberation Theology employs to judge *topoi* for conformance to the will of God, and to direct action to better shape *topoi* to conform to the will of God. In this sense, the Reign of God functions as *telos* for Liberation Theology.[102]

101   Doran's current major project, the book *The Trinity in History*, contains his vision of the Catholic systematic theology that will be constructed on such a foundation. Draft chapters of the book can be found at the collaboration-focused section of his webpage, Robert M. Doran, "Ongoing Collaboration" http://www.robertmdoran.com/Ongoing%20 Collaboration.htm (accessed 18-June 2011).

102   J.J. Mueller argues that Gustavo Gutiérrez possesses an understanding of a utopia that functions to guide action. He contrasts Gutiérrez's position with Doran's when he notes, "Where Gutierrez differs with Doran is in the explicit use of an ideal that projects a vision of what society can be. Most importantly, as it functions, the ideal enables us to make a comparison between where we are and where we want to be and thereby judge the adequacies or inadequacies of the present trajectory. An ideal, in this system, mediates the present and the future to each other. It allows the communication between religion and culture to take place in a practical way. Whereas the vision is an ideal, it can be a practical goal that people can commit themselves to and thereby galvanize their energies toward its actuation." J.J. Mueller, "The Role of Theological Symbols in Mediating Cultural Change," in *Communication and Lonergan: Common Ground for Forging the New Age*, ed. Thomas J. Farrell and Paul A. Soukup (Kansas,

This *telos*, of course, is not simply any idealized conception of society. Rather, to quote a paragraph of Sobrino's that was cited in Chapter 2 of this book,

> [I]t is the poor who will guide the fleshing out of what the Reign of God is today. Theoretically and historically, the concept of the Reign of God can be worked out in terms of other primacies than the poor. It can be developed from universal human needs, from the longing for freedom, from the desire for survival after death, from the utopia of continuous progress. This has actually been the point of departure for other theologies, and the differences among them in terms of their systematic concepts of the Reign of God are ultimately to be explained by the premises on which they read the Gospel text and current historical reality. In terms of the Option for the Poor, the systematic concept of the Reign of God plies a precise course: the Reign of God is the Reign of the poor.[103]

The question, here, is: can Doran's theology of history proffer hermeneutical tools that are both dialectical and at the service of the Preferential Option for the Poor?

To facilitate the discussion of Doran's work and the hermeneutics of the poor, it is helpful at this point to explain Lonergan's 'scissors analogy' of knowing. Knowing is dynamic, for Lonergan, and to capture this dynamism he claims that heuristic method possesses a scissors-like action. There are two distinct components to this action: the movement of both an upper and a lower blade. In recalling the operation of this action in classical physics, Lonergan notes that a lower blade exists which rises from the data up through measurements and curve fitting to formulae.[104] It is the kind of work that is commonly associated with science, the strictly empirical investigation. But there is also "an upper blade that moves downward from differential and operator equations

---

MO: Sheed & Ward, 1993), 310. From the above presentation of Doran's work, it can be asserted, in opposition to Mueller's stance, that the notion of a line of pure progress in *Theology and the Dialectics of History* functions to provide an heuristic tool that facilitates understanding the distortions in the present context and thereby it also guides corrective—redemptive—action in history as orthopraxis.

103   Sobrino, "Central Position of the Reign of God in Liberation Theology," 375.

104   Lonergan, *Insight: A Study of Human Understanding*, 337.

and from postulates of invariance and equivalence."[105] Among the physicist's pre-empirical assumptions are differential equations.[106] These equations are not arrived at via a process of observation or experiment, but are simply mathematical. They prefigure the formulae—the laws—physicists are seeking. "The differential equation, then, is an anticipation of the possible laws relevant to the formulation of a given thing that one is trying to understand."[107] In other words, the differential equation is part of the upper blade of the heuristic structure of classical physics,[108] and in this way it functions as a determinant from above upon the possible laws that can be found.[109] Moving back to the present context, the key point to remember is that elements of the upper blade act as a determinant on the insights one has into the data.

Doran's theory of history is part of the upper blade of the heuristic structure of historical process. In this manner, Doran's categories of the Reign of God, and the relationships between the categories, provide the general viewpoint for the analysis of history. As noted above, this viewpoint includes a conception of "an ideal line of pure progress"

---

105   Ibid.

106   One can also note that the physicist, in a manner akin to the algebraist's approach of letting an unknown equal x, names the unknown she is seeking by asking, 'what is the nature of...'? Further, the physicist also holds the *a priori* position that similars are similarly understood and the important intelligibility from a scientific perspective is of things in their relationships to each other. And one can also add the anticipation of invariance to the elements of a physicist's upper blade. See Lonergan, *Understanding and Being: the Halifax Lectures on Insight*, 67-68.

107   Ibid., 68.

108   To reiterate a note from the last chapter, an heuristic structure, "is a conjunction both of data on the side of the object and of an operative criterion on the side of the subject." Moreover, heuristic structures form an *a priori* in that they shape the content of what is to-be-known. Lonergan, "Christology Today: Methodological Reflections," 87. This is evident when the nature of an heuristic structure is understood as: data, question, insight, and judgment. In this process one aims to, "Name the unknown; work out its properties; use the properties to direct, order, guide the enquiry." Coelho, *Hermeneutics and Method: The 'Universal Viewpoint' in Bernard Lonergan*, 33. Thus the content of the "anticipated act of understanding is designated heuristically. The properties of the anticipated and designated content constitute the clues intelligence employs to guide itself towards discovery." Lonergan, *Insight: A Study of Human Understanding*, 126.

109   Lonergan, *Understanding and Being: the Halifax Lectures on Insight*, 69.

within history, progress that results "from the harmonious working of ... opposed principles."[110] These opposed principles are the poles pertaining to the dialectics of the subject, culture, and community, that is, the dialectics of history. And

> [t]aken together these three processes constitute ... the immanent intelligibility of the process of human history. History is to be conceived as a complex network of dialectics of subjects, communities and cultures. Insofar as these dialectics are integral, history is intelligible. Insofar as these dialectics are distorted, history is a compound of the intelligible and the surd.[111]

This general viewpoint developed by Doran needs to be coupled with concrete data before an understanding of the historical situation can be achieved. Nevertheless, in any given situation—that is, with any given set of historical data—because of the relations from below upwards, the integrity of the situation is always measured by the global (mal)distribution of vital values which is 'built in' to the upper blade of historical analysis. This is the irruption of the poor into history; it is the poor as the measure of the Reign of God; it is the partiality of an Option for the Poor that excludes no one in its universality.

From this it can be seen that Doran's work incorporates the Option for the Poor as the criterion by which the functioning of society is appraised. For Doran, the poor are the standard by which history is judged, and it is judged dialectically. His approach provides theologians with a theory of history that is not oblivious to the existence of both social and cultural sin, and that does not normalize sin as liberal-functionalist theories of history are wont to do. The ability to appraise sinful situations precisely as sinful is essential to any Liberation Theology. For example, because of the limitations in contemporaneous social theory, liberation theologians were forced to engage with—and seek to transform—Marxist social thought, often in the form of dependence theory, because the inadequacies of developmentalism that characterized the policies of the international community in the 1970s and 1980s could not be met by an engagement

---

110   Doran, *Theology and the Dialectics of History*, 77. Doran's added italics have been removed. The original quote is taken from, Lonergan, *Insight: A Study of Human Understanding*, 268-69.

111   Doran, *Theology and the Dialectics of History*, 144.

with structural-functionalism.[112] But in doing so, Liberation Theology was accused of operating out of what Michael Novak—echoing Magisterial sentiments, and prefiguring those of John Milbank—calls an ontology of darkness.[113] However, because of the distinction between dialectics of contraries and dialectics of contradictories, Doran avoids such pitfalls. Whereas dialectical social theory anticipates only dialectics of contradictories, such as perennial conflict between capital and labour until the end of history, *Theology and the Dialectics of History* anticipates decline, and also progress and redemption.[114]

4.3 THE PREFERENTIAL OPTION FOR THE POOR AND THE MISSION OF THE CHURCH: UNDERSTANDING HISTORY FOR THE SAKE OF PRAXIS[115]

As noted in the previous section, Liberation Theology employs an understanding of the Kingdom of God to judge *topoi* within history for their conformance to the will of God so that missional activity can be directed to better shape *topoi* to conform to the will of God. So it is that Liberation Theology seeks to direct the Church's mission in such a manner as to build a minimalist 'utopia of life' for the

---

112   Ormerod, "A Dialectic Engagement with the Social Sciences in an Ecclesiological Context," 832.

113   Gutiérrez, *A Theology of Liberation: History, Politics, and Salvation*, 49-57. See also Michael Novak, *Will it Liberate? Questions about Liberation Theology* (New York: Paulist Press, 1986), 109. And John Milbank, *Theology and Social Theory: Beyond Secular Reason* (Cambridge, MA: Blackwell, 1991), 278-325.

114   Joseph Carry makes a similar point with respect to Lonergan's functional specialization Dialectic as he critiques Liberation Theology: he asks do liberation theologians, in accepting the Option for the Poor, tacitly accept an ontology of violence? Doran's distinctions between dialectics of contraries and contradictories indicate that there is no necessary connection between the Option for the Poor and an ontology of violence. See Joseph B. Carry, "Methodical Creativity: The Foundational Contribution of Bernard Lonergan and Clodovis Boff Toward a Global Theology of Liberation" (Doctor of Philosophy, Fordham University, 2005), 295-97.

115   The dialectics of history could, of course, be applied to the Church in terms of guiding its ministry, but the focus here is the mission of the Church.

poor.[116] It is by this praxis of the Reign of God, that the Option for the Poor is concretely made manifest.[117] The question that remains is: does Doran's theology of history ground an understanding of the mission of the Church that meets the needs of liberation theologians and their commitment to the Option for the Poor? This section of the Chapter seeks to sketch a response to this question. Three points are made in response: (1) it is reiterated that, on the basis of Generalized Empirical Method, understanding moves towards action; (2) it is affirmed that the scale of values ensures the Church's mission is neither mystified to avoid political engagement nor reduced to the merely political; and, (3) it is demonstrated that the Church's cultural and social missions can be conceived of in a manner so as to integrate the Option for the Poor within their purview.

4.3.1 THE IMPERATIVE OF ORTHOPRAXIS: UNDERSTANDING MOVES TOWARDS ACTION

The first issue to raise is simply a reminder of a point that was made in earlier chapters: the converted subject acts in accord with Generalized Empirical Method in that she moves from affirming what is understood accurately to acting in a manner that corresponds to the true scale of values. For the integrally converted individual, Doran's heuristic structure of history also functions, effectively, as a 'diagnosis' in that an understanding of distortions in the dialectics of history will thus move one towards remedial action aimed at strengthening the proper functioning of the dialectics. This movement towards responsible transformation of the situation is also evident within theological method. As noted in the last chapter, in the last functional specialization—Communications—the meaning constitutive of Christianity is mediated to contemporary pastoral, interdisciplinary, and inter-religious situations.[118] That is to say, the upper blade of history, in Doran's understanding, not only includes a priority position for those who are denied vital goods—the hermeneutics of the poor—but in doing so it also helps direct ecclesial action in a manner that favors those denied

---

116   Sobrino, "The Centrality of the Kingdom of God Announced by Jesus: Reflections Before Aparecida," 81.

117   Sobrino, "Central Position of the Reign of God in Liberation Theology," 379.

118   Lonergan, *Method in Theology*, 125-368. And Doran, "System and History: The Challenge to Catholic Systematic Theology," 662.

vital goods. Concrete policy that addresses specific distortions, will, of course, need to be developed. But the understanding of history facilitated by Doran's theory ultimately functions to guide targeted courses of action across the spectrum of the dialectics of history.

4.3.2 AVOIDING THE TRUNCATION OF THE KINGDOM: AGAINST MYSTIFICATION AND POLITICAL REDUCTIONISM

Doran's theory of history—because of its explicit reliance on the integral scale of values—avoids two chief pitfalls regarding the manner in which the mission of the Church is often conceived. On one hand, Liberation Theology opposes any understanding of the mission of the Church that is oblivious, or overtly hostile, to social praxis. Sobrino's 'phenomenology of the 'more' in bread' is an expression of Liberation Theology's attempt to guard against mystification of the mission of the Church. Doran's approach, in the manner it employs the scale of values, provides a precise structure for this phenomenology. When the scale is read from below upwards, 'bread', whilst initially a vital good, becomes a social good when it encourages 'a spirit of community' and 'activity and toil'. Moreover, it emerges as a cultural good—including soteriological culture—when 'it becomes sacramental in the festival of maize where poetry and singing occur as bread opens out to art and culture'. Furthermore, it becomes a personal good when it needs to be shared with the group and within the group.[119] The material life is indeed the germ of a fuller life, and this is precisely why Liberation Theology speaks of integral liberation: social, cultural, and spiritual liberation are only possible if life exists.[120] On the other hand, Liberation Theology has been accused of reducing the Church's missional concerns to political values at the expense of the religious values.[121] In the

---

119   Sobrino, "Central Position of the Reign of God in Liberation Theology," 380-81.

120   Ibid., 381. One wonders how dissimilar the stance of Liberation Theology is to Pope Benedict's when he writes, "The book of nature is one and indivisible: it takes in not only the environment but also life, sexuality, marriage, the family, social relations: in a word, integral human development." See, at §51, Pope Benedict XVI, "Caritas in veritate". Benedict does, it should be noted, still use the term 'development' rather than 'liberation'.

121   See, particularly, the first Vatican notification as an illustration of such suspicions surrounding Liberation Theology. Congregation for the Doctrine of the Faith, "Instruction on Certain Aspects of the Theology of Liberation".

process of meeting such a *perceived* distortion, the Magisterium tends to assert an understanding of the Church's mission that emphasizes the scale of values from above downwards.[122] At worst, such a starting point can become a mystification of the Church's mission whereby the scale is truncated to religious, personal, and cultural goods. Liberation Theology, by contrast, tends to emphasize the scale from below-upwards, which, in the extreme, could involve a truncation of the Church's mission such that it becomes solely a political mission. Each side of the debate appears to fear that the other somehow neglects its own starting point. Doran's stance guards against both concerns.

Doran's stance provides a critically grounded theology of history that incorporates a normative scale of values—central to the thrust of *Centesimus annus* but not explicitly identified therein[123]—which also integrates a precise understanding of the nature of cultural and social praxis in terms of seeking to strengthen the dialectics of culture, and of community. That is, the Church's current missional activity can be conceived of in terms of the scale of values and the dialectics of history in a way that integrates theologically what previously could seem piecemeal. And fidelity to the normativity of the scale and the tensive integrity of the dialectics of history incorporate the Option for the Poor as part of its integrative achievement.

4.3.3 THE DIALECTICS OF HISTORY AND ORTHOPRAXIS: THE GLOBAL FOOD CRISIS AND THE PREFERENTIAL OPTION FOR THE POOR

It is clear that orthopraxis, when understood from the perspective of Doran's theology of history, has a precise character: it strengthens the tension of the dialectics of history. If one considers this understanding of praxis from below upwards along the scale—from vital, to social, to cultural, to personal values—it becomes evident as to how Doran's theory of history directs remedial action to meet the problem of global injustice. To demonstrate the potential of Doran's theory of history with respect to guiding orthopraxis, the issue of the Global Food Crisis is sketched in a rudimentary fashion below as a test case.

---

122   In the opinion of the current author, Liberation Theology—at least Gutiérrez and Sobrino—also assert the priority of God's grace, even if neither are clear on the relevance of cultural values.

123   The document occasionally uses the term 'hierarchy' instead of 'scale'. But explicit references are found to a hierarchy/scale at §§ 28, 29, 39, 41, 47. See Pope John Paul II, "Centesimus annus".

First, the problem: the Global Food Crisis involves a situation where, since 2008, food prices have spiked as global supply continues to fail to meet the global demand for staple foodstuffs. More than 942 million people are undernourished and the number continues to grow;[124] 2011's spike in food prices forced an additional 44 million people into poverty when compared with 2010's situation.[125] The situation, in the long term, will worsen. Indeed, "A modest but steady increase in global grain consumption, a more variable global grain supply due to weather, and a draw-down of stocks held by the major grain exporting countries have all combined to increase both uncertainty in global grain markets and broader food price volatility since 2005."[126] It is a case of over 13% of the world's population being denied 'bread', and thus being denied the 'more' that is 'in' bread.

If one considers the scale from below upwards, at the level of vital value, the Church's concerns are well known. It barely needs to be stated that the Church continually stresses the value of life—it engages consistently in cultural critique for the sake of the premier vital good—often most vocally in terms of opposition to abortion, but also, and no less importantly, in stances against war, against the death penalty, against famine, and more recently against ecological degradation. Some of the Church's most distinctly Catholic institutions, its hospitals and charities—such as the Ascension Health network of hospitals in the USA and the global Caritas organization—are social institutions that focus intently on ensuring the maintenance of vital goods that promote biological integrity. So, if one posits the problem of the Global Food Crisis, how would Doran's theory of history suggest remedial action be directed? From below, our attention moves to focus on the dialectic of community.

In its social teaching it is evident that the Catholic Church is aware of the dialectic of community, even if it does not use that terminology. Particularly, and more so after the collapse of Soviet Communism, the Church criticizes the tendency in capitalism to fracture the integral

124 The World Bank, "Food Crisis – The World Bank" http://www.world-bank.org/foodcrisis/ (accessed 3 July 2011).

125 The World Bank, "News & Broadcast – Global Food Crisis" http://web.worldbank.org/WBSITE/EXTERNAL/NEWS/0,content MDK:21928797~menuPK:34480~pagePK:64257043~piP-K:437376~theSitePK:4607,00.html (accessed 3 July 2011).

126 Ibid.

dialectic of community in the direction of practical intelligence. That is, because social-orthopraxis promotes the tension of the dialectic,[127] the Church stridently objects when economic matters are prioritized at the expense of authentic intersubjective bonds: when family units wilt under the stress of compulsory overtime whether paid or unpaid; when entire communities can be devastated as employment is outsourced to cheaper, and less protected, foreign labour 'markets'; and, increasingly in a globalized world, when whole nations remain in poverty as multinational companies treat them solely as a means of making profit without investing in the community.[128] Indeed, authentic solidarity with those most aggrieved by distorted dialectics of history is required to combat the Food Crisis. The Church's mission involves—as a matter of strengthening the dialectic of community—concerted attention focused upon the neglected pole of the dialectic, that is, encouraging the cultivation of intersubjective habits and stances that establish a global solidarity with those who are suffering because of the Crisis.[129]

In the absence of a genuine global intersubjective solidarity, it is apparent that the pole of transcendence—practical intelligence (polity, economy, technology)—has ceased to function in dialectical tension

---

127   Doran, *Theology and the Dialectics of History*, 415.

128   John Paul II's social encyclicals resound with such themes. Indeed, 'solidarity' is treated in its own section in the *Compendium of the Social Doctrine of the Church*, at §§ 192-208, "VI. The Principle of Solidarity". See Pontifical Council for Justice and Peace, "Compendium of the Social Doctrine of the Church".

129   Doran's stance provides a critical grounding for the Church's stance. Again, in the "Compendium of the Social Doctrine of the Church," one finds the claim, "The new relationships of interdependence between individuals and peoples, which are de facto forms of solidarity, have to be transformed into relationships tending towards genuine ethical-social solidarity. This is a moral requirement inherent within all human relationships. Solidarity is seen therefore under two complementary aspects: that of a social principle and that of a moral virtue. Solidarity must be seen above all in its value as a moral virtue that determines the order of institutions. On the basis of this principle the 'structures of sin' that dominate relationships between individuals and peoples must be overcome. They must be purified and transformed into structures of solidarity through the creation or appropriate modification of laws, market regulations, and juridical systems." See, at §193, ibid. There is not, however, in this excerpt, a clear understanding of the role of culture in ensuring the correct ordering of institutions.

with the pole of limitation. Practical intelligence has, in fact, been instrumentalized and elevated into the role of culture. That is, in the instance of the Global Food Crisis, the breakdown of the integral dialectic of community represents a distortion of the scale of values in which economic concerns, properly a matter of social value, are elevated into the role of cultural values that reinforce the distortions at the level of community: a case of the longer cycle of cultural decline exacerbating the shorter cycle of decline with its roots, particularly, in group bias. With respect to the Option for the Poor, the resultant distortions in technological, economic, and political structures are degrading the environment and contributing to the ongoing Global Food Crisis.[130] In such a situation, the social order has become structured to serve the economy rather than the economy being structured in a manner guided by genuine cultural values that are capable of facilitating dramatic living—which is, of course, only possible if one has bread—for all peoples on the globe.

It is with respect to cultural praxis that Doran's approach distinguishes itself most clearly from early Liberation Theology—Gutiérrez, Sobrino, Segundo, the Boffs—precisely because of his focus on culture as a distinct entity. It was noted in the last chapter that distortions in the dialectic of community are at the root of the shorter cycle of decline and that such imbalance has historically been the concern of Liberation Theology. Moreover, it was also noted that Liberation Theology rarely accords culture the significance that Doran gives to it: it is in the neglect of cultural integrity that the longer cycle has its genesis and in cultural integrity that the longer cycle is ultimately arrested and reversed. Doran's theology of history directs the attention of the Church's mission explicitly to the level of culture.

For Doran, theologians and philosophers are involved in orthopraxis as they strive to give voice to the soteriological cultural meanings and values needed to underpin the authentic social values that alone can ensure the global distribution of vital goods. Such theologians and philosophers may seek to emphasize either cosmological or anthropological meanings, depending on the prevailing distortion of the

---

130   Julian Cribb makes the point very clearly that the resolution to the Crisis involves technological, economic, political, and cultural challenges. See Julian Cribb, *The Coming Famine: The Global Food Crisis and What We Can Do To Avoid It* (Berkeley, CA: University of California Press, 2010), passim.

cultural dialectic in which they work. Discerning the nature of the distortion is precisely the first step in cultural orthopraxis.

From below, in terms of the Food Crisis, the integrity of the cultural dialectic is essential. Although it may seem unrelated, one can show that the need for the integrity of the cultural dialectic is operative in the recent surge in 'eco-theology' in Western Christianity. This surge is, arguably, indicative of a sense among theologians of a distortion in the global cultural dialectic towards anthropological meanings such that anthropocentricism has come to dominate much of the Western cultural horizon. Moreover, anthropocentrism, with its roots in the detachment of spirit from psyche, does not encourage solidarity among the members of the human species; rather, it fosters destructive competition and domination: the more 'rational' members of the species dominate the less 'rational'. Christian thinkers have thus sought to create cultural meanings to emphasize elements of revelation that redress this deformation of the integral cultural dialectic.[131] For example, Thomas Berry and Brian Swimme write of the need for a 'new story' of the universe.[132] This story is the creation of a renewed cultural horizon in which the psyche is enabled to play a key role in the recovery of the cosmological values that are required to help humanity overcome the distortions inherent in the 'technozoic' era. The 'technozoic' era involves, again, practical intelligence—technology—being elevated into the role of a culture and the earth, including its poor, being exploited for its resources.[133] Eco-theology, in this sense, functions as an element of the cultural orthopraxis that is required as a precondition for effective social praxis. For this reason, much of Leonardo Boff's work in the 1990s turned to the issue of the eco-crisis: the cry of the earth was also the cry of the poor and the fate of the earth was also the fate of the poor.[134] The liberation of the poor, for Boff, has spiri-

---

131   Thomas Berry, for example, seeks to argue for a biocentricism that combats anthropocentrism. See Thomas Berry, *The Dream of the Earth* (San Francisco: Sierra Club Books, 1988).

132   Brian Swimme and Thomas Berry, *The Universe Story: from the Primordial Flaring Forth to the Ecozoic Era—A Celebration of the Unfolding of the Cosmos* (San Francisco: HarperSanFrancisco, 1994). It is worth noting that Berry completed his doctorate in the history of cultures.

133   Ibid., 14-15.

134   See, for example, Leonardo Boff and Virgil Elizondo, eds., *Ecology and Poverty: Cry of the Earth, Cry of the Poor*, Concilium (Maryknoll, NY:

tual-cultural roots: a 'new-mysticism' is needed that reconnects people to the whole of creation. This new mysticism, it appears, includes new cosmological meanings/values, and intersubjective affect.[135] But even as he understands it, it points beyond the integrity of culture to the level of personal values.

The cultural and social dialectics depend, remotely, on the integrity of the individual. And indeed at the level of personal integrity, the Church has always been concerned with the spiritual and moral health of individuals. So, although one may be inclined to sin in terms of either carnality or scrupulosity, both inclinations are equally distortions of the basic dialectic of the subject. A comprehensive pastoral approach anticipates both distortions and develops a means of spiritual counseling to address them as they manifest.

So it is that, in terms of the dialectics of the subject—if one limits oneself to consideration of the first and second stages of meaning—it is a healthy relationship between bodiliness and spirit, between intentionality and psyche, that underpins the authentic functioning of the subject such that one can live in fidelity to the true scale of values and so be an originator of authentic cultural and social values. In the third stage of meaning, moreover, a healthy derived dialectic of the subject, as demonstrated in the last chapter, involves familiarity with the victimized nature of one's psyche (familiarity that results from reflexively appropriated psychic conversion). This familiarity establishes a point of "solidarity" between oneself and "the most victimized peoples of history."[136] Furthermore, in terms specifically of the West's response to the Global Food Crisis, the tensive strength of the derived dialectic of the subject, specifically the recovery of the role of the psyche, is required to both begin to overcome anthropocentrism—which has its roots in the disintegration of the dialectics of the subject, the detachment of spirit

---

Orbis Books, 1995). And also, Leonardo Boff, *Ecology and Liberation: A New Paradigm* (Maryknoll, NY: Orbis Books, 1995).

135   Boff, *Ecology and Liberation: A New Paradigm*, 139-62. Such emphases are at least partially in concert with Benedict's observations in *Caritas in veritate*, where he demonstrates an awareness of the fact that cultural distortions have social ramifications: economic systems that degrade the environment and, in the process, exploit the poor can only be healed by culture proportionate to the task. See, the document at §51.

136   Doran, *Theology and the Dialectics of History*, 252.

from psyche—and to facilitate the (re)establishing of one's affective bonds with all of creation and all of humanity.

The Church already directs its mission—as is evident in elements of Catholic Social Teaching—in such a manner as to attempt to address distortions in the dialectics of history and respond to some notion of a hierarchy of values. But it is not explicitly aware of the constitution of the dialectics of history or their interrelations. What Doran's theory of history offers, in terms of understanding the mission of the Church, is precisely this explicit formulation of the dialectics and the scale so that missional activity may be critically guided to include the Option for the Poor as an integral element in that mission. Doran is in concert with Liberation Theology's position and that of N.T. Wright when he insists, speaking soteriologically, that the Kingdom of God is a symbol of complete human flourishing. God's grace does indeed heal and redeem the individual. But the redeemed individual influences the dialectics of society such that the individual living the life of grace contributes to the redemption of culture and community. So it is that the focus on societal praxis, both cultural and social praxis, is by no means Pelagian: humans do not build the Kingdom. But a redeemed humanity does build *for* the Kingdom in anticipation of the New Heaven and the New Earth.

5. CONCLUSION

This chapter had a threefold purpose: (1) to introduce Doran's theology of history and the manner in which it grounds the Preferential Option for the Poor; (2) to introduce Liberation Theology's understanding of the mission of the Church, its stance on the role of the Kingdom of God, and the function of the Preferential Option for the Poor in that understanding; and, (3) to demonstrate that Doran's theology of history can meet the needs of Liberation Theology with respect to the Option for the Poor whilst simultaneously avoiding some of the limitations within liberation thought. This chapter has by no means exhaustively catalogued the relevance of Doran's thought, let alone demonstrated the sweeping scope of its relevance. But it has indicated that more than a cursory similarity exists between Doran's theology of history and the major liberationist foci in that he is able to critically ground the Option for the Poor in a manner that gives it its full force.

CONCLUSION

LONERGAN AND DORAN: TOWARDS AN INTEGRAL OPTION FOR THE POOR IN ALL THEOLOGY

The first two chapters of this book contained an historical account of the emergence, and subsequent bifurcation, of the doctrine of the Preferential Option for the Poor. Chapter 1 traced the trajectory of thought from Vatican II to CELAM's (The Latin American Episcopal Conference) meeting at Puebla, Mexico, 1979, at which the Preferential Option for the Poor was unambiguously affirmed in terms of conversion, hermeneutics, and praxis. Chapter 2 recounted the 'Bifurcation of the Preferential Option for the Poor' in which the understanding of the Option for the Poor splits into two distinct forms: an ecclesial form adopted by the Roman Magisterium and a theological form adopted by liberation theologians such as Gustavo Gutiérrez and Jon Sobrino. The former interpretation limited the Option for the Poor to the exercise of Christian charity, whereas the latter interpretation understood the Option in terms of conversion, hermeneutics, and praxis.

Chapter 3 introduced the thought of Bernard Lonergan and of Lonergan scholar Robert Doran. Specifically, it focused on the subject in her integrity and it: (1) summarized Lonergan's theory of conscious intentionality and introduced his understanding of patterns of experience and realms of meaning; (2) presented Lonergan's understanding of the horizon of the subject; and, (3) built on the previous two sections to outline Lonergan and Doran's combined stance on religious, moral, intellectual and psychic conversion.

Chapters 4 and 5 contained an answer to the question: how might one understand the Option for the Poor from Lonergan and Doran's perspective on the fourfold conversion of the subject? In constructing an answer to this question, the chapter focused on how conversion, initiated by divine grace, overcomes bias—in its egoistic, collective, general-intellectual, and psychic-affective forms—in history and how this process relates to the Option for the Poor. Moreover, this chapter provided a means of understanding the difference between the Magisterium's approach to the Option for the Poor and that adopted by Liberation Theology. Both conceive of the Option in terms of conversion. But for Liberation Theology it is a case of integral conversion, whereas for the Magisterium it is a matter of religious and moral conversion without extending the Option's relevance into the realms of intellectual and psychic conversion.

Chapter 6 concentrated more narrowly upon the issue of the Preferential Option for the Poor and the mission of the Church. This is an issue central to Liberation Theology: the development of a systematic account of the Reign of God that is able to guide the mission of the Church in a manner that incorporates the Preferential Option for the Poor. To illustrate the capabilities of Lonergan Studies to meet such an exigence, the final chapter presented Doran's theology of history and indicated some of its key abilities in this regard. Moreover, this theology of history was then related to the issue of the mission of the Church in terms of hermeneutics and praxis, both of which are integral to the theological understanding of the Preferential Option for the Poor.

The aim of this book, as stated in the Introduction, was to situate an understanding of the doctrine of the Preferential Option for the Poor within the field of Lonergan Studies. And while it has achieved that aim, it has by no means exhaustively discussed what Lonergan Studies can offer liberation thought. For example—and to again prescind from consideration of Lonergan's economic thought—two highly relevant issues that were not discussed in the book can be indicated here. First, Lonergan's understanding of the communal nature of the economy of salvation has yet to be fully explored and integrated into a liberationist perspective.[1] Secondly, the fact that Doran conceives of the 'unified field structure' of systematic theology in terms of the Trinitarian 'four-point hypothesis' raises another possibility of great significance for Liberation Theology. Doran writes of the hypothesis:

> The hypothesis thus speaks of four absolutely supernatural ways of imitating God through a created participation in the divine relations. One of these (the created term of the created relation of the humanity of Jesus to the eternal Word, a participation in the eternal relation of paternity) is peculiar to Christ. Two (sanctifying grace

---

1   See, for example, Chapter 6 of Bernard J. F. Lonergan, *The Triune God: Systematics*, ed. Robert M. Doran and H. Daniel Monsour, trans. Michael G. Shields, Collected Works of Bernard Lonergan, vol. 12 (Toronto: University of Toronto Press, 2007).

and charity, participating in active and passive spiration, respectively, and so in the entire life of the Trinity) are given to us in this
life. ... The final way (the light of glory, participating in filiation) is
promised to us in the life to come.[2]

On the basis of this approach, the identity of Christ and the Poor—
essential in the thought of the Group of the Church of the Poor and
indicated in Chapter 1 of this book—can perhaps be accorded its
proper place in systematic theology, that is, at the level of the base of
the *nexus mysteriorum fidei*. Can the Poor, along with the Church, be
understood as, in some sense, participating in the eternal relation of
paternity (clearly, as a non-hypostatic participation in paternity)?[3]
Such an approach can only be flagged at this point, because it moves
far beyond both the focus of this book and the present research conducted by its author.

To return to the direct focus of this book, it should be noted that,
in writing a book on the Preferential Option for the Poor, it becomes
apparent that one is treating subject matter of the utmost simplicity,
profundity and elegance: a great many consequences hinge upon the
doctrine. It is one of the great theological achievements of the twen-
tieth century. Indeed, the Option for the Poor remains at the core
of Liberation Theology such that Gutiérrez once noted, "If one day
someone posed the question, 'What is the most important perspective
in the theology of liberation?' I would reply that it is the Preferential
Option for the Poor. The theology of liberation could disappear, so
long as this option remains."[4] The Option does remain in Liberation
Theology. And even outside Liberation Theology, its presence is felt. It
is, in its explicit formulation, the gift of Liberation Theology and the
Latin American Church to the Universal Church.

---

2   Robert M. Doran, "The Trinity in History: The Starting Point" http://
    www.robertmdoran.com/Design/Assets/Text/The%20Trinity%20
    in%20History%202%20The_Starting_Point.pdf (accessed 21 July 2011).

3   Neil Ormerod suggests that such a relationship may be posited between
    paternity and: the Invisible Mission of the Son, the Real Presence of Christ
    in the Eucharist, and the Church as the Body of Christ. To these, the Poor
    as the Body of Christ can, perhaps, be added. See Neil Ormerod, "The Four
    Point Hypothesis: Transpositions and Complications," *Irish Theological
    Quarterly* 77:2 (2012): 127-140.

4   Gutiérrez, "Option for the Poor: Reviews and Challenges," 17.

In the final analysis, what I hope this book has achieved, is—inspired by the comments of the Very Reverend Dr. Adolfo Nicolás, SJ—to aid in Liberation Theology's continued 'process of maturation' by engaging liberation thought in a process of constructive dialogue.[5] In so doing, this book has sought to offer something in return to Liberation Theology and the Latin American Church for their gift of the Option for the Poor to the Universal Church.

---

5   Casabella, "Adolfo Nicolás: "No sé si abrir fosas y beatificar mártires ayudará a reconciliar"".

BIBLIOGRAPHY

Alberigo, Giuseppe. "Major Results, Shadows of Uncertainty." In *History of Vatican II: Church as Communion, Third Period and Intersession, September 1964 – September 1965*, edited by Giuseppe Alberigo and Joseph Komonchak, IV, 617-40. Maryknoll, NY: Orbis Books, 2003.

_____. *A Brief History of Vatican II*. Translated by Matthew Sherry. Maryknoll, NY: Orbis Books, 2006.

Allen Jr, John. "CELAM Update: The Lasting Legacy of Liberation Theology" http://ncronline.org/node/11128 (accessed 4 September 2012).

_____. "Sorting out the Results of the Latin American Bishops' Meeting" http://ncronline.org/node/11148 (accessed 4 September 2012).

Balthasar, Hans Urs von. "Theologie und Spiritualität." *Gregorianum* 50 (1969): 571-86.

_____. "Teología y espiritualidad." *Selecciones de Teología* 13, no. 50 (1974): 136-43.

Baum, Gregory. *Essays in Critical Theology*. Kansas City, MO: Sheed & Ward, 1994.

Beards, Andrew. *Method in Metaphysics: Lonergan and the Future of Analytical Philosophy*. Toronto: University of Toronto Press, 2008.

Berry, Thomas. *The Dream of the Earth*. San Francisco: Sierra Club Books, 1988.

Blackwood, Jeremy. "Sanctifying Grace, Elevation, and the Fifth Level of Consciousness: Further Developments within Lonergan Scholarship." In *West Coast Methods Institute* Loyola Marymount University, 2009.

Boff, Clodovis. *Theology and Praxis: Epistemological Foundations*. Maryknoll, NY: Orbis Books, 1987.

Boff, Leonardo. *Ecology and Liberation: A New Paradigm*. Maryknoll, NY: Orbis Books, 1995.

Boff, Leonardo, and Virgil Elizondo, eds. *Ecology and Poverty: Cry of the Earth, Cry of the Poor*, Concilium. Maryknoll, NY: Orbis Books, 1995.

Brown, Robert McAfee. *Gustavo Gutiérrez: An Introduction to Liberation Theology*. Maryknoll, NY: Orbis Books, 1990.

Byrne, Patrick H. "Ressentiment and the Preferential Option for the Poor." *Theological Studies* 54, no. 2 (1993): 213-41.

Cadorette, Curt, *The New Dictionary of Catholic Social Thought*. Collegeville, MN:Liturgical Press, 1994.

Calvez, Jean-Yves. "The Preferential Option for the Poor: Where Does it Come From for Us?" *Studies in the Spirituality of Jesuits* 21, no. 2 (March 1989): 2-35.

Canning, Raymond. *The Unity of Love for God and Neighbor in St. Augustine.* Heverlee-Leuven: Augustinian Historical Institute, 1993.

Carry, Joseph B. "Methodical Creativity: The Foundational Contribution of Bernard Lonergan and Clodovis Boff Toward a Global Theology of Liberation." Doctor of Philosophy, Fordham University, 2005.

Casabella, Jordi. "Adolfo Nicolás: "No sé si abrir fosas y beatificar mártires ayudará a reconciliar"" http://www.elperiodico.com/es/noticias/sociedad/adolfo-nicolas-abrir-fosas-beatificar-martires-ayudara-reconciliar-34712 (accessed 14-June 2011).

Casaldáliga, Pedro. *In Pursuit of the Kingdom/Writings*. Maryknoll, NY: Orbis Books, 1990.

Catholic Church: Extraordinary Synod of Bishops Rome 1985. *A Message to the People of God and the Final Report*. Washington D.C.: National Conference of Catholic Bishops, 1986.

Coelho, Ivo. *Hermeneutics and Method: The 'Universal Viewpoint' in Bernard Lonergan*. Toronto: University of Toronto Press, 2001.

Comblin, José. "The Church and Defence of Human Rights." In *The Church in Latin America 1492-1992*, edited by Enrique Dussel, 435-54. Maryknoll, NY: Orbis Books, 1992.

Congregation for the Doctrine of the Faith. "Instruction on Certain Aspects of the Theology of Liberation" http://www.vatican.va/roman_curia/congregations/cfaith/documents/rc_con_cfaith_doc_19840806_theology-liberation_en.html (accessed 4 September 2012).

_____. "Instruction on Christian Freedom and Liberation" http://www.vatican.va/roman_curia/congregations/cfaith/documents/rc_con_cfaith_doc_19860322_freedom-liberation_en.html (accessed 4 September 2012).

Conn, Walter. *Christian Conversion: A Developmental Interpretation of Autonomy and Surrender*. New York: Paulist Press, 1986.

Copeland, M. Shawn. "A Genetic Study of the Idea of the Human Good in the Thought of Bernard Lonergan." Doctor of Philosophy, Boston College, 1991.

Cox, Harvey. *The Silencing of Leonardo Boff: The Vatican and the Future of World Christianity.* Oak Park, IL: Meyer-Stone Books, 1988.

Cribb, Julian. *The Coming Famine: The Global Food Crisis and What We Can Do To Avoid It.* Berkeley, CA: University of California Press, 2010.

Crowe, Frederick E. *Old Things and New: A Strategy for Education.* Atlanta, GA: Scholars Press, 1985.

_____. "Bernard Lonergan and Liberation Theology." In *Appropriating the Lonergan Idea,* edited by Michael Vertin, 116-26. Washington, D.C.: Catholic University of America Press, 1989.

_____. *Lonergan.* Collegeville, MN: Liturgical Press, 1992.

_____. "'All My Work has Been Introducing History into Catholic Theology'." In *Lonergan Workshop 10,* edited by Frederick Lawrence, 49-81, 1994.

Dadosky, John. "Healing the Psychological Subject: Towards a Fourfold Notion of Conversion." *Theoforum* 35, no. 1 (2004): 73-91.

_____. *The Structure of Religious Knowing: Encountering the Sacred in Eliade and Lonergan.* Albany, NY: SUNY Press, 2004.

Deck, Allan Figueroa. "Commentary on *Populorum progressio* (*On the Development of Peoples*)." In *Modern Catholic Social Teaching: Commentaries & Interpretations,* edited by Kenneth Himes, 292-314. Washington, D.C.: Georgetown University Press, 2004.

Doran, Robert M. *Psychic Conversion and Theological Foundations: Toward a Reorientation of the Human Sciences.* Chico, CA: Scholars Press, 1981.

_____. "Theological Grounds for a World-Cultural Humanity." In *Creativity and Method: Essays in Honor of Bernard Lonergan, S.J.,* ed. M. Lamb, 105-22. Milwaukee, WI: Marquette University Press, 1981.

_____. "Education for Cosmopolis." *Method: Journal of Lonergan Studies* 1, no. 2 (1983): 134-57.

_____. "Suffering Servanthood and the Scale of Values." In *Lonergan Workshop 4,* edited by Frederick Lawrence, 41-67. Missoula, MT: Scholars Press, 1983.

_____. "The Analogy of Dialectic and the Systematics of History." In *Religion in Context: Recent Studies in Lonergan,* edited by Timothy P. Fallon and Philip Boo Riley, 35-57. Lanham, MD: University Press of America, 1988.

_____. *Theology and the Dialectics of History*. Toronto: University of Toronto Press, 1990.

_____. "Dramatic Artistry in the Third Stage of Meaning." In *Theological Foundations*, 1: Intentionality and Psyche, 231-77. Milwaukee, WI: Marquette University Press, 1995.

_____. "Jung and Catholic Theology." In *Theological Foundations*, 2: Theology and Culture, 129-87. Milwaukee, WI: Marquette University Press, 1995.

_____. "Primary Process and the Spiritual Unconscious." In *Theological Foundations*, 1: Intentionality and Psyche, 447-79. Milwaukee, WI: Marquette University Press, 1995.

_____. "System and History: The Challenge to Catholic Systematic Theology." *Theological Studies* 60, no. 4 (1999): 652-78.

_____. *What Is Systematic Theology?* Toronto: University of Toronto Press, 2005.

_____. "The Trinity in History: The Starting Point" http://www.robertmdoran.com/Design/Assets/Text/The Trinity in History 2 The_Starting_Point.pdf (accessed 21 July 2011).

_____. "What is the Gift of the Holy Spirit?" http://www.lonerganresource.com/pdf/contributors/20091029-Robert_Doran-What_Is_the_Gift_of_the_Holy_Spirit.pdf (accessed 19-May 2011).

_____. "Ongoing Collaboration" http://www.robertmdoran.com/Ongoing Collaboration.htm (accessed 18-June 2011).

Dorr, Donal. *Option for the Poor: A Hundred Years of Catholic Social Teaching*. Blackburn, Vic.: CollinsDove, 1992.

_____, *The New Dictionary of Catholic Social Thought*. Collegeville, MN:The Liturgical Press, 1994.

Dupont, Jacques. "Introduction aux Béatitudes." *Nouvelle Revue Théologique* 108, no. 2 (1976): 97-108.

Dussel, Enrique. *Philosophy of Liberation*. Maryknoll, NY: Orbis Books, 1985.

Eagleson, John, and Philip Scharper, eds. *Puebla and Beyond: Documentation and Commentary*. Maryknoll, NY: Orbis Books, 1979.

Eddington, Arthur. *The Nature of the Physical World*. Cambridge, UK: Cambridge University Press, 1928.

Elizondo, Virgilio. "Culture, the Option for the Poor, and Liberation." In *The Option for the Poor in Christian Theology*, edited by Daniel G. Groody, 157-68. Notre Dame, IN: University of Notre Dame Press, 2007.

Ellacuría, Ignacio. *Freedom Made Flesh: The Mission of Christ and His Church.* Translated by John Drury. Maryknoll, NY: Orbis Books, 1976.

_____. "Aporte de la teología de la liberación a las religiones abrahámicas en la superación del individualismo y del positivismo." *Revista Latinoamericana de Teología (San Salvador)* 10 (1987): 3-28.

Famerée, Joseph. "Bishops and Dioceses and the Communications Media (November 5 – 25, 1963)." In *History of Vatican II: The Mature Council, Second Period Intersession, September 1963 – September 1964*, edited by Giuseppe Alberigo and Joseph Komonchak, III, 117-88. Maryknoll, NY: Orbis Books, 2000.

Fesquet, Henri. *The Drama of Vatican II: The Ecumenical Council June, 1962 – December, 1965.* Translated by Bernard Murchland. New York: Random House, 1967.

Freire, Paulo. *Pedagogy of the Oppressed.* New York: Seabury Press, 1970.

Freire, Paulo, and Antonio Faundez. *Learning to Question: A Pedagogy of Liberation.* Geneva: World Council of Churches, 1989.

Fuellenbach, John. *The Kingdom of God: the Message of Jesus Today.* Maryknoll, NY: Orbis Books, 1995.

Gauthier, Paul. *Christ, the Church, and the Poor.* Translated by Edward Fitzgerald. Westminster, MD: The Newman Press, 1965.

Gudorf, Christine E. "Octogesima adveniens." In *Modern Catholic Social Teaching: Commentaries & Interpretations*, edited by Kenneth R. Himes, 315-32. Washington, D.C.: Georgetown University Press, 2005.

Gutiérrez, Gustavo. *The Power of the Poor in History: Selected Writings.* Maryknoll, NY: Orbis Books, 1983.

_____. *We Drink from Our Own Wells: The Spiritual Journey of a People.* Translated by Matthew J. O'Connell. Maryknoll, NY: Orbis Books, 1984.

_____. *A Theology of Liberation: History, Politics, and Salvation.* Translated by Caridad Inda and John Eagleson. Maryknoll, NY: Orbis Books, 1988.

_____. "Church of the Poor." In *Born of the Poor: The Latin American Church Since Medellín*, edited by Edward Cleary, 9-15. Notre Dame, IN: University of Notre Dame Press, 1990.

_____. *The Truth Shall Make You Free: Confrontations.* Translated by Matthew O'Connell. Maryknoll, NY: Orbis Books, 1990.

_____. "Option for the Poor." In *Mysterium Liberationis: Fundamental Concepts of Liberation Theology*, edited by Ignacio Ellacuría and Jon Sobrino, 235-50. Maryknoll, NY: Orbis Books, 1993.

_____."Option for the Poor: Reviews and Challenges." *Promotio Justitiae*, no. 57 (1994): 11-18.

_____. *The Density of the Present: Selected Writings*. Maryknoll, NY: Orbis Books, 1999.

_____."The Option for the Poor Arises from Faith in Christ." *Theological Studies* 70, no. 2 (2009): 317-26.

Harrington, Donal. "The Meaning and Function of Conversion in Moral Theology According to Bernard Lonergan." Doctor of Sacred Theology, The Pontifical University of Saint Thomas Aquinas, 1990.

Hebblethwaite, Peter. "Spiritual Points in Liberation Themes Basic to the Document: An Analysis." In *Liberation Theology & the Vatican Document: Perspectives from the Third World*, edited by Sonia R. Perdiguerra, 3, 85-95. Quezon City: Claretian Publications, 1987.

_____. *The Christian Hope*. Oxford: OUP, 2010.

Hefling, Charles C. "A Perhaps Permanently Valid Achievement: Lonergan on Christ's Satisfaction." *Method: Journal of Lonergan Studies* 10, no. 1 (1992): 51-76.

_____. "On the Possible Relevance of Lonergan's Thought to Some Feminist Questions in Christology," edited by Cynthia S. W. Crysdale, 199-219. Toronto: University of Toronto Press, 1994.

Hennelly, Alfred T. "A Report from the Conference." In *Santo Domingo & Beyond: Documents & Commentaries from the Historic Meeting of the Latin American Bishops' Conference*, edited by Alfred T. Hennelly, 24-36. Maryknoll, NY: Orbis Books, 1993.

Himes, Kenneth. "To Inspire and Inform." *America*, June 6 2005, 7-10.

Himes, Kenneth R. "Justitia in mundo." In *Modern Catholic Social Teaching: Commentaries & Interpretations*, edited by Kenneth R. Himes, 333-62. Washington, D.C.: Georgetown University Press, 2005.

Holland, Joe, and Peter Henriot. *Social Analysis: Linking Faith and Justice*. Maryknoll, NY: Orbis Books, 1983.

Hollenbach, David. "Gaudium et spes." In *Modern Catholic Social Teaching: Commentaries & Interpretations*, edited by Kenneth Himes, 266-314. Washington, D.C.: Georgetown University Press, 2005.

Kanaris, Jim. "Bernard Lonergan's Philosophy of Religion." Doctor of Philosophy, McGill University, 2000.

Lamb, Matthew L. "Methodology, Metascience and Political Theology." In *Lonergan Workshop 2*, edited by Frederick Lawrence, 281-403. Missoula, MT: Scholars Press, 1981.

_____. *Solidarity with Victims*. New York: Crossroad, 1982.

Latin American Episcopal Conference. *The Church in the Present-Day Transformation of Latin America in the Light of the Council: Conclusions.* Vol. 2., 2 vols. Bogatá: General Secretariat of CELAM, 1973.

_____. *The Church in the Present-Day Transformation of Latin America in the Light of the Council: Position Papers.* Vol. 1., 2 vols. Bogatá: General Secretariat of CELAM, 1973.

_____. "Conclusions: New Evangelisation, Human Development, Christian Culture." In *Santo Domingo & Beyond: Documents & Commentaries from the Historic Meeting of the Latin American Bishops' Conference,* edited by Alfred T. Hennelly, 71-155. Maryknoll, NY: Orbis Books, 1993.

_____. "Documento Conclusivo" http://www.celam.org/aparecida.php (accessed 3 September 2012).

Lawrence, Frederick G. *Communicating a Dangerous Memory: Soundings in Political Theology.* Atlanta, GA: Scholars Press, 1987.

_____. "Lonergan as Political Theologian." In *Religion in Context: Recent Studies in Lonergan,* edited by Timothy P. Fallon and Philip Boo Riley, 1-34. Lanham, MD: University Press of America, 1988.

Lee, Michael. *Bearing the Weight of Salvation: The Soteriology of Ignacio Ellacuría.* New York: Crossroad, 2008.

Lernoux, Penny. *Cry of the People: United States Involvement in the Rise of Fascism, Torture, and Murder and the Persecution of the Catholic Church in Latin America.* Garden City, NY: Doubleday & Company, Inc., 1980.

Liddy, Richard M. *Transforming Light: Intellectual Conversion in the Early Lonergan.* Collegeville, MN: Liturgical Press, 1993.

Linden, Ian. *Global Catholicism: Diversity and Change Since Vatican II.* New York, NY: Columbia University Press, 2009.

Loisy, Alfred. *L'evangile et l'eglise.* Paris: Picard, 1902.

Lonergan, Bernard J.F. *De verbo incarnato.* 3rd ed. Romae: Pontificia Universitatis Gregoriana, 1964.

_____. *Method in Theology.* London: Darton, Longman, and Todd, 1972.

_____. "Christology Today: Methodological Reflections." In *A Third Collection: Papers by Bernard J. F. Lonergan, S.J.,* edited by Frederick E. Crowe, 74-99. New York: Paulist Press, 1985.

_____. "Healing and Creating in History." In *A Third Collection: Papers by Bernard J. F. Lonergan, S.J.*, edited by Frederick E. Crowe, 100-09. New York: Paulist Press, 1985.

_____."Natural Right and Historical Mindedness." In *A Third Collection: Papers by Bernard J. F. Lonergan, S.J.*, edited by Frederick E. Crowe, 169-83. New York: Paulist Press, 1985.

_____. "Third Lecture: The Ongoing Genesis of Methods." In *A Third Collection: Papers by Bernard J. F. Lonergan, S.J.*, 146-65. New York: Paulist Press, 1985.

_____. *Understanding and Being: the Halifax Lectures on Insight*. Vol. 5 Collected Works of Bernard Lonergan, edited by Elizabeth A. Morelli and Mark D. Morelli. Toronto: University of Toronto Press, 1990.

_____. *Insight: A Study of Human Understanding*. Vol. 3 Collected Works of Bernard Lonergan, edited by Frederick E. Crowe and Robert M. Doran. Toronto: University of Toronto Press, 1992.

_____."The Origins of Christian Realism." In *A Second Collection: Papers by Bernard J. F. Lonergan, S.J.*, edited by William F. Ryan and Bernard Tyrrell, 239-62. Toronto: University of Toronto Press, 1996.

_____. "The Subject." In *A Second Collection: Papers by Bernard J. F. Lonergan, S.J.*, edited by William F. Ryan and Bernard Tyrrell, 69-86. Toronto: University of Toronto Press, 1996.

_____. "The Transition from a Classicist World-View to Historical Mindedness." In *A Second Collection: Papers by Bernard J. F. Lonergan, S.J.*, edited by William F. Ryan and Bernard Tyrrell, 1-9. Toronto: University of Toronto Press, 1996.

_____. "Unity and Plurality: The Coherence of Christian Truth." In *Philosophical and Theological Papers, 1965-1980*, Vol. 17 Collected Works of Bernard Lonergan edited by Robert C. Croken and Robert M. Doran, 70-104. Toronto: University of Toronto Press, 2004.

_____. "The World Mediated by Meaning." In *Philosophical and Theological Papers, 1965-1980*, Vol. 17 Collected Works of Bernard Lonergan, 107-18. Toronto: University of Toronto Press, 2004.

_____. *The Triune God: Systematics*. Translated by Michael G. Shields. Vol. 12 Collected Works of Bernard Lonergan, edited by Robert M. Doran and H. Daniel Monsour. Toronto: University of Toronto Press, 2007.

_____. *The Triune God: Doctrines*. Translated by Michael G. Shields. Vol. 11 Collected Works of Bernard Lonergan, edited by Robert M. Doran and H. Daniel Monsour. Toronto: University of Toronto Press, 2009.

Maldonado, Enrique Ruiz, ed. *Liberación y cautiverio: Debates en torno al método de la teología en América Latina.* Ciudad de México: Comité Organizador, 1975.

Marsh, James L. "Praxis and Ultimate Reality: Intellectual, Moral, and Religious Conversion as Radical Political Conversion." *Ultimate Reality and Meaning* 13, no. 3 (1990): 222-40.

_____. *Critique, Action, and Liberation.* Albany, NY: SUNY Press, 1995.

_____. *Praxis, Process, and Transcendence.* Albany, NY: SUNY Press, 1999.

Martin, Stephen. *Healing and Creativity in Economic Ethics: The Contribution of Bernard Lonergan's Economic Thought to Catholic Social Teaching.* Lanham, MD: University Press of America, 2008.

Martín-Baró, Ignacio. *Writings for a Liberation Psychology.* Cambridge, MA: HUP, 1994.

McCormack, John. "The Church of the Poor." *The Furrow* 17, no. 4 (1966): 10.

McLaughlin, Michael T. *Knowledge, Consciousness and Religious Conversion in Lonergan and Aurobindo.* Rome: EPUG, 2003.

Meier, John P. "The Bible as a Source for Theology." *CTSA Proceedings* 43, no. 1 (1988): 1-14.

Melchin, Kenneth R. *History, Ethics and Emergent Probability: Ethics, Society, and History in the Work of Bernard Lonergan.* Lanham, MD: University Press of America, 1987.

_____. "Democracy, Sublation, and the Scale of Values." In *The Importance of Insight: Essays in Honour of Michael Vertin* edited by John J. Liptay and David S. Liptay, 183-96. Toronto: University of Toronto Press, 2007.

Metz, Johannes Baptist. *Theology of the World.* London: Burns & Oates, 1969.

Milbank, John. *Theology and Social Theory: Beyond Secular Reason.* Cambridge, MA: Blackwell, 1991.

Mueller, J.J. "The Role of Theological Symbols in Mediating Cultural Change." In *Communication and Lonergan: Common Ground for Forging the New Age,* edited by Thomas J. Farrell and Paul A. Soukup, 294-311. Kansas, MO: Sheed & Ward, 1993.

Nickoloff, James B., *An Introductory Dictionary of Theology and Religious Studies.* Collegeville, MN:Liturgical Press, 2007.

Novak, Michael. *Will it Liberate? Questions about Liberation Theology*. New York: Paulist Press, 1986.

O'Brien, John, *The New Dictionary of Catholic Social Thought*. Collegeville, MN:Liturgical Press, 1994.

O'Grady, Desmond. *Eat from God's Hand: Paul Gauthier and the Church of the Poor*. London: Geoffrey Chapman, 1965.

Origen. *An Exhortation to Martyrdom; Prayer; First Principles: Book IV; Prologue to the Commentary On the Song of Songs; Homily XXVII on Numbers*. Translated by Rowan A. Greer. Mahwah, NJ: Paulist Press, 1979.

Ormerod, Neil. "Augustine's *De Trinitate* and Lonergan's Realms of Meaning." *Theological Studies* 64, no. 4 (2003): 773-94.

_____. "A Dialectic Engagement with the Social Sciences in an Ecclesiological Context." *Theological Studies* 66, no. 4 (2005): 815-40.

_____. "The Four Point Hypothesis: Transpositions and Complications." *Irish Theological Quarterly* 77:2 (2012), 127-140.

Ormerod, Neil, and Shane Clifton. *Globalization and the Mission of the Church*. New York: T&T Clark, 2009.

Panikkar, Raimundo. *The Cosmotheandric Experience: Emerging Religious Consciousness*. Maryknoll, NY: Orbis Books, 1993.

Pelletier, Denis. ""Une marginalité engagée: le groupe Jésus, l'Église et les Pauvres." In *Les Commissions Conciliaires à Vatican II*, edited by M. Lamberigts, C. Soetens and J. Grootaers, 63-89. Leuven: Peeters, 1996.

Pixley, George V., and Clodovis Boff. *The Bible, the Church and the Poor*. Translated by Paul Burns. Maryknoll, NY: Orbis Books, 1989.

Pontifical Council for Justice and Peace. "Compendium of the Social Doctrine of the Church" http://www.vatican.va/roman curia/pontifical councils/justpeace/documents/rc pc justpeace doc 20060526 compendio-dott-soc en.html (accessed 3 September 2012).

Pope Benedict XVI. "Deus caritas est" http://www.vatican.va/holy_father/benedict_xvi/encyclicals/documents/hf_ben-xvi_enc_20051225_deus-caritas-est_en.html (accessed 4 September 2012).

_____. "Message of his Holiness Benedict XVI for Lent 2006" http://www.vatican.va/holy_father/benedict_xvi/messages/lent/documents/hf_ben-xvi_mes_20050929_lent-2006_en.html (accessed 14-June 2011).

_____. "Inaugural Session of the Fifth General Conference of the Bishops of Latin America and the Caribbean: Address of His Holiness Benedict XVI" http://www.vatican.va/holy_father/benedict_xvi/speeches/2007/

may/documents/hf_ben-xvi_spe_20070513_conference-aparecida_
en.html (accessed 3 September 2012).

_____. *Jesus of Nazareth: From the Baptism in the Jordan to the
Transfiguration*. Translated by Adrian J. Walker. London: Bloomsbury,
2007.

_____. "Message of His Holiness Pope Benedict XVI for the Celebration
of the World Day of Peace" http://www.vatican.va/holy_father/benedict_
xvi/messages/peace/documents/hf_ben-xvi_mes_20061208_xl-world-
day-peace_en.html (accessed 4 September 2012).

_____. "Spe salvi" http://www.vatican.va/holy_father/benedict_xvi/
encyclicals/documents/hf_ben-xvi_enc_20071130_spe-salvi_en.html
(accessed 20-June 2010).

_____. "Caritas in veritate" http://www.vatican.va/holy_father/ben-
edict_xvi/encyclicals/documents/hf_ben-xvi_enc_20090629_cari-
tas-in-veritate_en.html (accessed 3 September 2012).

_____. "Message of His Holiness Pope Benedict XVI for the Celebration
of the World Day of Peace: Fighting Poverty to Build Peace" http://
www.vatican.va/holy_father/benedict_xvi/messages/peace/documents/
hf_ben-xvi_mes_20081208_xlii-world-day-peace_en.html (accessed 4
September 2012).

_____. "Message of His Holiness Pope Benedict XVI for the Celebration
of the World Day of Peace: Fighting Poverty to Build Peace" http://www.
vatican.va/holy_father/benedict_xvi/messages/peace/documents/hf_
ben-xvi_mes_20061208_xl-world-day-peace_en.html (accessed 17-May
2010).

Pope John Paul II. "Familiaris consortio" http://www.vatican.va/holy_father/
john_paul_ii/apost_exhortations/documents/hf_jp-ii_exh_19811122_
familiaris-consortio_en.html (accessed 4 September 2012).

_____. "Celebración de la palabra: Homilía del Santo Padre Juan Pablo
II" http://www.vatican.va/holy_father/john_paul_ii/homilies/1984/
documents/hf_jp-ii_hom_19841012_celebrazione-santo-domingo_
sp.html (accessed 5-April 2009).

_____. "Sollicitudo rei socialis" http://www.vatican.va/holy_father/
john_paul_ii/encyclicals/documents/hf_jp-ii_enc_30121987_sollicitu-
do-rei-socialis_en.html (accessed 3 September 2012).

_____. "Centesimus annus" http://www.vatican.va/holy_father/john_
paul_ii/encyclicals/documents/hf_jp-ii_enc_01051991_centesimus-an-
nus_en.html (accessed 4 September 2012).

_____. "Opening Address of the Holy Father." In *Santo Domingo & Beyond: Documents & Commentaries from the Historic Meeting of the Latin American Bishops' Conference*, edited by Alfred T. Hennelly, 41-60. Maryknoll, NY: Orbis Books, 1993.

_____. "Ecclesia in America" http://www.vatican.va/holy_father/john_paul_ii/apost_exhortations/documents/hf_jp-ii_exh_22011999_ecclesia-in-america_en.html (accessed 4 September 2012).

_____. "Fides et ratio" http://www.vatican.va/holy_father/john_paul_ii/encyclicals/documents/hf_jp-ii_enc_15101998_fides-et-ratio_en.html (accessed 3 September 2012).

Pope John XXIII. "Mater et magistra" http://www.vatican.va/holy_father/john_xxiii/encyclicals/documents/hf_j-xxiii_enc_15051961_mater_en.html (accessed 14-February 2011).

_____. "Radiomessaggio del Santo Padre Giovanni XXIII ai fedeli di tutto il mondo a un mese dal concilio ecumenico Vaticano" http://www.vatican.va/holy_father/john_xxiii/speeches/1962/documents/hf_j-xxiii_spe_19620911_ecumenical-council_it.html (accessed 3 September 2012).

Pope Paul VI. "Populorum progressio" http://www.vatican.va/holy_father/paul_vi/encyclicals/documents/hf_p-vi_enc_26031967_populorum_en.html (accessed 3 September 2012).

_____. "Octogesima adveniens" http://www.vatican.va/holy_father/paul_vi/apost_letters/documents/hf_p-vi_apl_19710514_octogesima-adveniens_en.html (accessed 4 September 2012).

_____. "Evangelii nuntiandi" http://www.vatican.va/holy_father/paul_vi/apost_exhortations/documents/hf_p-vi_exh_19751208_evangelii-nuntiandi_en.html (accessed 4 September 2012).

Raguer, Hilari. "An Initial Profile of the Assembly." In *History of Vatican II: The Formation of the Council's Identity, First Period and Intersession, October 1962 – September 1963*, edited by Giuseppe Alberigo and Joseph Komonchak, II. Maryknoll, NY: Orbis Books, 1997.

Richard, Pablo. *Death of Christendoms, Birth of the Church*. Maryknoll, NY: Orbis Books, 1987.

Ruggieri, Guiseppe. "Beyond an Ecclesiology of Polemics: The Debate on the Church." In *History of Vatican II: The Formation of the Council's Identity, First Period and Intersession, October 1962 – September 1963*, edited by Giuseppe Alberigo and Joseph Komonchak, II, 281-357. Maryknoll, NY: Orbis Books, 1997.

Segundo, Juan Luis. *The Liberation of Theology*. Maryknoll, NY: Orbis Books, 1976.

Shute, Michael. "The Origins of Lonergan's Notion of the Dialectic of History: A Study of Lonergan's Early Writings on History, 1933-1938." Doctor of Theology, Regis College and University of Toronto, 1990.

Smith, Marc. "Religious Language and Lonergan's Realms of Meaning." *Sophia: A Journal for Discussion in Philosophical Theology* 25, no. 1 (1986): 19-29.

Sobrino, Jon. "Puebla, serena afirmación de Medellín " *Christus* 44, no. 521 (1979): 45-55.

_____. "The Significance of Puebla for the Catholic Church in Latin America." In *Puebla and Beyond: Documentation and Commentary*, edited by John Eagleson and Philip Scharper, 289-309. Maryknoll, NY: Orbis Books, 1979.

_____. *Spirituality of Liberation: Towards Political Holiness*. Translated by Robert R. Barr. Maryknoll, NY: Orbis Books, 1985.

_____. "Central Position of the Reign of God in Liberation Theology." In *Mysterium Liberationis: Fundamental Concepts of Liberation Theology*, edited by Ignacio Ellacuría and Jon Sobrino, 350-88. Maryknoll, NY: Orbis Books, 1993.

_____. *Jesus the Liberator: A Historical-Theological Reading of Jesus of Nazareth*. Maryknoll, NY: Orbis Books, 1993.

_____. "The Centrality of the Kingdom of God Announced by Jesus: Reflections Before Aparecida." In *No Salvation Outside the Poor: Prophetic-Utopian Essays*, 77-98. Maryknoll, NY: Orbis Books, 2008.

_____. "The Crucified People and the Civilization of Poverty: Ignacio Ellacuría's 'Taking Hold of Reality.'" In *No Salvation Outside the Poor: Prophetic-Utopian Essays*, 1-18. Maryknoll, NY: Orbis Books, 2008.

_____. "Depth and Urgency of the Option for the Poor." In *No Salvation Outside the Poor: Prophetic-Utopian Essays*, 19-34. Maryknoll, NY: Orbis Books, 2008.

_____. *No Salvation Outside the Poor: Prophetic-Utopian Essays*. Maryknoll, NY: Orbis Books, 2008.

_____. "The Urgent Need to Return to Being the Church of the Poor" http://ncronline.org/news/justice/urgent-need-return-being-church-poor (accessed 4 September 2012).

Steinfels, Peter. "CELAM & The Vatican: Preferential Option for Dickering." *Commonweal*, 20 November 1992, 5-6.

Straßner, Viet. "Die Arbeiterpriester: Geschichte und Entwicklungstendenzen einer in Vergessenheit geratenen Bewegung" http://www.con-spiration.de/herwartz/texte/arge.html (accessed 30-March 2010).

Swimme, Brian, and Thomas Berry. *The Universe Story: from the Primordial Flaring Forth to the Ecozoic Era—A Celebration of the Unfolding of the Cosmos*. San Francisco: HarperSanFrancisco, 1994.

Tanner, Norman. "The Church in the World (Ecclesia ad Extra)." In *History of Vatican II: Church as Communion, Third Period and Intersession, September 1964 – September 1965*, edited by Giuseppe Alberigo and Joseph Komonchak, 4, 269-386. Maryknoll, NY: Orbis Books, 2003.

The World Bank. "Food Crisis – The World Bank" http://www.worldbank. org/foodcrisis/ (accessed 3 July 2011).

_____. "News & Broadcast – Global Food Crisis" http://web. worldbank.org/WBSITE/EXTERNAL/NEWS/0,,contentMDK: 21928797~menuPK:34480~pagePK: 64257043~piPK:437376 ~theSitePK:4607,00.html (accessed 3 July 2011).

Thistlethwaite, Susan Brooks, and Mary Potter Engle, eds. *Lift Every Voice: Constructing Christian Theologies from the Underside*. Maryknoll, NY: Orbis Books, 1998.

Tilley, Terrence. "Review of *Theology and the Dialectics of History* by Robert Doran." *Journal of the American Academy of Religion* 62, no. 1 (1994): 186-90.

Twomey, Gerald S. *The 'Preferential Option for the Poor' in Catholic Social Thought from John XXIII to John Paul II*. Queenstown, ON: The Edwin Mellen Press, 2005.

Vertin, Michael. "Lonergan on Consciousness: Is There a Fifth Level?" *Method: Journal of Lonergan Studies* 12, no. 1 (1994): 1-36.

Walmsley, Gerard. *Lonergan on Philosophic Pluralism: The Polymorphism of Consciousness as the Key to Philosophy*. Toronto: University of Toronto Press, 2008.

Whelan, Gerard. "The Development of Lonergan's Notion of the Dialectic of History: A Study of Lonergan's Writings 1938-53." Doctor of Philosophy, University of St Michael's College, 1997.

World Synod of Catholic Bishops. "Justitia in mundo" http://catholicsocials-ervices.org.au/Catholic_Social_Teaching/Justitia_in_Mundo (accessed 4 September 2012).

Wright, N. T. *Jesus and the Victory of God*. Minneapolis: Fortress Press, 1996.

_____. *Surprised by Hope: Rethinking Heaven, the Resurrection, and the Mission of the Church*. New York: HarperOne, 2008.

APPENDIX

THE PACT OF THE CATACOMBS:
A POOR SERVANT CHURCH

We, bishops assembled in the Second Vatican Council, are conscious of the deficiencies of our lifestyle in terms of evangelical poverty. Motivated by one another in an initiative in which each of us has tried to avoid ambition and presumption, we unite with all our brothers in the episcopacy and rely above all on the grace and strength of Our Lord Jesus Christ and on the prayer of the faithful and the priests in our respective dioceses. Placing ourselves in thought and in prayer before the Trinity, the Church of Christ, and all the priests and faithful of our dioceses, with humility and awareness of our weakness, but also with all the determination and all the strength that God desires to grant us by his grace, we commit ourselves to the following:

We will try to live according to the ordinary manner of our people in all that concerns housing, food, means of transport, and related matters. See Matthew 5,3; 6,33ff; 8,20.

We renounce forever the appearance and the substance of wealth, especially in clothing (rich vestments, loud colors) and symbols made of precious metals (these signs should certainly be evangelical). See Mark 6,9; Matthew 10,9-10; Acts 3.6 (Neither silver nor gold).

We will not possess in our own names any properties or other goods, nor will we have bank accounts or the like. If it is necessary to possess something, we will place everything in the name of the diocese or of social or charitable works. See Matthew 6,19-21; Luke 12,33-34.

As far as possible we will entrust the financial and material running of our diocese to a commission of competent lay persons who are aware of their apostolic role, so that we can be less administrators and more pastors and apostles. See Matthew 10,8; Acts 6,1-7.

We do not want to be addressed verbally or in writing with names and titles that express prominence and power (such as Eminence, Excellency, Lordship). We prefer to be called by the evangelical name of "Father." See Matthew 20,25-28; 23,6-11; John 13,12-15).

In our communications and social relations we will avoid everything that may appear as a concession of privilege, prominence, or even preference to the wealthy and the powerful (for example, in religious services or by way of banquet invitations offered or accepted). See Luke 13,12-14; 1 Corinthians 9,14-19.

Likewise we will avoid favoring or fostering the vanity of anyone at the moment of seeking or acknowledging aid or for any other reason. We will invite our faithful to consider their donations as a normal way of participating in worship, in the apostolate, and in social action. See Matthew 6,2-4; Luke 15,9-13; 2 Corinthians 12,4.

We will give whatever is needed in terms of our time, our reflection, our heart, our means, etc., to the apostolic and pastoral service of workers and labour groups and to those who are economically weak and disadvantaged, without allowing that to detract from the welfare of other persons or groups of the diocese. We will support lay people, religious, deacons, and priests whom the Lord calls to evangelize the poor and the workers by sharing their lives and their labors. See Luke 4,18-19; Mark 6,4; Matthew 11,4-5; Acts 18,3-4; 20,33-35; 1 Corinthians 4,12; 9,1-27.

Conscious of the requirements of justice and charity and of their mutual relatedness, we will seek to transform our works of welfare into social works based on charity and justice, so that they take all persons into account, as a humble service to the responsible public agencies. See Matthew 25,31-46; Luke 13,12-14; 13,33-34.

We will do everything possible so that those responsible for our governments and our public services establish and enforce the laws, social structures, and institutions that are necessary for justice, equality, and the integral, harmonious development of the whole person and of all persons, and thus for the advent of a new social order, worthy of the children of God. See Acts 2,44-45; 4;32-35; 5,4; 2 Corinthians 8 and 9; 1 Timothy 5,16.

Since the collegiality of the bishops finds its supreme evangelical realization in jointly serving the two-thirds of humanity who live in physical, cultural, and moral misery, we commit ourselves: a) to support as far as possible the most urgent projects of the episcopacies of the poor nations; and b) to request jointly, at the level of international organisms, the adoption of economic and cultural structures which, instead of producing poor nations in an ever richer world, make it possible for the poor majorities to free themselves from their wretchedness. We will do all this even as we bear witness to the gospel, after the example of Pope Paul VI at the United Nations.

We commit ourselves to sharing our lives in pastoral charity with our brothers and sisters in Christ, priests, religious, and laity, so that our ministry constitutes a true service. Accordingly, we will make an effort to "review our lives" with them; we will seek collaborators in ministry so that we can be animators according to the Spirit rather than dominators according to the world; we will try to make ourselves as humanly present and welcoming as possible; and we will show ourselves to be open to all, no matter what their beliefs. See Mark 8,34-35; Acts 6,1-7; 1 Timothy 3,8-10.

When we return to our dioceses, we will make these resolutions known to our diocesan priests and ask them to assist us with their comprehension, their collaboration, and their prayers.

May God help us to be faithful.[1]

---

1   Sobrino, "The Urgent Need to Return to Being the Church of the Poor."

INDEX